P9-BXZ-160

The Essential
Whitewater Kayaker

A Complete Course

JEFF BENNETT

MCGRAW-HILL
RAGGED MOUNTAIN PRESS

CAMDEN, MAINE • NEW YORK • SAN FRANCISCO • WASHINGTON, D.C. • AUCKLAND
BOGOTÁ • CARACAS • LISBON • LONDON • MADRID • MEXICO CITY • MILAN
MONTREAL • NEW DELHI • SAN JUAN • SINGAPORE • SYDNEY • TOKYO • TORONTO

This book is dedicated to my favorite shuttle bunny, Tonya.

Ragged Mountain Press
A Division of The **McGraw-Hill** *Companies*

8   10   9   7

Copyright © 1999 Jeff Bennett

All rights reserved. The publisher takes no responsibility for the use of any of the materials or methods described in this book, nor for the products thereof. The name "Ragged Mountain Press" and the Ragged Mountain Press logo are trademarks of The McGraw-Hill Companies. Printed in the United States of America.

Library of Congress Cataloging-in-Publication Data

Bennett, Jeff, 1961–

The essential whitewater kayaker : a complete course / Jeff Bennett.

p.   cm.

Includes bibliographical references (p.) and index.

ISBN 0-07-134327-X

1. Kayaking.   2. White-water canoeing.   I. Title.

II. Title: Essential white water kayaker.

GV783.B458   1999

797.1'224—dc21   98-33127

CIP

Questions regarding the content of this book should be addressed to

Ragged Mountain Press

P.O. Box 220

Camden, ME 04843

Visit us at www.raggedmountainpress.com

Questions regarding the ordering of this book should be addressed to

The McGraw-Hill Companies

Customer Service Department

P.O. Box 547

Blacklick, OH 43004

Retail customers: 1-800-262-4729

Bookstores: 1-800-722-4726

Design by Eugenie S. Delaney

Production by Deborah Evans, Pentagöet Design

Edited by Tom McCarthy and Jerry Novesky

All photos and illustrations by Jeff Bennett unless otherwise noted. Many illustrations are based on techniques shown on *Just Add Water*, courtesy of Joe Holt Productions, P.O. Box 97, Almond, NC 28702. Front cover photo of kayaker Kevin McEvoy by Christopher Smith Photography, courtesy of Perception, Inc. Back cover photo of champion kayaker Scott Shipley by Jed Weingarten.

WARNING: This book is not intended to replace instruction by a qualified teacher or to substitute for good personal judgment. In using this book, the reader releases the authors, publisher, and distributor from liability for any injury, including death, that might result.

Contents

Acknowledgments

Insights from the Pros

The sport of kayaking is developing faster than you can say *eddy out*. New boats spring from the minds of inventive paddlers, wind their way onto rivers, and blast open tricks and techniques never before imaginable. Like many aspiring kayakers, I've paddled up to some hot paddlers and asked, "How'd you do that?" Much to my pleasure, they've almost always been willing to share some insight and help me improve.

If you've ever felt too intimidated to talk to the big guns on the paddling scene, don't worry. This is your chance to hear what they have to say. I've even polled paddlers who have surfed the front edge of kayaking—people who have seen the sport evolve, pushed it into the future, and who have taken the time to share their passions with the newest generations of paddlers.

In this book, you'll find tips and quotes from a veritable who's who of whitewater kayakers. The elite list of kayakers who contributed to this book not only inspire awe wherever they paddle, they're infinitely in tune with the nuances of kayaking. Still, as impressive as their résumés are, they are open, friendly, and able to translate their knowledge and experience into simplified concepts and tangible images. They've inspired me, given me ample incentive to improve at kayaking, and can do the same for you.

Shane Benedict. Shane grew up in Knoxville, Tennessee, but matured as a paddler on the Chattooga River near Highlands, North Carolina. An instructor at the Nantahala Outdoor Center and the Academy at Adventure Quest Rodeo Team, Shane has competed on the rodeo circuit since 1991 and has designed kayaks for Perception. Shane appears in *Just Add Water*, the freestyle instructional video by Joe Holt Productions that was used for many of the illustrations in this book.

Sam Drevo. By the time Sam had barely turned 22, he had already accumulated a long, impressive list of accomplishments. He had been to three world whitewater championships, made the 1995 U.S. Ocean Surfing team, had been a two-time Olympic Festival medalist, and was a Junior Nationals medalist in both slalom and wildwater. Paddling now for Wave Sports, he still competes in slalom and wildwater while chalking up many top finishes on the rodeo circuit.

Dan Gavere. Based in Salt Lake City, Utah, Dan's paddling career started with open canoes at age 11, then moved into kayaking at age 13. Since then, Dan has paddled throughout Europe, South America, Japan, and Costa Rica. An avid photographer and videographer, Dan has produced or coproduced such videos as *Paddle Quest, We Come to Play, Paddle Frenzy*, and *Kavu Day*. In rodeo circuits, Dan took second place in the hole-riding competition at the 1993 World Championships, first in the 1996 WKF Extreme World Championship, and third overall in the 1997 National Organization of Whitewater Rodeos (NOWR) circuit. When not kayaking,

Dan also does snowboard modeling, research, and development for a variety of companies.

Cathy Hearn. Cathy is a passionate all-around paddler, but her résumé speaks for itself. She has earned 12 medals in slalom and wildwater at world championships, was first on the U.S. National Team in 1977 (and a team member ever since), and raced in both the 1992 and 1996 Olympics. In 1997, she ranked third overall in the World Cup and third in the World Championships. Finally, Cathy has managed to become a two-time world champ in long-distance outrigger canoeing. When not racing, Cathy coaches at the Bethesda Center of Excellence near her home outside Washington, D.C.

Lars Holbek. Lars paddled plenty of first descents on rivers throughout California, Middle America, and South America when firsts were plentifully available and only a few makes of plastic boats existed. He has authored *The Rivers of Chile*, appeared in *Canoe & Kayak* magazine, and appeared in the video *Wild Americans*. He also recently completed the third edition of *A Guide to the Best Whitewater in the State of California*. Sometimes a kayak instructor and guide, Lars now works as a kayaking model and stuntman in film and print.

Brandon Knapp. From his home base in southern Oregon, Brandon and his brother Dustin manage to spend a ton of time paddling around the world. While competing on the rodeo tour and putting together videos like *Good to the Last Drop* and *Liquid Lifestyles*, he has checked out rivers in Mexico, Guatemala, Chile, Canada, New Zealand, Austria, Germany, Switzerland, and Italy. A member of Team Dagger, he placed ninth at the 1997 World Championships—and has many first descents to his name.

Dustin Knapp. Like his brother Brandon, Dustin has squeezed in a ton of paddling into an illustrious paddling career. Having traveled from Europe to South America and from New Zealand to the four corners of North America, he has amassed an unbelievable number of extreme descents. A top finisher in many rodeos, he paddles for Team Dagger and shows up in videos like *Good to the Last Drop*, *Liquid Lifestyles*, *Water of Wisdom*, and *Full On*.

Jamie Simon. Whenever the words *female paddler* and *extreme paddling* occur in the same conversation, Jamie's name always comes to mind. A 1995–96 world champion in freestyle kayaking, 1997–98 silver medalist in freestyle kayaking, and the top U.S. female freestyle kayaker since 1995, she has also held the record for waterfall descents by running drops over 40 feet. While paddling for Wave Sports, she manages to show up in videos like *Dashboard Burrito*, *Good to the Last Drop*, and *Paddle Quest*, hanging it out on wild Class 5 creeks and incredible extreme descents.

James Snyder. Jim's been paddling rivers since 1965 and was a pioneer raft guide, steep creeker, and squirt boater. Jim turned a generation of paddlers onto squirt boating with *The Squirt Book* and his video *Certain Squirtin'*. He also has appeared in *Class Five Chronicles*, *Paddler* magazine, and *Canoe & Kayak* magazine. Jim invented the mystery move and was largely responsible for popularizing the 45-degree feather paddle. Jim apprenticed with Keith Backlund in 1975 and has been making custom, hand-crafted wooden paddles since then. A kayak designer since 1981, he has well over 40 kayak designs to his name and now designs for Perception and New Wave.

John "Tree" Trujillo. A native Oregonian, Tree left Oregon in the 1990s to head east and train with the U.S. Canoe and Kayak Team. While away, he chalked up a silver medal in K-1 at the 1992 Worlds in Norway, a couple of medals at the Olympic Festivals, and even made it to the 1995 world surfing competitions with the 1995 U.S. Kayak Surf team. Semiretired from competition (he's coming back), Tree turned his focus to the business side of paddling in 1996, returned to Oregon, and opened Cascade Whitewater Company in Hood River with brother Adam.

The Rest of the Gang

I owe an enormous debt of gratitude to my fellow paddlers and other members of the paddling community for keeping me stoked, wet, and, on occasion, sane.

American Canoe Association (ACA) Certified Instructors Kenny Bavoso, Ron Blanchette, Jim Heise, and Andrew Wulfers helped blend their knowledge of ACA techniques with my own twisted views on kayaking to help make this book a useful tool for all levels of paddlers.

Many thanks to Eugene Buchanan, Fryar Calhoun, Bob Carlson, Jim Cassady, Bill Cross, Jay "JD" Davies, Jenny Goldberg, Veronica Griner, David Harrison, Nancy Harrison, Joe Holt, Phyllis Horowitz, Eric Jackson, Steve Jordan, Dan Jursnick, Jay Kincaid, Robert Koch, Mike Lawson, Glenn Lewman, John Lovett, John Mason, Jack Nelson, Jan Nesset, Taylor Robertson, Eric Southwick, Gary Stott, Bryan Tooley, Jed Weingarten, Tom Windham, and Chan Zwanzig, who kept my head full of ideas.

Finally, a bunch of organizations, magazines, manufacturers, outfitters, and suppliers kept me immersed in everything from up-to-date information to top-quality gear while this book was evolving. Thanks to *Adventure Journal*, Alder Creek Kayak Supply, Alpenbooks, American Canoe Association, AT Paddles, *Canoe & Kayak*, Cascade Whitewater Company, Cascade Outfitters, Colorado Kayak Supply, Columbia Sportswear, Dagger, Extrasport, Four Corners River Sports, Glacier Gloves, Joe Holt Productions, Impex International, Kavu, Kokatat, Lidds, Lightning Paddles, Lotus Designs, Mountain Surf, Nantahala Outdoor Center, New England Whitewater Center, North American River Runners, Northwest River Supplies, Pacific River Supply, *Paddler* magazine, Patagonia, PD Designs, Perception, Pyranha, *River* magazine, Rivers and Mountains, Salamander, Seals, Sierra South Mountain Sports, Silver Creek Paddles, Stohlquist Waterware, Subaru, Swan Enterprises, Waterwalker, Wave Sports, Werner Paddles, Wildwater, and Yakima. *The Essential Whitewater Kayaker* is truly the culmination of the efforts and insights provided by all these individuals and companies.

Introduction

If there are two ways to learn something new, I'll take the hard way first. It's not intentional or anything—I'm just funny that way. So, the school of hard knocks seemed to be the natural course to follow when it came to kayaking.

I came to river running first through canoes, later through rafts and inflatable kayaks. Always envious of the light, nimble kayaks that skittered around me, I did everything I could to cajole one particular paddling buddy of mine out of his kayak just long enough so I could try it. His boat was an antiquated beast—an old-fashioned fiberglass kayak two sizes too small for my lumbering, 6-foot frame—but still a delicate swan compared to my opulent raft. When I finally wore my friend's resistance down, I leaped at my first opportunity to jump in a kayak. Still wearing my size 11 sneakers—common river-wear for river runners in the old days—I straddled the kayak's back deck, dropped my legs into the cockpit, and crammed myself into the hull. Within moments the spray skirt was fitted to the deck and I was bobbing in an eddy.

I paddled my buddy's kayak precisely 10 feet before I hit an eddy line and flipped. With no clue how to exit a kayak, I twisted, kicked, and clawed until I finally popped free of the boat. I swam back to the bank, crawled barefooted onto the rocks, and gave my friend his boat back. I'm sure he wanted to say something witty, but he was laughing too darned hard.

I set upon searching the riverbank for my missing sneakers while my buddy began to work his way back into his boat. "What'd you do to my boat?" he asked.

"What do you mean?"

"It doesn't fit anymore."

"How should I know? It's your boat." I was a bit perturbed with his attitude, if you don't mind me saying.

My friend huffed his way out of his boat, kneeled next to the cockpit, and glared into the bow's dark recesses. Up there, nestled firmly against the footpegs, was a pair of size 11 sneakers jammed tightly within the hull. In my haste to exit the kayak I had climbed right out of my shoes.

More than 15 years and thousands of river miles have faded behind me since that first experience. Amazingly, I'm still kayaking! I quickly came to my senses after my first trip and learned to kayak from a qualified instructor. I paddled easy rivers until I got the basic kayaking techniques under control, then gradually worked my way up to Class 5 descents. I even bought some wetsuit booties so I wouldn't look like a dweeb.

I took up whitewater kayaking as an extension of other river pursuits such as rafting and fishing. Forever the adrenaline freak, I trembled with delight the first time I crashed through a standing wave and plunged over my first tiny ledges. At the same time, kayaking brought me into closer touch with the wilderness and opened up riparian worlds I never would have seen otherwise. It let me see places I used to explore only by foot or raft while doing something I loved.

Since my first kayaking trips more than a decade ago, I have explored rivers from Maine to California, from British Columbia to Costa Rica. And, no matter where I paddled, I always learned something new. There was always a smoother way to surf a wave, a more subtle way to catch an eddy. I gleaned tips and techniques from amateurs and pros alike and incorporated them into my paddling adventures. I may have never matched their grace, but I knew what I was aiming for.

As the years have passed I have met scores—if not hundreds—of kayakers who possess extraordinary skills. I've joined them on first descents and watched in awe as they pulled off the latest rodeo moves with style and panache. Whether sailing over waterfalls, shredding lightning-fast waves, or simply kicking back in a calm section of a beautiful canyon, we all have found common ground: a keen awareness of the inner solace that only river running can produce. For all of us, kayaks have been our perennial companions, veritable magic carpets granting our every river wish. Nimble, rugged, and sleek, our kayaks have traversed chasms we never would have seen any other way.

As a long-time whitewater instructor, river guide, swiftwater rescue technician, and author (*A Guide to the Whitewater Rivers of Washington; The Complete Whitewater Rafter, Class Five Chronicles*; and contributions to many other books), my river-running passions have blended self-indulgent paddle fests with joyful days turning on new paddlers to the wonders of kayaking. I still live vicariously through the eyes of beginners, sharing the stoke they feel when they hit their first roll, and feeling their elation as they sail through a picture-perfect train of rolling waves. I've never adopted the word *teacher* as part of my vocabulary but have always considered myself a conduit of information. Borrowing information from my predecessors, I strive to share my knowledge with other paddlers in the hope that somewhere, someday, they'll paddle up to me bursting with their own water-soaked tales of whitewater adventures.

Cathy Hearn displays the skill and determination that helped her become one of the world's top competitors.

What Are You Getting Yourself Into?

The phrase *whitewater kayaking* evokes a broad liquid canvas upon which a rainbow of emotions can be painted. From the peaceful babble of a small, woodsy stream to the deafening roar of a monstrous, thundering river, whitewater kayaking means many things to many people. Whether your penchant is for languid floats or raucous, high-gradient descents, whitewater kayaks can take you there.

If you have any friends who have gone kayaking, you already know how much fun the sport can be. You also can see it in magazines, television commercials, even on the pages of corporate advertisements or on cereal boxes. Still, all kayakers come from humble beginnings, flipping upside down in quiet pools, learning the intricate techniques that make up the Eskimo roll, and cultivating a set of skills that allow them to enjoy rivers in safety. And, a vast majority of kayakers are just like you: eager to learn, excited about water, and passionate about the outdoors.

Ultimately, whitewater kayaking is whatever you, the kayaker, make of it. Your kayak will bring you back in touch with our world's natural splendors, provide you with an opportunity to grow, and push your limits. With the enormous flexibility of kayaking, you always will have a fantastic array of choices at your disposal, from the equipment you use to the type of rivers you paddle.

Why Whitewater Kayaks?

Kayaks are the sports cars of the whitewater world. They are to rivers what mountain bikes are to dirt and what snowboards are to snow. They dare you to have fun and beg you to seek excitement. Kayaks can be found in the Grand Canyon and on your backyard creek. They can survive a 40-foot plunge and surf a wave with willowy grace. Today's crop of kayakers are aquatic acrobats and aging sightseers. They're granola heads and desk jockeys. Kayaks provide a common ground for all walks of life and turn walking itself into a trivial regimen relegated to the annoying time slots between river trips.

Instructors and Paddle Schools

Analogies run deep in kayaking. It is like skiing, riding a bike, swinging a golf club: It looks effortless in the hands of a skilled paddler, but it takes a bit of practice to become at least marginally proficient.

The best way to learn kayaking is from a qualified instructor. In the United States, the American Canoe Association (ACA) trains and certifies kayaking instructors, thereby providing newcomers with a solid measure of

Eric Southwick gives kayaking the thumbs-up after a great rodeo event.

Pool sessions are one way to learn basic kayaking skills in a safe, comfortable environment.

If gear isn't readily available through your kayaking school (or if you want to bring your own gear to class), check out the equipment chapter later on in this book. It'll provide you with plenty of solid advice for selecting everything from riverwear to boats and paddles. To start, you can rent boats or borrow them from friends. But ultimately you'll want to procure your own kayaking gear because each person's kayak is as individualized as his or her body shape and attitude.

their teachers' qualifications. On the other hand, many outstanding instructors honed their skills merely by paddling challenging streams over the course of many years. Never hesitate to interview potential schools and instructors, ask for references, or check with the ACA before signing up for classes. Find out who makes you feel comfortable, then get set to get wet.

What about Gear?

One of the best aspects of kayaking schools is free gear. Well, almost free. Many kayak schools provide kayaks, paddles, and paddling gear during class time; some schools even have enough kayaks to allow each student an opportunity to select one boat best suited to his or her physique and/ or paddling style. So, while you go to school to learn a bit about kayaking, you may pick up a "try-before-you-buy" program as an added benefit, especially if you're taking classes through a retail shop.

Clubs and Organizations

Once you have gleaned basic skills from your instructor, you will be able to look toward clubs, whitewater organizations, and college outdoor programs for advice, paddling companions, and organized river outings. If kayaking is on your agenda, you need only call your local outdoor store, visit the local paddling shop, or ask the kayaker down the hall how to get started. You'll be amazed by just how easy it is to get wet.

You're never too young to start paddling. Just ask Dane Jackson, the son of world-class paddler Eric Jackson. Dane (at the top of the picture) is shown here paddling at the ripe young age of 5!

How to Use This Book

This book is arranged in a simple, user-friendly format, one that takes you from the showroom of your local paddle shop to the put in of your favorite river. It is a complete course in river running, with each chapter designed to build upon the ideas learned in the preceding chapter. As you float through this book, you will embark upon a journey that leads you through all aspects of kayaking. After an introductory look at equipment and accessories, you will explore rivers, probing their underwater currents, surface hydraulics, and the many forces that make up whitewater rapids. Next, river running will be covered, from basic maneuvers to the advanced techniques used on Class 5 rivers and when playboating. As you move from chapter to chapter, you'll learn about safety and rescue, how to plan river-running expeditions, and much more.

If you have never paddled a kayak before, start with the first page and keep reading. As you progress from chapter to chapter, you will learn new concepts and acquire new skills that will carry you into later chapters. After a day on the river, come back to where you left off, read some more, then go paddle again. Experienced kayakers can jump to later chapters and pick up the information they need to break through learning plateaus or learn the latest moves.

Though this book teaches kayaking with descriptions, photographs, and diagrams, it is ultimately still a book—little more than frozen glimpses of a fluid sport. The techniques taught here work best when you have competent guides or more-experienced paddlers to demonstrate and coach you through each skill. Also, it is up to you to *start easy* and to *progress slowly!*

Ultimately, this book will exercise the most important part of your body—your brain. Through imagery and explanation, *The Essential Whitewater Kayaker* will give you the mental tools you need to get down the river safely and efficiently. With the time you spend in your kayak—learning by both mistake and triumph—you will advance faster and more efficiently than you had ever dreamed possible.

So, read this book, find a great instructor, and dive into kayaking. A wet, wild world of fun awaits.

> "One of the best things any beginner can do to improve is to watch better paddlers, especially the pros. Try to imitate and mock what they do and don't be afraid to ask, "How do I do that?" The more you ask, the more you learn. The more you watch, the more you learn. And don't be afraid to flip over. Don't be afraid to make mistakes. Don't be afraid to swim. Everybody's been there. Pay your dues now, and soon you'll get where you want to be."
>
> —JAMIE SIMON
> WORLD FREESTYLE CHAMPION

Equipment

Don't Leave Home without It

When I first began kayaking, fiberglass boats were common, Hollowforms (one of the first mass-marketed plastic kayaks) still appeared on roof racks, and Perception's Mirage (a 13-foot, 2-inch kayak that was considered cutting edge for its time) had just recently emerged on the paddling scene.

Well, the days of the Hollowform and Mirage have gone the way of bellbottoms and tie-dyed T-shirts. Fiberglass now is usually reserved for specialty boats; Hollowforms have been turned into backyard planters; and Mirages have been replaced by many generations of shorter, higher-performance plastic boats.

Today's kayaks provide a snapshot of an evolutionary process that is ongoing and dynamic. They range from fat, stubby boats specially designed to handle the rigors of steep creeks, to low-volume, sharp-edged craft built to catch submarine currents or cartwheel about the river surface. There are still 13-footers out there, but they usually are used more for slalom and downriver events than for anything else. If you look around long enough, you'll find a boat for almost every river and every river runner.

Kayak Anatomy

KAYAK ANATOMY 101

No matter what type of whitewater kayak you select, all boats have some common components. Most modern whitewater kayaks consist of a *hull*, a *seat*, *footpegs* or *footbraces*, and may be supported from the inside by vertical *pillars* or *bulkheads*. The entry hole in the deck is known as the *cockpit*, while the cockpit's flared lip is frequently known as the *coaming*. Just inside the cockpit, *thigh braces* (sometimes called *thigh hooks*) nestle beneath the front deck and provide a contact point for your thighs and knees. The handles near the *bow* (the front of the boat) and *stern* (the back of the boat) are usually known as *grab loops*, while the extra-sturdy deck loops mounted closer to the cockpit (designed to make rescues easier and provide a way to lock the kayak to your car) are known as *broach loops*. Finally, some kayaks come outfitted with *backbands* or *lumbar pads* for lower-back support, and *drain plugs* for fast, efficient bailing.

No matter how your kayak is put together, take a look at the diagram on page 2 and spend some time learning the terminology for the parts. Learning the names for each part of a kayak will help a lot when it comes time to selecting and fine tuning your boat.

Materials used in the construction of whitewater kayaks generically fall into two major categories: plastic and fiberglass. Polyethylene (which can be *linear, cross-linked, rotation-molded,* or *blow-molded*) appears in many top brands, while fiberglass (which may be mixed with materials like Kevlar and Spectra Glass) appears in a handful of specialized whitewater kayaks, such as racing boats and squirt boats.

There you have it. Kayak Anatomy 101. Now, if you want to keep up with the campfire chatter, you might want to learn a little bit more about things like *edges* and *chines, displacement hulls* and *planing hulls.* Interested? Read on.

KAYAK ANATOMY 201

Stack a dozen different kayaks up side by side and you'll notice a variety of subtle differences. Besides being fat, skinny, short, or long, kayaks vary in ways that aren't so obvious to the untrained eye. The key variances are in *length, width, deck height, volume,* and *rocker.*

Now, before I say anything about design features, let me emphasize that this is a very tricky topic. There are so many design features that go into each boat that no one (including me) can make generic design comments and be right all the time. On the other hand, I can provide you with plenty of material

for campfire conversation on your next river trip. So, let's dive into it anyway.

Length. Whitewater kayaks generally range from 7 to just over 13 feet long. The longer the boat, the straighter it usually tracks and the faster it will usually feel. Longer boats often feel better in big water, too, thanks in part to their ability to bridge big waves and deep troughs. Shorter boats generally spin faster and fit on small waves better when surfing, but they may feel slower on the water when forward or back paddling.

Width and Deck Height. These are design features that balance out your kayak's hull design by providing enough room to seat the paddler while simultaneously achieving whatever paddling effect the designer was looking for. Most kayaks are 23 to 25 inches wide; wider boats often feel more stable on the water, while narrower boats feel faster but less stable. Deck heights, which frequently range from 10.5 to 12.5 inches near the cockpit, often are matched to the predicted size of the paddler in order to provide comfortable seating while holding the kayaker's legs in the proper position.

Volume. Volume is a measure of how much water the kayak would displace if it was completely submerged. High-volume boats (as you might guess) float higher in the water, making them more suitable for larger paddlers. Depending on the boat's overall shape, corky high-volume boats can bob quickly to

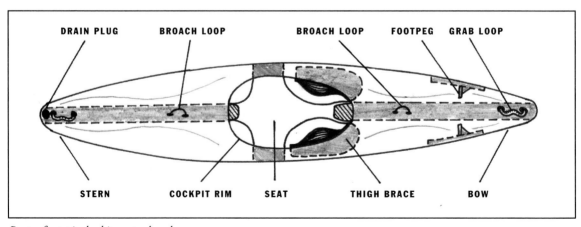

Parts of a typical whitewater kayak.

the surface on steep creeks, or they may get stuck in the recirculating backwash of certain holes on other streams. Small-volume boats, on the other hand, often offer increased maneuverability and performance, but at a cost: They often fit small paddlers better but may require more skill to paddle, especially if they have sharp, current-catching edges.

Rocker. One of the most common design topics at campfire chats is *rocker*. Rocker is the bananalike curvature of the hull of many boats. Think of a rocking chair: The curved slats that rest on the floor are perfect examples of what boaters call rocker. Rocker helps a boat spin and it makes it easier to affect your boat's end-to-end trim by leaning forward or backward. At the same time, increased rocker creates more of a "bulldozer" effect, slowing your forward or backward speed when paddling.

KAYAK ANATOMY 301

Here we are. You've passed Kayak Anatomy 101 and 201, and words like volume and rocker are now passé. You're going for your master's degree in boat design. Well, kick back and mull over a few new words: We're now going to talk about the design features normally reserved for the tech-heads back at your favorite manufacturer's boat factory.

Chines. The *chine* is the area where the side of the kayak bends to meet the bottom. This transition between the bottom and side of the hull can be *sharp* (combining a fairly flat bottom with somewhat vertical sides) or soft (more gradual, rounder curves). *Sharp-chined boats* feel stable and secure when flat on the water (often known as having high *initial stability*), but they become less stable when leaned toward one side. *Soft-chined boats* have less initial stability, but they have more *secondary* or *final stability* (also known as *reserve*), since there are no sharp corners to grab any unpredictable cur-

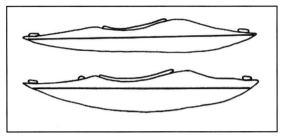

Rocker describes the curvature of the bottom of the hull from bow to stern. The top kayak displays little rocker (which can help the kayak travel straighter), while the bottom kayak displays lots of rocker (which can help the kayak spin easier).

rents. (Once again, we're talking in generalized terms here.) The amount of chine can—and will—vary along the length of the hull from bow to stern.

Displacement and Planing Hulls. In years past, all kayaks had round, cigar-shaped *displacement hulls* that were designed to push and cut through water. They were forgiving and easy to roll, and every kayak had them. However, as playboating was refined, kayak designers started to look at surfboard technology as a way to incorporate better designs into river-running craft. Soon, boats with surfboardlike *planing hulls* began to appear, and a new generation of playboats emerged. Planing hulls are sometimes slower then their displacement-hull counterparts, but they can surf well on waves and in holes once they're on top of the water. Today, both displacement and planing hulls occupy places on the river scene; many boats blend characteristics of both design schools to

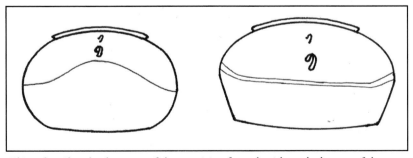

Chine describes the sharpness of the transition from the side to the bottom of the kayak. This diagram shows a kayak with soft chines (left) and one with hard chines (right).

generate boats that perform a variety of tasks relatively well. Only time will tell which designs predominate, and only you'll know which hull designs suit your paddling style best.

Choosing the Right Kayak

OK, I've got to admit it—I'm a *grass-is-greener* type of guy. Give me a low-volume kayak and I'll wish it had more volume; give me a forgiving hull design and I'll seek higher performance. Almost any kayak is a compromise, and choosing the right boat can be a challenging—albeit welcome—task. If you're in the market for a new kayak, here are a few things to know before you go.

Kayaks generally can be stuffed into a handful of categories: *creek, rodeo, squirt, slalom, wildwater,* and *all-around*. While few boats can be perfectly pigeonholed in any one category, it helps to understand what the categories are.

Once you know what types of kayaks are available, you'll at least know which ones to steer away from. Are you an absolute beginner? Chances are slalom and wildwater boats would be poor choices.

Are you fairly aggressive in your athletic pursuits? You may opt for a rodeo boat even though it demands better paddling technique than some creek and all-around boats do. Undecided? You can't go wrong purchasing an all-around boat until you know what type of paddling you'll be doing in the future.

No matter what your motivating forces are—style, color, logo—pick a boat that *fits!* While you may be able to cram your 250-pound frame into a diminutive rodeo boat, you may wish you'd chosen something a tad more comfortable. Looking for a boat for a 90-pound 12-year-old? They exist! In fact, most kayak manufacturers supply recommended weight ranges for most every boat they sell. Factor it into your purchasing decisions and you'll be a much happier paddler.

Kayak Outfitting

Have you ever tried running along a rocky trail wearing oversized running shoes? If you're normal, you answered no: You already know that properly fitting footwear provides the critical interface between you and the ground. Without it, you react slowly and stumble often.

Boat	Length	Volume	Intended Use	Other Benefits
creek	7–10.5'	medium-high	running steep boulder gardens, ledges, and waterfalls	the boat's bulbous, round shape is often forgiving for beginners
rodeo	7–10'	low-medium	playing in hydraulics	often used as an all-around boat by veteran paddlers and experts
squirt	9–12'	low	playing in hydraulics (excels in doing sub-surface maneuvers)	teaches paddlers how to view rivers as three dimensional and to understand the subsurface currents
slalom	13'2"	low-medium	racing with gates	High-performance characteristics help hone fine paddling skills
wildwater	13'2"	medium-high	racing without gates	hmmm—ask a wildwater racer
all-around	8–12'	varies	a variety of uses	a *one-boat-fits-all* type

Kayak design groups.

Now, can you imagine running a river in a sloppy, oversized kayak? If you're a whitewater kayaker, your answer should still be no. But why? If you think about it for a moment, the river's watery trail can be wilder and less predictable than the average hiking path, and it's often much less forgiving when it trips you up. So, why would anyone paddle a kayak that doesn't fit correctly?

Kayaks are meant to be worn like ski boots, not ridden like sleds. Loose, comfortable boats feel good on a showroom floor and on flatwater, but they can make *leaning* and *bracing* quite difficult. If you think that "wearing" a kayak sounds intimidating, cast your fears aside: A well-padded boat that provides a close, body-hugging fit still allows for easy exits while dramatically improving your performance level. The same rule applies to all levels of kayakers, whether they're paddling flatwater or whitewater, big-water runs or creeks. Customized outfitting helps transfer the river's aquatic signals through the kayak's hull to your body by providing more contact between your lower body and the boat. This, in turn, helps you sense changes in currents, make critical maneuvers, and maintain your balance.

Before you undertake any outfitting project, evaluate your knowledge of kayaking. Is this your first kayak? Take a look at other customized kayaks, talk to other kayakers, and suck up as much advice as you can. Many paddling shops, instructors, and expert paddlers will share tips and tactics for outfitting your boat. They'll tell you how to avoid making mistakes and how to get the most out of your outfitting. Listen to them and don't undertake any outfitting project based merely upon some book.

And remember, kayak outfitting is rarely a one-shot deal. A winter's worth of relaxation can change the shape of your body, or the addition of some cold-weather gear can change the way your kayak fits. However, once you know how good it feels to paddle a boat that mirrors the curves of your lower body, you'll come to enjoy tinkering with your boat and seeing just how good control can really feel.

TOOLS AND PARTS

Seasoned experts can customize a whole boat with one block of minicell foam, some carving tools, and glue. I've even outfitted kayaks with camp pads, duct tape, and kitchen knives—and had them work well for years. On the other hand, many shops carry pre-cut pads specially designed to fit kayaks. A knife, a Surform or some Dragonskin (special foam-carving tools), and some waterproof contact cement is all you need to glue pads to your cockpit, while items such as backbands may require some drilling. Again, your local shop rep can advise you and sell you the tools and parts you need to do it on your own.

GETTING STARTED

The first time you get in a new kayak, you'll notice that the seat found in many kayaks is molded to fit a generic butt. My skinny little butt isn't generic, and yours probably isn't either. Fortunately, you can modify the way your seat fits by installing *backbands*, *hip pads*, and *seat pads*. The *thigh pads* might not fit you right, but they can be customized, too.

Since kayakers press against the boat's inner hull with the small of their backs, butts, hips, thighs, and feet, these areas of the cockpit are most often customized to help match the shape and size of the paddler. Let's break the cockpit into sections and tailor each part to give you top-notch control of your boat.

Seat and footbraces. The first step in outfitting a kayak is to adjust the seat and footbrace positions so that your boat rests level and trim from bow to stern. If the boat sits unevenly in the water, the seat may be moved forward (toward the bow) or backward (toward the stern) until the boat is balanced. This usually involves loosening a few screws, adjusting the seat, then retightening the screws to hold it in place. Footbraces (footpegs and bulkheads) provide a solid position for your feet and help you push the rest of your lower body tightly into position. When the footbraces are perfectly adjusted, the balls of your feet will rest comfortably against them. But once you apply a little muscle pressure (by flexing your foot forward just slightly), your thighs, hips, butt, and back press slightly harder against their respective pads without feeling cramped or uncomfortable. Remember, you can keep shifting seat and footbrace positions until you start honing in on a perfect whitewater fit.

Backbands. Backbands and lumbar pads nestle against the small of your back, preventing you from sliding backward off your seat and holding you forward against your footbraces. They also provide some welcome lumbar support, easing the strain maneuvering imparts on your lower back. After-market backbands are designed to be threaded through holes cut into the seat walls or bolted onto the seat itself for a solid connection. You can decide which backband is best for you by sitting in a couple of boats already outfitted with them. Many paddlers opt for backbands with solid nylon or polyester straps and foam pads for maximum comfort and durability. Whichever backband you select, follow the manufacturer's instructions for installation.

Hip pads. If your seat is wide enough to slide a hand between your hips and the seat walls, you're probably going to need to add customized minicell foam or neoprene hip pads. Hip pads help you tilt and lean your kayak when you're rightside up, and they help you stay inboard and roll when you're upside down. After you customize your hip pads (provided you don't make the shims too tight), you'll notice that your boat will comfortably grab your hips and your level of control will skyrocket dramatically.

Seat pads. Thin foam or rubber seat pads are remarkable leg savers. They help prevent leg numbness by spreading your weight over broader parts of your butt while simultaneously increasing the friction between your butt and the seat. Some folks even swear they keep your bottom warm on midwinter paddle trips. Remember that *thin* is an important word when selecting seat pads. Thick seat pads raise your center of gravity and make it harder to balance in your boat. Fortunately, most manufacturers know this and build pads perfectly designed for kayak seats.

Crotch pads. In the late 1990s, kayakers started gluing foam triangular wedges to the seat just in front of their crotch. Soon, the pads became standard equipment on many kayaks. As scary as the thought of a crotch pad sounds (cough), they help improve paddling posture while keeping you back in your seat. And, unlike some recent findings regarding bicycle seats, fears about decreased fertility have yet to find clinical support in the paddling community.

Thigh braces. Little more than a decade ago, I dreaded the thought of casting aside an old custom-outfitted kayak and picking up a showroom-fresh model. The old models came with primitive thigh braces that were good for, well, nothing. However, my painstakingly customized foam interiors ultimately wrapped around my thighs like fur on a beaver. Now, an ever-increasing number of manufacturers offer adjustable or interchangeable thigh braces that can be matched to the size and shape of your upper legs. All you have to do is to pick the boat design you like and swap thigh braces until one fits you just right. I call this the Goldilocks approach to boat buying, and it works great.

Thigh pads. Every time you lean or roll, one of your thighs tends to sneak toward the centerline. Left to its own, it'd slip free from its thigh brace and cause you more control problems than you want to contemplate. Foam or neoprene thigh pads not only cushion and comfort your connection with your thigh braces, they provide the friction necessary to keep a solid grip on your boat. If your thigh pads don't fit you quite right, you can increase or decrease the amount of foam around your thighs until your legs meld into your cockpit perfectly. You can even build foam "hooks" along the insides of your knees if your thigh braces lack these features, or shave small cups for your kneecaps to give you the ultimate fit and control.

Screws. Here's one item many paddlers forget to check when a customizing a kayak. Screws hold many parts of your kayak in place, from the seat to the footbraces. They also take a lot of stress, so they tend to get loose on occasion. Check your boat's screws frequently, make sure they're tight, and they'll stay where they're supposed to be when you need them most.

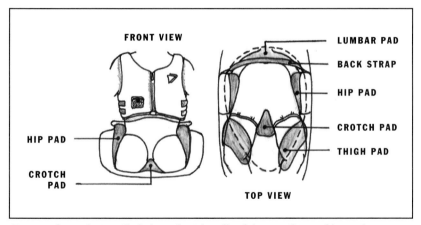

FRONT VIEW

LUMBAR PAD
BACK STRAP
HIP PAD
CROTCH PAD
THIGH PAD

HIP PAD

CROTCH PAD

TOP VIEW

Foam pads can be installed along the sidewalls of the seat (hip pads), on the seat bottom (butt pads), between your legs (crotch pads), and on the thigh braces (thigh pads), to achieve a customized fit. Kayaks also can be fitted with lumbar pads and/or back pads.

Keeping It High and Dry

I can't begin to count how many nonkayakers have come up to me and asked, "So, how do you keep the water out of that boat?" It's a pretty good question, actually. I mean, the gaping hole that you and I call a cockpit does look like it'd take on some water the second you hit a rapid.

SPRAY SKIRTS

An ingenious device known as a *spray skirt* (or *spray deck*) looks like a high-tech neoprene tutu for kayakers. (There are spray skirts made from other materials, but neoprene is the most popular for whitewater kayaking.) The spray skirt is pulled on like a skirt, with the tall body tube wrapping around your lower torso and the deck flapping out in front of you. A rubber rand—made of bungy cord or stretchy rubber—wraps around the perimeter of the deck and is used to seal the spray skirt to the cockpit rim (the *coaming*).

Every spray skirt has some type of release strap—known as a *grab loop*—that allows you to pull the spray skirt free when exiting the kayak. *Always* make sure the release strap is *outside* the cockpit so it is available when you need it, and learn to pull it forward toward the bow and upward to disengage it quickly.

FLOAT BAGS

Though a kayak bobs like a cork when the spray skirt is in place, it becomes downright unmanageable when full of water. *Float bags*—sturdy balloons shaped to the interior of the hull—help kayaks float higher when swamped and make rescues much easier when floating through rapids. Without them, you're simply relying on your

Spray skirts are worn around the paddler's waist, then attached to the cockpit to provide a watertight closure.

kayak's foam accessories (bulkheads, pillars, hip pads, etc.) for flotation—and asking for trouble.

Any time you add float bags to your kayak, follow the manufacturer's installation guidelines and secure them in place and away from your legs. Also, take care not to puncture them with gear stowed behind your seat. If you ever plan to carry overnight gear or any cargo that requires more than a little space, consider using *stow-floats*. These specialized float bags may be just what you need.

Paddles

There are scores of quality kayak paddles on the market today. Quality kayaking paddles are constructed from wood, fiberglass, and aluminum and can have *flat* or *dihedral blades*, *feathered* or *unfeathered* blades, *symmetrical* or *asymmetrical blades*, and *oval* or *round shafts*. Curved blades—also known as *spoon blades*—enter the water more easily, improve your bite on the water, and make paddling easier than do flat blades.

Feathered blades—offset or turned 30 to 85 degrees from each other—help make the paddle less wind resistant and increase the biomechanical efficiency of each stroke. Feathered paddles come in *right-* or *left-hand control* models to match the angle of the blades to your *control hand*. A right-hand control model is the most popular type—your right hand remains stationary on the shaft and determines the angle of the blades. When you take a stroke on

Float bags fill the bow and stern with air in order to provide extra flotation for swamped kayaks. (Photo courtesy of Northwest River Supplies, Inc.)

your left side, your right hand rotates the shaft through your left hand so that the left blade can bite the water. (In a left-hand control model, your left hand does all of this.) *Oval shafts* (also known as *indexed shafts*) make all of this easier by letting you home in on your blade angle by feel even when you can't see your blades.

SELECTING A PADDLE

Every kayaker has a different concept of the perfect paddle. Some paddlers like fiberglass; others like wood. Some like their blades feathered 60 degrees; others opt for 30-degree offsets. There's lots of room for debate on blade shapes and sizes. Still, one of the most important steps you'll take when selecting a paddle will be to determine your optimum *paddle length*.

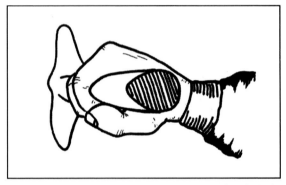

A right-hand control paddle with an oval (indexed) shaft.

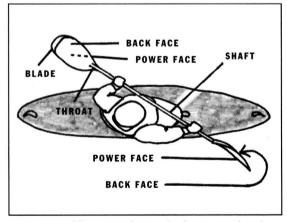

Learning paddle terminology makes learning to kayak easier.

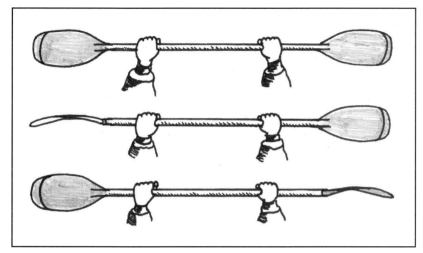

Paddles can be unfeathered (top) *or feathered* (bottom) *and come in left-hand control* (center) *or right-hand control* (bottom).

Ideal paddle length takes into account your height, arm length, kayak size, and paddling style. The paddle-length chart will provide you with a starting point for paddle selection. If you are quite tall, have a large kayak, or seek some extra support from your paddle, opt for a slightly longer paddle. On the other hand, shorter paddles are lighter, faster, and fit into tight spaces on narrow rivers.

Don't skimp on quality when purchasing a kayak paddle! Some inexpensive paddles may seem like good deals, but they are easy to break or bend, and they tend to make paddling more fatiguing. Get the best paddle you can afford, put your name on it in case you lose it, and take good care of it.

Here's a rough primer for selecting your first paddle. If you grab a paddle within the recommended range and try the hand-positioning technique shown on this page, the paddle will be properly sized if you can fit one fist between your hand and the butt of the blade. Later, you can select a paddle length that best suits your paddling style.

Riverwear

The first layer of protection between you and the river environment is your personal gear: helmet, life jacket, and clothing. Carefully designed and selected riverwear not only improves the quality of your river experience, it makes kayaking safer. Wetsuits, drysuits, life jackets, and helmets protect you from the debilitating effects of hypothermia, keep you afloat in powerful currents, and protect you from injury amid rock-strewn channels.

CLOTHING

Novice kayakers frequently are astonished when they first discover how cold many rivers are. Whether fueled by snowmelt, rainfall, or dam releases, the water temperature in many popular rivers is cold enough to require some form of outerwear, even on the warmest days.

When choosing riverwear, select garments that provide comfort, flexibility, and sufficient insulation to ward off the onset of hypothermia. Shorts or a bathing suit may be sufficient when the river is forgiving and the air is warm, but this is often the exception to the rule. Consider river and air temperatures, the type of river you'll be kayaking, and your expected level of activity to determine clothing requirements.

The three Ws—*wick, warmth,* and *weather*—provide an easy way to remember how to dress for

PADDLER'S HEIGHT OR ARM SPAN	RECOMMENDED PADDLE LENGTH, CM
Under 5 feet	188–92
5' to 5'6"	194–98
5'6" to 6'	202–6
6'+	204–8

General measurements for your first paddle.

paddling. Polypropylene underwear and sweaters work in conjunction with other items like drysuits, wetsuits and paddle jackets to provide warmth. Use a thin inner layer of polypro near your skin to wick sweat away; add a second, thicker layer outside of that to trap heat; and cover it all up with a paddle jacket, dry top or drysuit to ensure a full day of warm paddling.

WETSUITS

Wetsuits made of body-hugging neoprene have been a favored form of insulation for many years. A *farmer John*–style wetsuit—which leaves the arms and shoulders uncovered—provides the first layer of insulation, with pile sweaters and paddle jackets or dry tops for the outer layers. (A neoprene wetsuit also gives you some extra grip on your boat.)

The wetsuit works by trapping a thin film of water between the suit and your skin. Once water fills the suit it is warmed by your skin and insulated from the river by the suit itself. Wetsuits also provide some extra flotation and padding—nice things to have if you're swimming a boulder-strewn river.

When selecting a wetsuit, try not to get the same type of suit worn by scuba divers. A kayaker's higher activity level and increased range of motion demands a thinner wetsuit than one preferred by divers. A thickness of 2 to 3 mm provides both warmth and flexibility. Also check for proper fit—a properly fitted farmer John wetsuit will follow the contours of your body without being too tight.

PADDLING JACKETS AND DRY TOPS

Paddling jackets and dry tops are high-tech rain jackets similar to the upper half of a drysuit. They provide an outer waterproofing layer over a wetsuit, and they help prevent chilling blasts of cold water from finding their way down the front of your wetsuit. On warm days, paddle jackets and dry tops can provide enough protection to keep kayakers warm with nothing more than a wetsuit underneath, while on colder days they can often keep kayakers warm by allowing a synthetic sweater to be worn underneath.

The main difference between paddling jackets and dry tops is in their ability to shed water. The more-affordable paddling jackets combine loose layers of waterproof cloth with water-resistant neoprene or Lycra closures at the neck and wrists. A dry top, on the other hand, incorporates waterproof latex closures at the neck and wrists. While the paddle jacket lets some water in, the dry top does not (at least most of the time). Though both paddle jackets and dry tops are effective when you're sitting up in the kayak, either one can let water in through the waist when you're swimming.

DRYSUITS

Drysuits differ dramatically from wetsuits in both appearance and function. Instead of trapping water next to the skin, the drysuit keeps water off your body by enclosing you in a loose-fitting layer of waterproof fabric. The suit has a large waterproof zipper or flap closure that allows you easy entry and exit, and it is made totally waterproof with tight-fitting latex gaskets at the neck, wrists, and ankle openings.

Though drysuits lack the insulating qualities of wetsuits, they are baggy enough to fit over inner layers of clothing. (As mentioned above, the best way to choose clothing that will keep you warm inside your drysuit is to layer wicking and warmth layers: The innermost layer should wick sweat away from your skin, while the next layers should be warm and absorbent.) Since the drysuit will seal in body moisture, it is important to choose synthetic materials like nylon or polypropylene fleece for inner layers.

LIFE JACKETS

A life jacket—also called a *personal flotation device* or *PFD*—*must* be worn on any river. It increases your buoyancy, provides some extra insulation on cold days, and even provides some welcome body armor in the event of a swim.

The main purpose of a life jacket is to keep your mouth and chin above water long enough to let you breathe. Life jackets do this on some fairly basic principles. An average person is surprisingly buoyant

Riverwear can be tailored to match the weather and water temperature. Here, paddlers are wearing a wetsuit (left), a paddle jacket (center), and a drysuit (right).

(weighing only 10 to 12 pounds when immersed in water—less if you're thin; more if you're heavy), and anything that attaches to your body and provides more upward lift than your body's sinking weight will increase your buoyancy.

When choosing or purchasing life jackets, you must consider two important factors: *flotation* and *fit*. Most paddle shops can help you figure out how much flotation you'll need by evaluating your body type, paddling abilities, river selection, and even the clothing you intend to wear underneath the life jacket (a wetsuit can add 6 to 8 pounds of buoyancy; an air-filled drysuit can add more).

A properly fitted life jacket is comfortable enough to wear all day and doesn't interfere with paddling or swimming. It will cinch snugly around your torso and won't ride up over your face or head in rapids. Many life jackets are available in different sizes (from extra-small child sizes to extra-large adult sizes) and allow you to achieve a customized fit through the use of flexible, contoured-foam panels and cinch straps.

To make sure you're getting the best fit possible, try on a few life jackets. Put on a jacket that has ties or straps that tighten at the waist, and cinch them down until they're comfortably tight. Now, have a friend yank on the jacket's shoulders: It should only budge slightly while remaining comfortable. Next, wear the life jacket while sitting in your boat. Does it allow you a full range of motion? (You'll need flexibility on the river!) Also, keep in mind that you may be adding bulky layers of riverwear under the jacket, so make sure there's enough space left to accommodate your clothing.

Life jackets should be comfortably snug yet allow freedom of movement.

HELMETS

Helmets are de rigeur for kayakers on whitewater rivers. Helmets consist of a sturdy outer shell, a shock-absorbing liner, and a chin harness designed to keep the helmet on your head. A correctly shaped and well-fitted helmet covers your entire head—including the top, temples, and ears—but remains unobtrusive to the wearer. Some helmets even have face guards to protect against facial injuries caused by rocks, flailing paddles, or collisions with other paddlers.

When selecting a helmet, check out the *liner.* You may prefer foam padding over a suspension-type shock-absorbing system, but either system works well.

Finally, make sure the helmet fits your head comfortably: The chin strap should hold the helmet securely in place so the helmet won't ride up and expose your forehead or slide down and block your vision.

CLOTHING ACCESSORIES

Booties, gloves, pogies, and *insulating caps* vastly improve the quality of your kayaking experience on cold rivers. Thick neoprene booties with semirigid soles keep your feet warm and provide decent traction during slippery portages. In warmer climates, specially designed river sandals (with extra straps to hold them securely on your feet) can work great as long as you don't mind having exposed feet when walking or portaging. Waterproof caps help you retain an enormous amount of body heat by providing an extra layer of insulation over your head.

Your hands can be kept comfortably warm with neoprene gloves or pogies. Pogies attach directly to the paddle shaft, forming a water-resistant cocoon. Your bare hand slips into the pogie and grabs the paddle shaft without any barrier to affect your "feel" for the shaft. Gloves, on the other hand, cover your entire hand and palm. Though you lose some feel this way, gloves also provide some protection from injuries.

Finally, ear plugs and nose plugs are great ideas for every paddler—they help preserve your sinuses and hearing while preventing vertigo and ice-cream headaches (that feeling you get when you eat something cold too fast).

Helmets come in many shapes and sizes. Pick one that offers plenty of protection and fits your head snugly. (Courtesy of Alder Creek Kayak Supply)

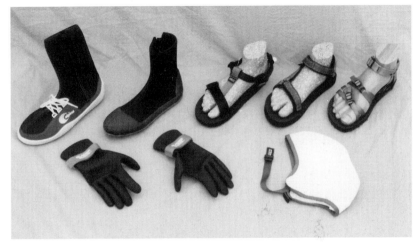

From neoprene booties to specialized river sandals, from neoprene gloves to head-hugging helmet liners, a variety of riverwear accessories can make your paddling adventures more comfortable.

2

Climbing Aboard Your Kayak

No matter how you slice or dice it, kayaking is physical. Though seasoned paddlers can finesse their moves like aquatic ballerinas, beginners are more akin to wrestlers than dancers: They pull harder on their paddles and expend a lot more effort trying to master the fundamentals.

Before You Get in the Water

STRETCHING AND WARMUP

Before you enter your boat, take a few minutes to stretch your shoulders, arms, chest, back, waist, and legs. Do some light jogging or jumping jacks to get your blood flowing and your heart pumping. All of your muscles should be loose and warm before you ever start to paddle. You'll feel better on the river (and you'll consume far less ibuprofen later on).

CARRYING YOUR KAYAK

The most common way to carry your kayak is to rest the cockpit on your shoulder (place your shoulder near the seat's hip pad) while extending an arm inside the boat to steady it as you walk. An even easier way to carry your kayak is to have a friend hold the bow while you hold the stern. Whatever method you use to get your kayak to the river, use your leg muscles for lifting to avoid back strain, and *don't drag your boat on the ground!* Today's boats are tough and resilient but they'll wear down quickly if you drag them often.

DON YOUR SKIRT

After you've suited up in your riverwear, don your spray skirt. Make sure the deck flap is in front of you, that the tunnel extends neatly from the bottom of

Many kayakers carry their kayak by lifting it onto one shoulder while holding the inside of the cockpit for balance and stability.

your chest down to your waist, and that your paddle jacket, dry top, or drysuit's spray skirt tunnel covers the skirt's tunnel so water doesn't filter in through the top of the spray skirt.

Getting into Your Kayak

Ever seen a butterfly emerge from a cocoon? Well, slipping into a kayak is something like getting halfway back into the cocoon after you're already free.

If you have a sturdy kayak (don't try this with fragile boats), practice entering it on dry land first. Set it on flat ground (the softer the better) and don

your spray skirt with the flap facing forward. When you're ready, sit on the rear deck, extend your legs into the cockpit, and slip forward into the cockpit until your lower body nestles firmly into place. If your boat is too tight (making entry difficult or impossible), or too loose (your feet and thighs don't touch the braces or your hips are too loose in your seat), revisit the equipment chapter and consider re-tuning the kayak.

One way to get in your kayak is to place it in the water parallel with the bank and use your paddle like an outrigger for stability (don't try this with a fragile paddle). To do this, lay the paddle shaft just behind the cockpit rim with one blade on the shore and the other one lying just past the outer edge of the boat. Now, face the front of your boat and simultaneously grab the shaft and the backside of the cockpit rim with the hand nearest the river. With your other hand on the shore side of the shaft, step into the cockpit, keeping your weight just slightly toward the shore (you wouldn't want to snap your paddle). Finally, slide your legs into the hull, sit down, and relax. All you need to do now is attach your spray skirt and you'll be ready to paddle.

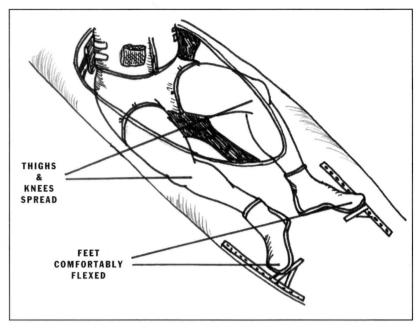

THIGHS & KNEES SPREAD

FEET COMFORTABLY FLEXED

When sitting in a properly fitted kayak, your knees and thighs will splay comfortably outward where they'll nestle in the thigh braces, and your feet will remain comfortably flexed when the balls of your feet are pressed against the footpegs or bulkhead.

A paddle can act as a stabilizing outrigger as you enter a kayak. Use the hand nearest your kayak to hold both the paddle and cockpit rim, and use the hand nearest the bank to hold the paddle shaft for stability. To avoid damaging your paddle, keep most of your weight toward your kayak when using this technique.

ATTACHING THE SPRAY SKIRT

Once you're comfortably seated in your kayak, lean back, reach behind the small of your back, and grab the back of your spray skirt. Hook it over the back part of the cockpit coaming, then work your hands, forearms, and elbows forward along the coming, snapping the skirt into place as you go. If you can hook only the back and front of the skirt first, that's OK—you can hook the sides last. Also, don't be afraid to ask a friend for help (I do it all the time, especially when I'm nervous). Finally, *make absolutely sure the grab loop stays outside of the cockpit.* You'll need quick access to the grab loop any time you need to get out of your boat. Check your skirt one last time before entering the water.

Don't be surprised if it takes a little practice to get your spray skirt seated properly. Use your forearms like extra hands and have a friend help seat your skirt if you have problems initially.

Otter Launching

If you boarded your boat on the water, you're all ready to paddle and don't need the following advice. If you boarded your boat on land, on the other hand, you're ready to execute an *otter launch.*

In an otter launch, you slip off the bank into the water by first positioning your boat so it rests on the bank and extends partway into the water. You enter your kayak as you normally would, attach your spray skirt, then push your way into the water. This technique can impose a fierce licking to boats—especially when the shoreline is rocky and sharp.

Getting Out of Your Kayak

So, you're doing well so far. You're in your boat, on the water, and you've come back to the bank without flipping and swimming. Now you're ready to exit your boat.

One way to exit is simply to run it up onto the bank, pop off your spray skirt and exit the way you entered. Or you can exit from the water using your paddle as an outrigger for stability—the same technique you used to enter the boat. Either way, first

With modern, durable kayaks and smooth banks you can enter your boat onshore, then slide into the water once you're ready to paddle. Enter your kayak by first extending your legs into the cockpit, then sliding your lower body into place (top). Once you're comfortably seated, attach the spray skirt by snapping it over the back of the cockpit and working it around the sides of the coaming to the front of the cockpit (center). After you check your spray skirt to make sure it is firmly attached with the grab loop on the outside, push off the bank into the water (bottom). Don't try this technique with fragile boats or on sharp surfaces.

pull the spray skirt grab loop upward and toward the bow to release it, then exit your boat the same way you slid in.

On the other hand, you can join a cast of thousands of paddlers who didn't stay upright their first trip out and had to *wet exit*. Wet exiting—exiting your boat upside down—is a crucial skill and must be learned early. The wet exit makes it possible to safely disembark your kayak from an upside-down position. Done correctly, it's as easy as taking off your pants; done incorrectly, it will leave you tired, breathless, or even trapped. So, take some time to learn the wet exit the *right way* and you'll be better off when your body's tipped the *wrong way*.

Attempt your first wet exit in a deep, calm pool. Take a deep breath, then simultaneously tuck your torso forward as you flip the boat upside down. Keep your nose on the deck, one arm wrapped in front of your head, your paddle to one side of the boat. (Later, this position offers a ton of protection from shallow rocks and can form the basis for initiating Eskimo rolls.) When you're relaxed and ready, let the paddle go with one hand and use that free hand to pull the grab loop on your spray skirt. (Remember, your grab loop must be pulled up and away from the cockpit rim to release the skirt.) Now, put your hands on the boat near your hips, relax your legs, and push out of the boat as if you were taking off your pants. (Somersaulting forward is usually the best way to go.) Keep going until your legs are free, then head for the surface and breathe. Aaaah!

Once you can combine your knowledge on how to outfit and carry your boat, fasten your spray skirt, and climb aboard, it's time to start paddling. Are you ready? Good! Let's go!

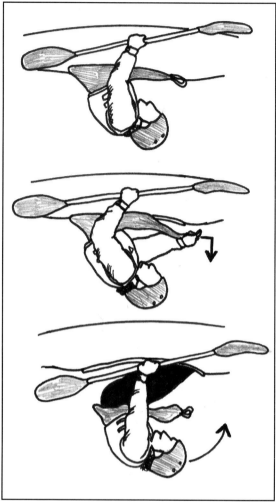

The wet exit allows kayakers to exit their kayaks while upside down quickly and efficiently. Start by getting your bearings (top). Next, release your spray skirt by pulling the grab loop forward and away from the cockpit (middle). Finally, somersault forward out of the boat (bottom). Practice releasing your spray skirt while upright before attempting your first wet exit, and try to hold your paddle during the wet exit.

3

Propulsion Basics

Different Strokes to Move Your Boat

As terrestrial beings, humans long ago adapted to their environment by learning to crawl, walk, and run. Rivers provide a unique escape from these mundane modes of travel. Relax on the land and you just become part of the scenery. The world becomes static. Float along in your kayak and you become one with the river, part of a process in which rain and snow follow a downhill route back to the ocean. Paddling lets you tune this descent and adapt to the river. It allows you to adjust to currents, change your position on the river's surface, and travel faster or slower. Ultimately, paddling will even increase your stability and, when done properly, keep you out of trouble.

Paddling a kayak through whitewater embraces two very distinct activities acting in harmony: *reading rapids* and *executing the proper set of maneuvers*. Watching a skilled paddler run difficult rapids reveals both the simplicity of individual strokes and the complexity of whitewater maneuvers.

In this chapter we'll explore the basic techniques for paddling your kayak: power and turning strokes. From the fundamentals of the forward stroke to the intricacies of the duffek stroke, this chapter will provide you with your first glimpse of the techniques you'll need to paddle whitewater successfully. You'll put your hands on the wheel and feel what it's like to drive a floating sports car on the river.

How Paddling Works

The first person to figure out how paddling works was the renowned physicist Isaac Newton (the same guy who described the principle of gravity). Even though Newton wasn't a river runner, he understood a basic law of physics—one he aptly called the *third law of motion*.

Newton's third law is simple: *For every action there is an equal and opposite reaction.* Kayakers supply the action every time they take a paddle stroke—this applies force from your body to the water. Your body reacts by moving in the opposite direction from the force of the stroke. Thus, when you pull back on a forward stroke your body—and the kayak attached to your body—moves forward; push forward on a back stroke and your kayak moves backward.

The best way to put Newton to work for you is to imagine the river as a giant bowl of heavy cement. Every time you plant your blade in the river during a power stroke, the paddle gets caught in the cement—hence the kayaker's term for this part of the stroke: *the catch*. Make sure you feel the blade catch in every stroke described in this chapter.

Pulling on your paddle from the catch position causes your boat to slide toward the paddle, not vice versa. In other words, your blade remains stuck in the heavy bowl of wet cement while your boat glides along the river's slippery surface.

Once you grasp the basics of Newton's third law, you will discover that you can change the amount of force you apply to the water by changing the angle of your paddle blades: Turn the blade perpendicular to the current and you'll feel a lot of force; turn the blade parallel with the current and you'll feel very little force. This *feel* is what will later help you fine tune your paddling repertoire.

Holding Your Paddle

Earlier, we discussed a variety of paddle designs: feathered and unfeathered paddles, flat and dihedral blades, oval and round shafts. Now it's time to learn how these features work.

Maximize the power of each paddle stroke by planting your paddle blade in an imaginary block of wet cement, then moving your boat and body toward the blade, not vice versa.

POWER FACES

Let's start off by looking at the blades. Curved blades enter and bite the water better than flat blades, but they can be a little confusing to first-time paddlers. The concave side of the blade is called the *power face*; the opposite side is called the *non-power face* or *back face*.

When you start forward paddling, the power face will face the stern and press against the water. If the paddle is unfeathered, finding both power faces will be easy, but if you're using a feathered paddle, the offset blades will pose a bit of a quandary: How do you get both blades to work the same way? The answer lies right in the palm of your hand. Your *control hand*, that is.

CONTROL HAND

Your control hand always maintains a solid, relaxed grip on the shaft and rotates the shaft within the other hand (the non-control hand). If you're using a right-hand control paddle (the most common), your right hand grips the paddle so that the top of your hand, wrist, and forearm are 90 degrees to the blade. Your right wrist stays that way when you stroke with the right blade, but cocks upward and outward to set the left blade for a left-side stroke. (You'll later find many occasions when an inward/downward cocking of your wrist will come in handy.)

Don't worry if this wrist movement feels funny at first; it will soon become second nature. If you have a paddle with an oval shaft, the shaft will nestle snugly in your control hand and impart a feel that your brain will become used to. (If you don't have an oval shaft, you can customize your round shaft. Spread Shoo Goo, Aquaseal, or fiberglass putty in a long strip on the shaft under the palm of your control hand, or tape a thin dowel in the same location.) Even if you're a slow learner, resist the urge to rotate the shaft partially with both hands—you'll have a more difficult time learning advanced paddle strokes, and you'll never develop quite the same feel for the water.

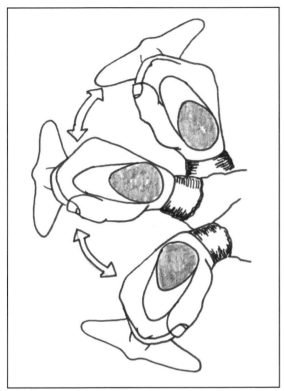

Cocking your wrist upward (to ready the opposite blade for a stroke or high brace) or downward (to ready your opposite blade for a low brace) is an essential skill.

Hand placement is the final element in the paddling formula. It ensures that you'll transfer plenty of power through your paddle while maintaining your reach and control.

To find your proper hand placement, rest the paddle on your head, parallel to the ground. Now, hold the paddle so that your elbows are facing forward and are bent at 90 degrees. Finally, make sure that your hands are equidistant from both blades, then slide both hands in an inch or so. Using this as your starting point, you can widen or narrow your grip slightly to suit your paddling style. Keep in mind, however, that big variations in your hand placement may reduce your power, efficiency, control, or reach.

Body Talk

There's much more to paddling than sticking your paddle in the river and moving it around. Every stroke you take is only as good as the foundation for that stroke. This foundation consists of many factors, including posture, balance, lean, and paddle control. Let's take a look at a few of these items before we start paddling.

One way to find your optimum hand position is to hold your paddle on your head with your elbows bent 90 degrees, then slide each hand inward an inch or so. Lower the paddle in front of you and get ready to paddle.

PADDLING POSTURE

Some poorly fitted kayaks are the whitewater equivalent of a lounge chair: They're comfortable, cozy, and just beg you to sit back and relax. That's fine if you're floating gentle rivers, but serious whitewater calls for a more upright posture.

Sitting upright in your kayak will increase your paddling power, flexibility, range of motion, and balance. It allows you to rotate your torso during each stroke and to use your big, strong trunk muscles to propel the paddle. While your arm muscles may tire out quickly after some intense paddling, your torso muscles can keep providing power to your paddle stroke after stroke.

Sitting upright and rotating your torso also keeps your chest and shoulders facing your hands. This, in turn, reduces the chance of shoulder injuries by keeping your arms in front of your body.

Finally, if the techno side of the posture formula doesn't interest you, just keep in mind that you'll look better and feel more confident if you're sitting upright.

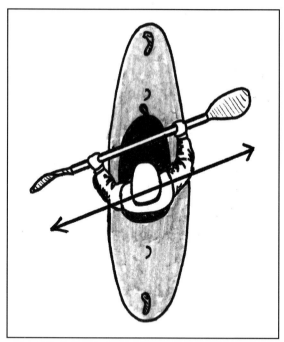

To prevent shoulder injuries, never let your arms drift behind an imaginary line passing through your chest and shoulders.

LEVERAGE AND RELAXATION

It sounds paradoxical, but you can simultaneously be both a powerful and a relaxed paddler. The key to powerful strokes is *leverage*, not just strength. Fully extend your arms and use that torso. At the same time, *relax*. You don't have to tense every muscle in your body to stroke effectively, just the ones that are moving your paddle. Also, relaxing between strokes will save energy for when you need it.

> **"A**s I travel around to different rivers, I often see a lot of beginners leaning back in their boats. We call this *sitting in the back seat*. Sitting in the back seat, you're unstable and stiff. By sitting up straight and using good posture, you'll have better balance and be able to paddle a lot easier. **"**
>
> —BRANDON KNAPP
> FREESTYLE KAYAKER

BALANCING AND LEANING

Good balance and an effective lean will help keep you upright and paddling long after lazy paddlers flip.

Balancing blends the upright and relaxed posture described above with the bobbing motion of your kayak. When you relax your stomach muscles, your upper body floats independently of your lower body. That lets the boat dance beneath you while your upper body remains steady. *Leaning*, on the other hand, counteracts the tipping forces associated with hydraulics and obstacles. In some cases—when you're broadsiding a hole or boulder, for example—leaning will even help prevent flips and broaches. It is one of the most important skills you'll ever learn and is a basis for all successful river maneuvers.

There are many ways to lean while kayaking: You can lean your upper body to one side (using loose hips to allow the kayak to remain flat) or tighten torso muscles (to tilt your boat onto one edge).

These techniques have their time and place, but the best way to lean is with a technique called the *J-lean*. The J-lean—named for the shape your spine takes on during a proper lean—lets you tilt your boat on edge while simultaneously keeping your weight centered over your kayak. (In fact, *tilting* is a much better word than *leaning* and makes much more sense.) It lets your upper and lower body work independently and helps keep your paddle free for paddling rather than for bracing.

To do a proper J-lean, lift one knee upward while simultaneously pressing down on the opposite butt cheek. Keep your body weight centered over your boat by flexing your midsection, pinching your ribs and hips together opposite the lowered butt cheek. As you do this, your boat will tilt onto one edge with your weight balanced over that edge. Try rocking back and forth from one J-lean to another, testing your boat's stability as you proceed. Try it first without a paddle so you can concentrate on the way your lower body feels. Later, try your

The J-lean lets you tilt your kayak on one edge by pinching one hip to your ribs. Your spine takes on a J-shape, letting you balance on edge without using your paddle for support. With practice, you can hold the position shown here for many seconds.

Once your body leans out over the water, balance becomes more difficult and tenuous.

J-leans with your paddle and build up to paddling with your boat on edge. (If you flip, remember your wet exit!)

The Three Types of Strokes

Now that you have figured out how to hold your paddle, it's time to learn *how* to paddle. Amazingly, there are almost an infinite number of ways to move your paddle through the water. Fortunately, we can sort every imaginable stroke into just a few categories: *power strokes*, *turning strokes* (also known as *correctional strokes*), and *braces* (also known as *recovery strokes*).

Power strokes—like the *forward stroke* and *back stroke*—move your boat forward and backward. Turning strokes,—such as *sweeps* or *duffek strokes*—spin your boat while moving across the water. Finally, braces help keep you upright by using your paddle for support and stability (more about them in the next chapter).

Despite the chaos around him, a J-lean helps keep this paddler in an aggressive paddling position instead of forcing him to rely on a brace.

> **"W**hen watching top kayakers, you'll see that they all have good balance. Their bodies are always over their boats, and there's not a lot of excess movement. Staying balanced involves both your lower body and your upper body. Anticipating what the water can do lets you call upon your hips, thighs, knees, and butt to flatten or edge your boat whenever necessary. The other part of balance involves keeping your upper body centered over that package. Even if the boat is tilted to the left, your body should remain centered over the left edge and left butt cheek. If you are leaning off of that, you're going to have to use a brace or flip over and roll.**"**
>
> —SHANE BENEDICT
> KAYAK DESIGNER/INSTRUCTOR

Turning Strokes

Many instructors find it handy to teach turning strokes first. This keeps students in one place near the shallow end of a pool or lake and within ear shot of helpful directions.

Finding your kayak's *pivot point*—a balance point around which the kayak spins—is the first step in learning how to turn your kayak. As you learn about turning strokes, always use the pivot point as a reference: The farther your turning stroke is from the pivot point, the more effective your turns. Don't want to turn? The closer you paddle to your pivot point, the less you'll turn.

At rest, the pivot point is the point at which your kayak is trim from bow to stern and from edge to edge. The pivot point also sits deepest in the water, causing it to resist any kind of turn or spin. As you move your body, the pivot point moves with you. Lean toward the bow, and the pivot point moves forward; lean back, and the pivot point moves toward the stern. Stand your kayak on its bow and the pivot point moves to the front of your boat.

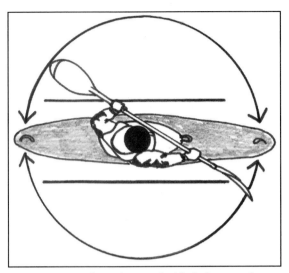

A pivot point is shown here as the black dot near the center of the kayak. The farther your paddle moves from the pivot point (shown here as the circular lines), the easier it is to turn. To travel straighter, keep your paddle closer to the side of your kayak (shown here as straight lines). Bear in mind that your pivot point can travel forward, backward, and side to side as your kayak's angle changes.

FORWARD SWEEP

The *forward sweep* is the most basic of all turning strokes, and it works great in a variety of situations.

In the forward sweep, the blade traces a wide, arcing path from the bow to the stern. It works by pushing the bow away from the paddle during the first half of the stroke, and then pulling the stern toward the blade during the last half of the stroke.

To execute the forward sweep, keep your hands low and the shaft nearly horizontal. Wind up your torso into the stroke to gain plenty of reach, flexibility, and power without leaning forward, then unwind your torso during the stroke.

To execute a right-side forward sweep in still water, first wind up your torso by extending your right arm, rotating your right shoulder forward, and planting the right blade near the bow. Your left hand starts out close to your chest with your right arm comfortably extended and reaching. During the power phase, unwind your torso by sweeping the

To execute a forward sweep on your right side, first wind up your torso by comfortably extending your right arm, rotating your right shoulder forward, and planting the right blade near the bow. Let your left arm remain comfortably close to your chest.

To complete the forward sweep, unwind your torso by sweeping the right blade 180 degrees from bow to stern while keeping your right arm comfortably extended. Keep your chest and shoulders parallel with the shaft throughout the stroke to avoid injury. Finish the stroke by rotating your right shoulder back, pulling the stern toward your blade with your hip and ab muscles, and bending your right elbow down.

right blade 180 degrees from the bow to the stern with your right arm comfortably extended. At the same time, let your left arm drift diagonally across the front of your body while keeping your chest and shoulders almost parallel with the shaft. Finally, finish the stroke by rotating your right shoulder back, pulling the stern toward your blade with your hip and ab muscles, and bending your right elbow down.

Now let's apply forward sweeps to moving water. Although the forward sweep is often taught as a big, broad stroke starting at the bow and ending at the stern, the first part of the stroke has very little turning effect once you're paddling downriver. Picture a sailboat or powerboat—these boats don't steer from the bow, do they? That's because steering from the stern is physically easier when moving through the water. (The theory here is that your pivot point moves toward the bow when you're moving forward. This lets the stern move more freely.) When using forward sweeps on moving water, the last third of the sweep is

> "With a sweep stroke your torso rotation is directly proportional to the amount of power your stroke has: The more you rotate and get your paddle away from your boat and body on your sweep stroke, the faster and more powerfully you will turn. Also, on forward sweeps think about planting your paddle, leaving your paddle in one spot, and moving your feet as far away from the paddle as possible. Look in the direction that you want to go."
>
> —JAMIE SIMON
> WORLD FREESTYLE CHAMPION

the part of the stroke that helps you turn. We'll isolate this part of the stroke and discuss it later as a *stern draw*.

THE REVERSE SWEEP

The *reverse sweep*—also called a back sweep—retraces the path of the forward sweep, but in reverse. During your first reverse sweeps, look back at the paddle blade as you plant it behind you near the stern. Once again, wind up your torso, keep your sweep arm extended, and unwind during the stroke. Remember to keep your hands low and to sit upright.

THE STERN DRAW

Though the name is new, the *stern draw* is really just the last third of a forward sweep and has the same effect: It pulls the stern toward the blade without moving the boat forward. On the other hand, though an extremely important stroke for maintaining angles during maneuvers and making minor course corrections, it's an easy stroke to execute improperly. Let's isolate it and do it correctly from the start.

1. The first key to a proper stern draw is the *blade angle*. Keep the blade perpendicular to the water during the stern draw—be careful not to shovel water upward. Keeping your grip on your front hand loose and relaxed and really twisting your torso toward the

THE CLEAN SWEEP

There are several subtleties that will make your forward sweep stronger and more efficient. First, firmly *plant* the blade (without drowning it) at the catch, and keep the blade (not the shaft) vertical throughout the stroke. Next, *extend* the paddle—reach out! If your sweep arm is severely bent, your turn will be compromised. A couple of tricks that will improve your stroke include watching the blade and keeping constant pressure on the blade throughout the entire stroke. Finally, *use your entire body* to provide power to the stroke: Use your abs to force your legs away from the blade at the start of the stroke and toward the blade at the end of the stroke; don't lean backward (especially toward the end of the stroke); and keep your shoulders and chest parallel with the shaft while sitting upright (to help ward off shoulder injuries).

The stern draw is essentially the last part of the forward sweep—it pulls the stern toward the blade without moving the boat forward. Stern draws can help you maintain proper angles and make minor course corrections when maneuvering.

Think of a bow draw as being similar to the last quarter of the reverse sweep (in which your blade moves in a wide arc from your stern to your bow), but use outwardly cocked wrists so the power face of the blade faces inward toward the bow. Executed properly, it turns the bow toward the paddle.

PRY STROKES

Plant your blade behind you as if to initiate a reverse sweep, then push it through just the first foot or so of the reverse sweep. Your stern and paddle move away from one another as if being pried apart. Get it? That's why it's called the *pry stroke* (in this case a *stern pry*). Try the same thing with a bow plant and the first foot or so of the forward sweep and you'll have a *bow pry*.

Pry strokes feel a little funny at first, but they become very useful when you start playboating. They help initiate all sorts of spins and add another useful stroke to your paddling arsenal.

drawing side will help you maintain a vertical blade angle.

2. Position your hands properly to facilitate the stroke. Keep your front hand about chin high and toward the side of the boat you're working on, your back elbow pointed down.

3. Use your torso muscles to execute the stroke, pulling and pushing the boat toward and away from the blade using your abdominal and leg muscles.

4. When you first start exploring this stroke, follow the back blade with your eyes and head as it works near the stern. This will help you check blade angles and make sure your stroke is working correctly.

5. To avoid shoulder injuries, never let your back hand pass the plane of your chest.

THE BOW DRAW

Some instructors incorporate bow draws in their teaching regimen. Others just teach the duffek stroke (discussed later in this chapter). Whichever school of thought you attend, the bow draw is easy to explain and provides a good primer for the duffek.

The stern pry is the opposite of a draw. It can be used to push the stern away from the blade without moving the boat forward.

Power Strokes

A power stroke can be as simple or as complex as you want to make it. In the most basic forward stroke, all you have to do is plant one blade near the bow with the power face facing the stern, then pull back on the shaft to drive the kayak forward. Paddlers who thrive on simplicity can get away with this technique on gentle rivers without any problems. However, you'll become a much better kayaker if you spend a few minutes reading about the forward stroke, then practicing your paddling techniques on the river.

FORWARD STROKE

The forward stroke has four phases that blend into one fluid stroke: the *reach*, *catch (plant)*, *power*, and *recovery*. Let's start with a forward stroke on the right side of your kayak and see how these phases work.

Reach. Extend your right arm and rotate your right shoulder forward. This winds up your torso, extends your reach, and gets you ready for the catch.

Catch. Plant the blade near the bow, keeping the shaft vertical and the blade submerged up to the throat. Feel it grab before starting the power phase.

Power. In the power phase of the forward stroke, think of your upper shoulder as the engine driving your upper hand forward and your torso as the engine pulling the lower hand back. (Your arms connect this engine to the paddle, but they do not supply much power to the stroke.) Drive your left hand (upper hand) forward between forehead and shoulder, level with your left shoulder, and pull your right hand (lower hand) toward your right hip with an unwinding motion of your torso. Minimize any forward "punch" in your upper arm, and let your lower arm remain nearly straight throughout the power phase. When this stroke is done correctly, your blade will trace a straight path from your feet to your hips alongside the boat, and you'll feel a tug on your paddle blade throughout the stroke.

Recovery. Start the recovery by lifting your lower hand and slicing the blade out of the water just behind your hip. Notice how your left arm is extended and your left shoulder is rotated forward—that's the perfect position for starting a forward stroke on your left side.

The forward stroke begins with the reach and catch. Rotate your right arm and shoulder to wind up your torso, extend your reach, and plant the paddle blade near your feet. Keep the shaft fairly vertical and take a moment to feel it catch as it sinks into the water.

During the power phase, unwind your torso to supply energy to the stroke. Keep your lower arm fairly straight (this keeps the paddle's pivot point high toward the upper hand). By tracing a straight path from your feet to your hips alongside the boat you'll feel the tug on your paddle blade throughout the stroke.

The recovery phase starts by lifting your lower hand and slicing the blade out of the water just behind your hip. Notice how your left arm is now extended and your left shoulder is rotated forward.

You are now ready to reach and catch on your opposite side.

THE BACK STROKE

The back stroke is similar to a forward stroke—in reverse. It moves your kayak backward, which can buy you some extra time before paddling over a drop, and it can make some maneuvers easier to execute.

To start a back stroke, plant one blade just behind your hip (your lower hand will be near your hip) with the power face of the blade facing the stern. Now, *push* the blade toward the bow while pulling your upper hand toward your shoulder. Your lower arm will end up stretched forward, with your upper arm ending up near your shoulder.

To keep your back strokes smooth and powerful, remember the basics you learned in forward paddling: Wind and unwind your torso during each stroke; keep the paddle vertical; and don't let your hands cross your centerline. Also, just look over one shoulder—not over both—if you need to see behind you. That will help keep you from getting disoriented each time you swivel your head.

Advanced Strokes

There are infinite variations and combinations of the basic turning and power strokes. Some you'll just make up as you're running the river, others have a real identity and name.

Your first forward strokes are as likely to spin your kayak as to drive it forward. That happens to everybody—even top paddlers. However, the best kayakers know how to anticipate and counteract spins before they happen.

There can be many reasons why your kayak spins when you're forward paddling, but two common forward-paddling mistakes show up repeatedly: sweeping your paddle outward and paddling harder on one side than the other. If your kayak is turning with each forward stroke, you might be making one of these mistakes.

Remember how the forward sweep stroke worked? Your paddle traced an arc from bow to stern in order to make your boat turn. Well, the more your forward stroke resembles your sweep stroke, the more you'll turn. Keep your paddle vertical and moving parallel with the long axis of your kayak during the power phase of each

stroke, and you'll start paddling straighter than ever. Revert to those arcing sweeps only when you want to turn.

Paddling harder on one side of your kayak than the other is both common and curable. Watch which way your boat turns most often and be sensitive to the power you're exerting during each stroke. In time, your paddling power will balance out on both sides and your boat will start traveling straighter.

Once you work the basic kinks out of your forward stroke, begin to concentrate on a *smooth stroke* from start to finish. Make the end of one stroke the beginning of the next. You don't need to lean forward and backward to execute each stroke—the winding and unwinding of your torso will provide reach and power. As you put all of this together, you'll be on your way to smooth, efficient paddling!

To initiate the back stroke, plant the blade just behind your hip (your lower hand will be near your hip) with the power face facing the stern. Now, push the blade toward the bow while pulling your upper hand toward your shoulder. Your lower arm will end up stretched forward, while your upper arm will end up near your shoulder.

RUDDERING

Though it's not really a *stroke*, by planting the paddle blade vertically in the water near the stern and leaving it there, you can use the paddle the same way a sailor uses a rudder. Sounds easy, huh? Amazingly, most paddlers don't even come close to executing picture-perfect rudders.

Keep both hands on the same side of the boat (just like they were at the end of the forward sweep) with your back hand low. With the blade sliced vertically into the water near the stern of your boat, either pull the paddle toward the stern (like a stern draw) or push it away from the stern (like a stern pry).

THE DRAW TO THE HIP

Draw strokes are a tad tricky at first. They require a solid feel for blade angles, and they can flip you over if you're not paying attention. Fortunately, you don't even need draw strokes to get down easy rivers. Still, they're great strokes to know, and they'll become increasingly important as your overall skills develop.

> **"A** lot of beginners get frustrated right away with the fact that they can't paddle their boats in a straight line, especially when they're watching their instructors paddle straight. Whitewater kayaks are not designed to go in a straight line: they're actually designed so that when you're out on the river you will be mobile and able to avoid obstacles. Later on you'll appreciate that. Right now, just work on improving your forward stroke and you'll soon be paddling straight like the pros. **"**
>
> —JOHN "TREE" TRUJILLO
> 1992 WORLD MEDALIST

The *draw to the hip* (often called a *lateral draw stroke* or simply a *draw stroke*) is used to move your kayak sideways across the water toward the paddle blade. It's very useful in eddies, steep chutes, or narrow slots when a quick lateral adjustment is needed.

This is the proper position for a right-side rudder stroke. Note that the rear paddle blade is planted vertically near the stern, both hands are on the same side of the boat (similar to the position they were in at the end of the forward sweep), and the back hand is low near the water. From this position, you can pull the paddle toward the stern to turn the bow left or push it away from the stern to turn the bow right.

To start a draw stroke, plant one blade at a right angle to your kayak, even with your hip, with the power face facing the boat. Hold the shaft vertical by placing your top arm across your forehead and your bottom arm close to the side of the kayak (this is easier if you turn your torso to face your paddle). Now, execute the draw by pulling the blade in toward the kayak. Before the blade reaches your hip, twist your wrists inward to slice the blade away from the kayak or out of the water. (If the blade hits the side of the kayak, it might pull under and pop out of your hands.)

SCULLING DRAW

The *sculling draw*—or *feathering draw*—lets you move your kayak sideways for longer periods of time. The trick is getting used to slicing your paddle blade back and forth with correct blade angles while simultaneously pulling on the shaft. This takes a bit of finesse, but it will ultimately improve your boat control once you've mastered it.

Start the sculling draw by planting the blade slightly closer to the side of the boat than you would with an ordinary draw stroke. Next, twist the blade so that one edge angles out from the tube 20 to 30

The proper starting position for the draw to the hip (or the draw stroke). Note that the paddler's torso is rotated outward, the shaft is vertical, and his hands are placed one on top of the other.

degrees. Whichever edge is facing outward will become the *leading edge*. Slice the paddle a couple of feet in the direction of the leading edge while pulling on the shaft. The blade will want to travel away from your boat, but your pulling motion will pull the kayak toward the blade. At the end of the first slice, twist your wrists to reverse the blade angle, then slice it in the opposite direction. Keep changing the blade angle and direction while slicing the blade back and forth to keep the sculling draw going.

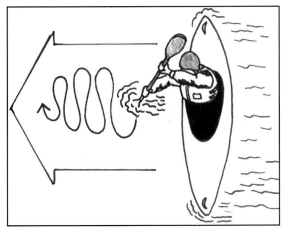

During a sculling draw, keep moving sideways by slicing your paddle back and forth while pulling the kayak toward your paddle. The blade's leading edge must be turned outward to supply the pulling pressure during this stroke.

THE DUFFEK STROKE

The *duffek stroke*—named after Czechoslovakian paddler Milo Duffek—is a fascinating blend of some techniques you have already learned. It may be more challenging to learn than other strokes, but it will let you turn faster and smoother than you ever dreamed possible.

Before practicing the duffek stroke, keep two new points in mind: First, your paddle blade *always stays to your front*—never behind; second, your *upper-arm position always stays low*—usually across your forehead, chin, or neck. (Letting your upper arm rise above your head invites shoulder dislocations.)

There are two ways to do a duffek stroke. Let's learn the *static duffek* first. Plant the blade as if you were doing a draw stroke, but plant it near the bow and turn the leading edge of the blade *outward* at a 45-degree angle (this is called an *open blade angle*). Your lower arm will be fully extended, your upper forearm horizontal across your forehead, and your upper wrist turned outward. As with the draw, both hands will be over the edge nearest the inside of the turn.

Practice planting the paddle in the static duffek position a couple of times with your kayak stationary. Once you learn what the plant feels like, first paddle forward, then plant the paddle again as just described. If you have done this correctly, you'll feel like a kid grabbing and spinning around a pole. Essentially, you're doing the same thing that you did when ruddering near the stern, except that now you're doing a *bow rudder*.

Once you have the static duffek down, you can experiment with blade angles and boat speeds. The more open your blade angle, the faster your turn, and vice versa. Once you're quite comfortable with the static duffek, you're ready for the *dynamic duffek*.

The dynamic duffek—also called a *bow draw*—starts as a draw stroke by your side, then travels

DOCTORING YOUR DUFFEKS

Duffek strokes take time and practice to perfect. When practicing, look at your paddle shaft: If it isn't vertical, reach farther across your forehead with your upper arm. Next, check out your blade angle: If you don't open your blade angle enough, it may slam into the side of the boat and throw you off balance. On the other hand, if you turn your blade out 90 degrees from your boat, it will act like a brake instead of a rudder. Practice your duffek strokes slowly at first, setting a 45-degree blade angle each time. As your confidence and ability grow, you can modify your blade angles and add speed to your turns.

diagonally toward the bow. If you froze the stroke midway, it would look like the static duffek already pictured, but the dynamic duffek calls for more paddle movement. You simultaneously slice and pull the blade toward the bow with a slightly open blade

angle (just like the starting position for the static duffek). As the blade travels diagonally toward the bow, the bow turns toward the blade. Again, you can experiment with different blade angles and boat speeds to adjust your turns.

The duffek stroke—which follows a C path from plant to recovery—provides a great way to make fast, powerful turns. Note that the blade is planted near the bow

(similar to a draw stroke near the bow), but that it turns into a forward stroke as it nears your hip.

4

Bracing

When You Need a Paddle to Lean On

Once you start paddling whitewater, you'll become addicted to the feeling of water on your face. Your first big surprise, though, will come when your face ends up in the water. Flips and swims happen to everybody sooner or later, but there are techniques that will lower your chances of getting dunked. These techniques are called *braces* (or *recovery strokes*) and *rolls*. They turn your paddle into a sort of outrigger, provide support when the river threatens to upset your kayak, and give you a way to flip upright when the river nearly flips you upside down.

As we discuss braces, think of your paddle blades as water skis: When they're sitting still, they sink easily and can't hold you up, but when they're moving they'll plane along the water's surface and offer incredible support. As long as the forward edge of the ski or paddle blade is kept at a climbing angle, you'll get lift; let it dive and you'll dive, too.

The easiest way to experience this concept is to walk out into some waist-deep water and skim one paddle blade across the surface while pressing down on the shaft. (Remember to keep the leading edge at a climbing angle to keep the blade skimming.) As your technique improves, lean harder on the shaft, or experiment starting with the blade beneath the surface. It's amazing how much pressure your paddle can take before the blade starts to sink.

You can do the same thing in your kayak by setting the blade at a climbing angle while doing a

> "I'm actually an anti-bracer as far as teaching. I am more into aggressively paddling with a purpose. The idea is that my strokes are propelling me where I want to go and are giving me some support if I am a little bit off balance. Bracing means that I have actually taken my weight off the top of my boat and have to recover it. It may also mean that I'm not on line, that I'm missing my target, and that I've had to rely on a recovery stroke as opposed to relying on aggressive, positive strokes and goals. So, the more I can paddle, be over my boat, and aggressively paddle toward my goal, the less the chance of me using a brace."
>
> **—SHANE BENEDICT**
> **KAYAK DESIGNER/INSTRUCTOR**

forward sweep stroke. Tip your kayak slightly to one side, then sweep your blade on that same side while pushing down. Provided you keep the blade at a climbing angle, you'll get some forward movement along with a lot of support from your paddle.

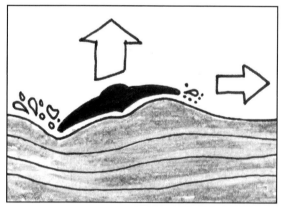

The key to braces is to keep your blade at a climbing angle. This helps keep the blade at or near the surface and provides a lot of upward lift.

Low Brace

The *low brace* often is the first choice for restabilizing your boat. It is a very stable brace that is used more for stability than recovery, and it can be used for resting in holes, practicing eddy turns, or regaining your balance in rapids.

The low-brace position starts with your paddle just above the deck of your kayak, with your elbows high. From this position, you can *slap* the non-power face (the backside) of the blade on the water and move it on the surface for stability (remember to keep the leading edge of the blade climbing toward the surface). At the same time that you slap the water, pull the hip and knee nearest the bracing blade up while pushing your opposite butt cheek down, and force your shoulder down over the bracing hand. Resist the urge to pull your head and shoulders away from your bracing hand—by keeping the shoulder nearest the bracing blade over your bracing hand you will maximize your leverage on the paddle.

Bracing offers stability in an unstable environment.

The low-brace position starts with your paddle just above the deck of your kayak, with your elbows high.

From this position, you can slap the non-power face (the backside) of the blade on the water and move it on the surface for stability.

At the same time that you slap the water, pull the hip and knee nearest the bracing blade up while pushing your opposite butt cheek down, and force your shoulder down over the bracing hand. Resist the urge to pull your head and shoulders away from your bracing hand.

High Brace

The *high brace* is a powerful recovery stroke. It can be used in rapids or in holes—anywhere that you need to keep from flipping. It is used more often than low braces, but it can be a real shoulder tweaker if done incorrectly.

The high-brace position places the paddle higher than in the low-brace position and it puts the power face down on the water. You can find this position by first resting the paddle across the deck in front of you, then flexing your elbows to bring the paddle to your chest. Now, extend the paddle out to one side of your kayak and rotate your control wrist back to turn the power face toward the river surface.

Once again, brace by slapping or pushing down on the water with your paddle, moving your paddle to keep it on the surface, and lifting the hip and knee near the side you're bracing. Your head relaxes and

GET YOUR BODY INVOLVED

Your hips, knees, and head complement your paddle in every brace. If you have great balance, you'll hardly need your paddle for anything more than momentary support when bracing. Still, your hips, knees, and head can help increase the mechanical advantage on the paddle blade and bring your kayak back to a balanced position.

You do this by lifting the hip and knee on the side you're flipping toward and driving the opposite hip and knee downward. Remember your J-leans? You're trying to restore them here and get back into paddling position. At the same time you're bringing up the brace-side hip and knee, you let your head drop toward the brace-side shoulder. Confused? Just think of pulling your ear, hip, and knee together with a rubber band on the side you're lifting, then sliding your head back upright once you've regained your balance.

drops toward your brace so that your boat can rotate upright as you execute the brace.

To maximize the power of the high brace, keep your upper hand lower than your chin and your elbows close to your body. Keeping your high brace low and in front of you helps put the blade flat on the water and helps prevent shoulder injuries.

Sculling Brace

The *sculling brace* (also called a *sweeping brace*) is bracing's equivalent of the sculling draw. It works by constantly changing the blade angle and by sweeping the blade back and forth. If you're paddling well, you'll never need it—in fact, you should try to avoid ever having to use it—but it does make for an interesting pool trick and it's something to think about if you just want to lay one ear in the water for a while.

To execute a sculling brace, set one blade on the water in either the low- or high-brace position at right angles to your boat (you'll need the high brace if you want to lean over and get that ear wet). Angle the blade so that the leading edge is climbing, then sweep the blade in that direction. (If you're right handed, it may be easier to relax your right grip and guide the blade angle with your left

The high-brace position places the paddle higher than the low-brace position and puts the power face down on the water. You can find this position by first resting the paddle across the deck in front of you, then flexing your elbows to bring the paddle to your chest. Now, extend the paddle out to one side of the kayak and rotate your control wrist back to turn the power face toward the river's surface.

Brace by slapping or pushing down on the water with your paddle, keeping it on the surface, and lifting the hip and knee near the side you're bracing.

hand when working on your left side.) After sliding the blade a foot or two, reverse the blade angle and sweep the blade in the opposite direction. Keep practicing this motion, sweeping the blade back and forth, until you can press down on the shaft while keeping the blade on the water's surface. The better you become at this, the longer you can keep yourself from flipping over.

Your head relaxes and drops toward your brace so that your boat can rotate upright as you execute the brace. To maximize the power of the high brace, keep your upper hand lower than your chin and your elbows close to your body. Keeping your high brace low and in front of you helps put the blade flat on the water and helps prevent shoulder injuries.

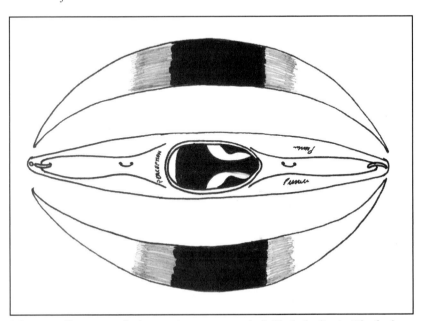

The most effective area for bracing is nearest your body (dark shading). *The farther your brace moves away from your body the less effective it becomes* (gray shading).

5

The Eskimo Roll and Beyond

Despite our amphibious tendencies, we are still land animals, firmly entrenched in our terrestrial ways and forever compelled to breathe clean, fresh air. That makes upside-down kayaking a bit of a challenge. Fortunately, Eskimos figured this stuff out many centuries ago and devised a remarkable technique for righting a capsized kayak: the Eskimo roll.

Rolling is a mandatory skill for any whitewater kayaker. It not only provides a means for safely recovering from upsets, it vastly enhances your whitewater experience by allowing you to play in holes and on waves without fear of swimming. Many people look at the roll as some sort of mystical art handed down in veils of secrecy and bestowed upon only the best paddlers.

Actually, the roll is remarkably easy—as long as you're willing to take the time to learn the techniques correctly. It combines much of the knowledge you already have, especially bracing techniques, and adds a few extra building blocks to complete the rolling package.

Whatever you do, *learn to roll from a qualified instructor.* Instructors can help you learn to roll more quickly by correcting defects in your style and technique, provide physical support so you avoid expending too much energy doing wet exits, and can help you avoid some of the injuries that could take place if you roll improperly.

The easiest place to learn the roll is in a warm pool or in a clear, shallow pond. By practicing rolls in a pool, you will have a familiar, safe environment that won't mess with your psyche, and you'll have built-in tools for practicing techniques such as the hip snap.

The Hip Snap and Eskimo Rescue

There are some challenging aspects of learning to roll. Much of the rolling technique is done with your body underwater, so you must think three dimensionally instead of two dimensionally, and it is easy to place too much emphasis on the negative upper body movements that detract from your roll. So, we need to instill some confidence in your ability to re-right your kayak by practicing *hip snaps* and *Eskimo rescues* first.

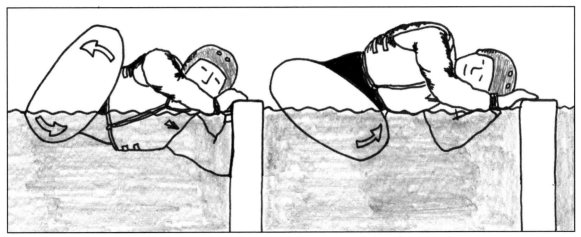

The hip snap aids in righting your boat in braces and rolls. Shown here at the side of a pool, the kayaker starts with his boat flopped nearly upside down (left). He then snaps his hips by relaxing his right knee and lifting his left knee using the muscles in his torso, hips, and thigh. Note that his head stays low and his arms are relaxed throughout the motion.

THE HIP SNAP

To learn the *hip snap*, place your hands near the water on a kick board, on the bow of a friend's boat, on a pool wall, or in an instructor's hands. Next, lay your head near your hands with your ear touching the water. While leaving your head at water level, roll your boat upside down and right side up using your knees, hip, and waist muscles. (Don't let go of whatever you're holding onto!) As you become more comfortable, leave your face in the water and continue practicing this boat-righting technique until it becomes swift and effortless.

As you practice the hip snap, concentrate on the location of your boat. Use your abdominal muscles to prevent it from swinging wildly and try to keep the bow pointed slightly toward the pool wall. Also, decrease the pressure on your hands as your ability to right the boat increases. Gradually, you should be able to right the boat with very little pressure on your hands at all.

THE ESKIMO RESCUE

Once you master the hip snap, you can practice the technique by placing your hands on the bow of a friend's boat. Again, keep your head on the water and near your hands, and use your hips, knees, and abdominal muscles to right your boat—don't use your arms. If you press too hard on your hands or lift your head during the hip snap, your friend's bow will sink, signaling poor technique.

After mastering this first part of the Eskimo rescue, try holding your friend's bow with just one hand. Completely submerge your head and body. Once you're in this position, you can reach and place your second hand on your friend's bow, bring your head up to your hands, and finish righting your boat with a solid hip snap. Try this slowly at first, and strive for smooth, fluid motions. Think of pulling your knee toward your head during the hip snap, and leave your head near the surface of the water until your boat nearly completes its upright rotation.

To perfect the Eskimo rescue, flip completely upside down without holding your friend's boat at all. Signal your rescue call by leaning forward onto your front deck, reaching out of the water around the sides of your hull, and slapping the bottom of the hull with both hands. Stay relaxed and move your hands forward and backward so that you'll feel your friend's bow pull into position. As your friend paddles toward your hands to present his bow, grab the bow and right your boat using the techniques you just learned.

The Eskimo rescue is a great technique for pool sessions. If you have to use it on the river, try to hold your paddle with one hand while using the other to complete the rescue. This will require you to learn how to snap your hips and execute Eskimo rescues on both sides of your boat, so practice to get a jump start on your rescue techniques.

Bang on the bottom of your boat to call for an eskimo rescue.

Elements of the Eskimo Roll

There are many ways to roll a kayak. We'll discuss the two main methods of rolling—the *C-to-C roll* and the *sweep roll*—and briefly touch upon other rolls, such as *reverse-sweep rolls* and *hand rolls*. Fortunately, these rolls have three things in common: the *setup*, the *sweep*, and the *hip snap/recovery*. These elements appear in the same sequence during every roll. So, as you learn about each roll, look for the setup, sweep and hip snap/recovery phases, and see how they make each roll work.

The setup position for a left-side C-to-C or sweep roll. The kayaker's face is down on the deck, and the paddle is parallel with the edge of the boat, power face up. Place your hands on the left side of the boat for a right-side roll.

THE C-TO-C ROLL

The *C-to-C roll* is named after the two arcs your body carves as you proceed through the roll: one horizontal arc from your bow out 90 degrees to your side, and a second vertical arc from an upside-down to a rightside-up position. Many instructors teach the C-to-C roll first because it is

The setup for the C-to-C roll. Note that the paddle is entirely above the water and that the paddler is bent forward onto the front deck of the kayak.

The first C: The front blade (the blade nearest the bow) has been swept out at a right angle from the boat and is still on top of the water. The kayaker's back arm has wrapped up and over the hull to give him space to maneuver.

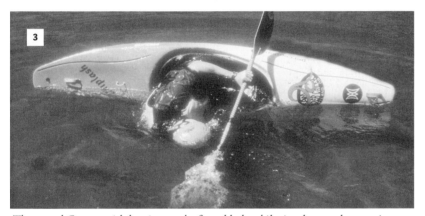

The second C starts with bracing on the front blade while simultaneously executing a hip snap to right the boat. The kayaker is using his hips, knees, and abdominal muscles (not his arms) to right the boat, and he's keeping his head low and relaxed. Also note that his left arm is tucked close to his body to prevent shoulder injuries.

The ending position for a C-to-C roll.

easy to teach, easy to learn, and leaves you in a protected position when upside down.

The setup. The setup for the C-to-C roll puts your head and torso in the same position you used in Eskimo rescues and wet exits, but adds some arm-position changes to accommodate your paddle. Start the setup by tucking your face down onto the deck and placing your paddle parallel along the left edge of the boat, power face up. (This sets you up for a right-side roll, where your body will emerge on the right side of your boat; a left-handed paddler can place the paddle on the right side of the boat to set up, and roll up on the left side.) With your right arm positioned in front of your head, your nose on the deck, and your paddle properly in place, you are ready to flip upside down in the setup position.

The sweep. Hold the setup position momentarily, feeling which torso muscles it takes to keep you in a protected position. Then, once you have your bearings, sweep your front blade (the blade nearest the bow) out at a right angle from your boat. Keep that front blade on top of the water, sweeping with a climbing angle, and your front hand as high and dry as possible. As your front blade sweeps into position 90 degrees from your boat, your back arm will need to wrap up and over the hull to give you space to maneuver. Keep in mind that the C-to-C sweep is not necessarily used to right yourself (as it will be in the sweep roll), but a poor sweep now will make the hip snap/recovery phase very difficult. So, have your instructor guide you through the sweep motion repeatedly until it begins to feel comfortable and familiar, then try it on your own. If your blade dives during the sweep, you probably have it set at a diving angle (cock your wrists downward more) or you failed to start with your blade on the surface (reach higher during the setup). Again, patience and practice make perfect. You have now completed the first C in the C-to-C roll.

The hip snap/recovery. With your front blade at a right angle to the boat, start the second C by bracing on the front blade while simultaneously executing a hip snap to right the boat. Remember all the keys to the hip snap and Eskimo rescue here: Use your hips, knees, and abs, not your arms, to right the boat; keep your head low and relaxed until your boat has righted itself; and try to be fluid and graceful in your motions. Also, keep your left arm (for right-side rolls) tucked close to your body to prevent shoulder injuries.

Instructors can help you through the final C motion, letting you work on muscle memory and correct technique before trying the full C-to-C roll on your own. Pay close attention to your instructor's guidance and you'll advance quickly.

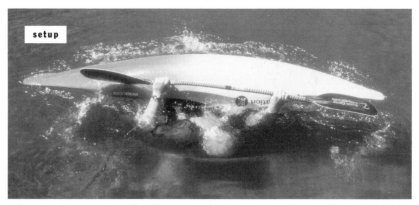

The setup for the sweep roll is the same as for the C-to-C roll. Note that the paddle is entirely above the water and that the paddler is bent forward onto the front deck.

In the sweep roll, the hip snap begins just after the sweep has begun. The active blade must be kept at a climbing angle so it stays on the surface during the sweep.

The Sweep Roll

Sweep rolls are remarkably similar to C-to-C rolls, but they are a bit easier for stiff, inflexible paddlers to execute. The only real difference between the sweep roll and the C-to-C roll is the timing of the hip snap. Here, the hip snap begins just after the sweep has begun. One perceived disadvantage of this roll is that it leaves you temporarily exposed to rocks and subsurface obstacles.

The Extended-Paddle Roll

The best way to learn to roll is the right way. Want to ride a bike? You must learn to balance on two wheels. Having trouble balancing? Try training wheels.

The *extended-paddle roll* is not a type of roll, it's a

> 2

Still sweeping the paddle, the kayaker is now executing a hip snap to right the boat, again using hips, knees, and abs to right his boat, his head low and relaxed. Again note that his left arm is tucked close to his body to prevent shoulder injuries.

> 3

The final position for the sweep roll.

training wheel for kayakers—a crutch to get you through the hard times but a liability if you stick with it. Just as you wouldn't keep your training wheels on your bike, you must learn to avoid extended-paddle rolls. (That's why many instructors won't even teach it to their students and the reason why I hid it back here after the roll discussions.) On the other hand, it adds leverage to C-to-C and sweep rolls by letting paddlers *choke up* on their paddle shafts, and it

may make the difference between successful rolls and swims early in the game.

To execute extended-paddle rolls, scoot the paddle forward in your hands so that your back hand nestles on the shaft right against the back blade. (For an even longer extended-paddle roll, you can grasp the back blade with your back hand, keeping your thumb outside and away from the boat, and your fingers inside the blade and nearer the boat.) This not only lets you feel your blade orientation more easily, it juts the front blade farther out, making it easier to keep it on the surface and to brace against.

Extended-paddle rolls make for great campfire debate. Some instructors like extended-paddle rolls because they're easier for students to learn; some despise them because they imprint a technique that is less than optimal (just think how much time you'll spend underwater adjusting your

One way to set up for an extended-paddle roll.

hands on the paddle shaft). Whether you're into extended-paddle rolls or not, take time to learn the C-to-C and sweep rolls the *right way* and your extended-paddle rolls will fade into the past.

The Reverse-Sweep Roll

The *reverse-sweep roll*—which goes by other names such as the *back-deck roll*, *back roll* and *rodeo roll*—is particularly useful when you're pasted against your back deck, and it teaches you how to roll when playboating. On the other hand, it exposes your shoulders to injuries. If you're going to try this roll—and you should—make sure you keep your elbows in close or risk dislocations!

To set up for the reverse-sweep roll, lean back onto the rear deck and point your sweeping blade toward the stern. Keep the shaft parallel to your boat and right in front of your face, and turn the power face of the sweeping blade down. From this position, flip upside down, get your bearings, then simultaneously sweep your torso and paddle forward while righting your boat with a low brace.

This motion is going to feel really strange at first. The boat interferes with the

setup

Reverse-sweep rolls—sometimes called rodeo rolls or back-deck rolls—come in handy on occasion but expose paddlers to shoulder injuries. To set up for the reverse-sweep roll, lean back onto the rear deck, and point your sweeping blade toward the stern. Keep the shaft parallel with your boat and right in front of your face, and turn the power face of the sweeping blade down.

From the setup position, flip upside down, get your bearings, then simultaneously sweep your torso and paddle while righting your boat with a low brace.

The ending position for the reverse-sweep roll.

"For river running and playboating, it's best to be able to roll up no matter what position you are in. Sometimes taking the time to actually lean forward, set up, sweep, and roll takes too long and you run into a rock or flush out of the hole you were playing in. So, I think you need to be able to automatically roll up instinctively from any position. In a hole, for example, it seems like you often roll when you're on your back deck because if you're leaning forward you're usually balanced and upright. Also, you can just go with the flow of the water and come up automatically in holes. All of this takes time to develop, but it really helps later on. **"**

—DUSTIN KNAPP
RIVER EXPLORER/VIDEOGRAPHER

roll and everything seems to be backwards. But, once you understand the dynamics of the C-to-C and sweep rolls, you will be able to feel what changes you need to make to your reverse-sweep roll so that it works on the river. If you perfect it in controlled situations, it may surprise you how well it works when rolling in a hole.

Offside Rolls

What? Another roll? Not really. *Offside rolls* are just normal rolls on the opposite side of the boat. In theory, you shouldn't even have an offside roll: You should be equally adept at rolling on both sides of your boat. In practice, though, many kayakers roll better on one side than on the other.

Let's say you're a right hander with a preference for coming up on the right side. You know how to do a right-side roll. Your offside roll—a left-side roll—starts with a setup on the right side of the boat so you can come up on the left side. The whole offside rolling motion will feel weird at first because you have already ingrained a series of motions suited only to the onside of your boat. Also, the feathering (or offset) of your paddle blades will make the paddle respond differently during an offside roll. You'll have to cock your wrists very little at the setup and rotate them upward toward the end of the roll.

Practice offside rolls frequently and make sure you have them down. They'll come in handy when your onside roll isn't working, and they can save you from swimming time and time again.

The Hand Roll

Ah, yes. The Holy Grail of rolls. The roll that impresses all the newcomers at the local paddle pool. The only roll that'll save your butt should you ever lose your paddle in the middle of a rapid!

Hand rolls can be executed in a variety of ways. Here, the kayaker starts with his body and hands near the surface and his hands close together (left). From this position, he can develop the downward hand pressure needed to initiate the roll. As he pushes down on his hands, he simultaneously executes a strong hip snap to flip the kayak upright while shifting his upper body low across the deck (center). To finish the roll and regain balance, he throws his left arm across the deck to the opposite side of the boat (right).

The *hand roll* is not nearly as mysterious as it sounds. In fact, you practically know it already. Remember those hip-snap sessions on the side of the pool? Those were hand rolls with some cement for support! Eskimo rescues? Hand rolls with a boat bow for support!

There are many ways to hand roll, but many paddlers find it easiest to let their body float up on their preferred rolling side, locking their thumbs together to form a big, webbed fin out of both hands, then slapping the water with the cupped hands while simultaneously executing a hip snap.

Any defects in your body position or hip snap will become readily apparent in your hand roll. If your head comes up too fast, you'll sink; if your hip snap is lame, you'll never hit your roll. Fortunately, you can borrow a friend's bow again, practice with your hands on a life jacket, or go back to the side of a pool to work out these kinks. Then keep practicing your hand roll until you have it down pat.

6

The Dynamics of Running Water

River Morphology

To the ordinary landlubber, whitewater rapids are a primal source of fascination. Flowing like unbridled liquid avalanches, rapids are breathtaking in their beauty yet awe inspiring in their power.

To an experienced river runner, though, rapids are predictable and orderly. Obstacles, constrictions, and changes in volume and gradient have definite and reliable effects on the river's character. The seasoned paddler understands these effects intimately and can anticipate how currents and rapids will affect a kayak.

In this chapter we will disassemble and examine rivers. Rather than looking at the big picture, we'll dissect rapids into tangible components, like pieces of a puzzle. Then, once we've gained an understanding of how the pieces work and fit together, we'll reassemble the puzzle and form complete rapids—much like the ones you'll see on your next river trip.

A Look beneath the Surface

Kayaks were designed to float on the river's surface. And, if you're doing things right, you'll spend most of your time there. But the surface is just the skin of the aquatic beast, the face of the river. Smooth or twisted, supple or furrowed, it tells you a lot about what's going on *inside* the stream.

Some paddlers spend years on the river without ever learning to see beyond the river's surface or grasping a full understanding of river morphology. But learning this stuff is not only easy, it helps you tie the whole river package together—from the surface to the river bottom—and to understand it as a single, fascinating unit.

WATER MECHANICS

Ask average river runners how water moves and in what state, and they're likely to respond, "It moves downstream in West Virginia." Well, yeah, that's a correct response. But ask hydrologists about water movements and they'll mention three very different states: *laminar*, *turbulent*, and *chaotic*. Each state describes a different pattern of currents and each appears at different places within the river system.

Laminar flow

For many kayakers, *laminar flow* is the most comfortable type of current to experience, for it is the most safe and predictable. Laminar flows show up on smooth, straight riverbeds where, if we sliced the river from bank to bank, we would find some distinct patterns. As the diagrams illustrate, rivers have multiple sheets of water, each moving at a different speed. The small circles and long arrows represent the fastest moving sheets—located near the center of the river below the surface. Large circles and short arrows represent slower sheets, their downstream progress hampered by friction from the riverbed, banks, or air. Between each sheet there's a zone of mild shearing, better described as an interface between two laminar sheets moving independently and at different speeds.

To feel the differences between laminar sheets, let your kayak float freely on the main current. If you plant your paddle deep in the river, you will feel a forward tug. That tug is caused by subsurface laminar sheets moving forward faster than the sheets on the surface. If you've ever exited your kayak in a big, powerful river, you may have experienced a *tunnel effect*, as if you were trapped inside a giant horizontal tube that wouldn't let you go. That's because the core of the river (just below the surface) is an independent laminar sheet totally separated from its surrounding sheets. Once you are in the tunnel, the shear zones hold you inside until your life jacket finally propels you back toward the surface.

Turbulent flow

Turbulent flows arise wherever obstacles obstruct the current. An obstruction forces too much water into too little space, which in turn forces one laminar sheet into another. When this happens, the laminar sheets begin to break up, leaving smaller ribbons of

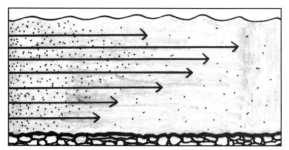

Laminar currents are fastest just beneath the surface and slowest near the river bed. The longer arrows designate the fastest water.

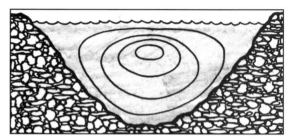

Laminar currents slow as they drag against the bank. The smaller circles designate the fastest currents.

current that seek their way independently through the neighboring currents.

Kayakers should look for turbulence at places like *chutes*, where the independent ribbons slip free and create ripples or waves on the river surface. Turbulence also appears in *eddies*, where an obstacle compresses the laminar sheets together as they slip around the obstacle. The turbulent zone is created behind the rock where the laminar sheets break up. The zone of turbulence (the eddy) is separated from the passing laminar sheets (the main current) by an abrupt boundary kayakers call an *eddy line*.

Chaos

At the extreme end of water-behavior patterns—just as with many kayakers' behavior patterns—there is *chaos*. Simply put, chaos is a state of utter confusion: The river's normal flow lines disintegrate and bounce around randomly. Interestingly, this commotion cancels itself out, leaving little real movement of water at all. Probably the best example of chaos is the ordi-

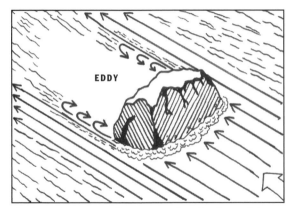

As the main current slips past an obstacle, the straight lines (laminar currents) shear off and rotate behind the obstacle (turbulent currents). In this example, the result is an eddy.

nary *hole* (discussed later in this chapter): At the base of a steep slide (like at the back of a rock or ledge) too little water tries to fill too large a space and thus settles on trying to be everywhere at once—chaos. Though the water explodes randomly throughout the hole, the water in the hole itself ends up being stationary.

Helical currents

Within any river, other universal patterns emerge. *Helical currents* flow outward from the bank along the surface until they collide with the main current. There they spiral downstream, dive and work their way back toward the bank under the surface. (If you have ever swum a river, you may have noticed that the last few feet to the shore seemed harder to swim than anything else. That's because helical currents were pushing you away from the bank, out toward the center of the river.)

Meanders

In the main current you'll find *horizontal* and *vertical meanders*. In horizontal meanders, the main current weaves back and forth across the river, trying to make one complete trip from bank to bank and back again in a distance equal to 11 times the channel width. In vertical meanders, the main current climbs from deep pools to shallow riffles and back again at a rate equal to 3 to 7 times the channel width.

Since meanders can be confusing, a couple of examples are in order. Let's start off with horizontal meanders. First, pick a bend in the river. Next, measure the river's width and multiply it by 11. Now, if you proceed downstream that distance, you would theoretically find another bend in the river where the current completes a horizontal meander. For vertical meanders, measure the distance across the river at a pool, multiply by 3 to 7, float that distance downstream, and—*voilà*—another pool. (Now, before you go try out these experiments, I've got to add a caveat: Currents don't always get their way. Banks are constantly eroding and rerouting the main channel. So it's a constant battle between the hydrodynamics of water and the impediments of new boulders.)

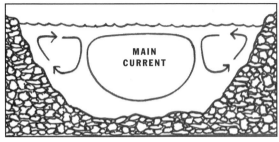

Helical currents flow away from the bank on the surface, meet the main current, then dive. Next, they work their way back to the bank and rise to repeat the cycle. Finally, helical currents corkscrew their way downstream along the banks, repeating this process over and over again.

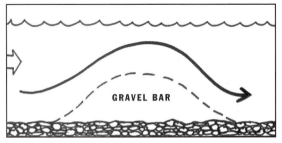

Vertical meanders rise and descend as water flows downstream. This cycle can eventually create shallow gravel bars and deep pools.

So, what does all of this scientific mumbo-jumbo mean for river runners? Well, each of these well-defined properties influences the shape and feel of rivers in ways that kayakers can see and understand. For example, the forces that determine the river's meander route cause it to lean against any bank that gets in its way. As the river continues to lean on that bank, the water's erosive power gradually carves out a new bend. Next, something different happens: Since water only travels in a linear course, the current piles up on the outside of the bend, where it has to travel faster than the water on the inside of the bend in order to reach the same point downstream. At the same time, the outer flow hits the bank, dives, and creeps along the bottom toward the slower currents at the inside of the bend.

The net effect of all this activity is that the fast-moving water on the outside of the bend keeps acquiring erosive power, continues to gnaw at the outer bank, and slowly pulls part of the bank into the current. At the same time, the slow water along the inside of the bend loses its ability to support the eroded particulates and deposits them on shallow bars. If the process continues, deeply undercut cliffs, exposed roots, and overhanging trees begin to appear along the outside of the bend, while the inside bend becomes increasingly shallow.

River Characteristics

Rivers outwardly display a broad range of emotions—at times calm and soothing, at other times an-gry and riotous. But inwardly, rivers are lazy by nature. Water can be compared to a train running lazily along a track. It just keeps rolling in the same direction unless something comes along and knocks it off course. Water, just like a train, follows a path of least resistance as it is pulled downhill by its natural engine—gravity. So, why do *rivers* and *rapids* look so different from each other?

There is much more to whitewater rivers than water's natural tendency to follow a course of least resistance. Obstacles clutter river channels, riverbeds descend at different rates, and water levels fluctuate with seasonal rains, snowmelt, or droughts. In the end, three factors have a profound effect on the intensity and character of whitewater rivers: *volume*, *gradient*, and *changes in river structure*.

VOLUME

River volume is measured in cubic units per second. In the United States, the foot is used for the cubic unit, and the correct term is *cubic feet per second*, or *cfs*. (In most other countries, the meter is used in place of the foot, so river volumes are measured in *cubic meters per second*, or *cms*.) Simply stated, cfs and cms measure the volume of water that passes a specific point each second. The proper formula is the river's width times its depth times the current's velocity. Using this formula, you can see that adding more water to a given channel—say from a recent rain or from a tributary swollen with snowmelt—increases the speed of the current dramatically.

Changes in volume or velocity have some important effects that kayakers need to understand. Since water is *heavy*—8.33 pounds per gallon, or 62.4 pounds per cubic foot—the addition of a few cubic units or an increase in velocity causes a big change in the amount of force that water exerts on a kayak or swimmer.

Let's look at this by slicing a long rod of water one foot wide

Horizontal meanders work back and forth across the river, continually pressing against the outside bank. Left to its own accord, the meander will erode the outside bank until the riverbed matches the serpentine shape of the meander.

by one foot high out of the river. Make that rod the same length as the river's flow in cfs. (For example, if the river is flowing at 1,000 cfs, make the rod one square foot wide by 1,000 feet long.) Now, the weight of that long pillar of water flowing past a designated point in the river doesn't have a force of just 62.4 pounds—it is backed by the force of 1,000 cubes of water, or *62,400 pounds!* Fortunately, the fluid property of water lets much of that force slide around a kayak, rock, or body unnoticed. However, a kayak (or a swimmer) held in place against the main current— say, during a *broach*—can prove just how powerful and heavy the river really is. The broached kayak is held tight by hundreds of pounds of pressure, making it very difficult to remove.

Up until now, we've assumed that rivers move downstream at a constant rate of speed. However, as you'll discover, rivers flow *upstream* in places and at *differing speeds* within the same section of river. In an eddy, reverse currents can flow upstream toward an obstacle just as fast as the main current's downstream velocity. This makes the velocity differential between the two currents as much as *double* that of the main current and creates powerful *rotational* or *twisting* forces. Kayakers caught on the interface between the currents have to fight the current's desire to spin their kayaks wildly. Rotational forces also are found where fast and slow currents meet: As the faster currents pass the slower currents, friction

MORE ON VELOCITY

A change in velocity—whether from an increase in gradient, a narrowing of the river channel, or an increase in volume—changes the river's force dramatically. It works like this: For every doubling of the current's velocity, the force exerted by the water quadruples. This added force can exert itself on anything in the water's path, or it can be used to support debris suspended in the river's current. That is why flooded rivers can lift and displace giant boulders or transport giant logs like overgrown corks.

pulls pieces of both currents free and causes them to rotate. The interface between the two currents is not as dramatic as those found in eddies, but it's still strong enough to spin your kayak around unless you fight to keep it straight.

RIVER SIZE
Without even looking at a river up close, kayakers can get some idea how *big* a river is by looking at its average flow. In a very general terms, rivers can be categorized as small, medium, or large. Small rivers can range from a few hundred cfs up to about 1,000 cfs; medium-sized rivers can range from 1,000 to 6,000 cfs; and some large rivers can exceed 100,000 cfs. Still, this description is pretty subjective: One kayaker's *small* may be another kayaker's *big* depending on point of view. Also, rivers grow and shrink in size and power with seasonal water fluctuations or dam releases.

GAUGES
Many governmental agencies monitor river flows. Kayakers can obtain water-level information by finding out which agency monitors the rivers they plan to run and asking that agency for the information. If

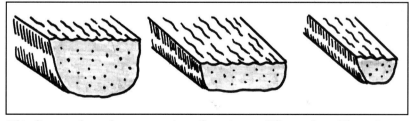

This diagram shows three cross sections of one river at different places. The section on the left is broad, deep, and slow. The center section is the same width, but shallower, forcing the current to move faster. Finally, the section on the right is both shallow and narrow, forcing the current to move the fastest.

you're not quite sure which agency to contact, check out the guidebooks in the Appendix—many list the phone numbers.

One problem I've run into with gauges is that many agencies monitor water levels on a *gauge-height* basis. Rather than indicating the flow in cfs or cms, you'll get a gauge height in feet or meters. All this information tells you is how high a river has climbed up an oversized ruler placed in the river at a location. To use this information you'll have to know the river intimately or ask someone to correlate the gauge height with river flow. Many guidebooks explain how to do this, but the correlations between the gauge height and actual water levels can change frequently. Just beware, rely on good judgment, and get the most up-to-date information available.

FLOW VERSUS DIFFICULTY

Trying to correlate changes in water volume uniformly with the river's difficulty rating is nearly impossible. On most rivers, rapids become more difficult as water levels rise, while rapids disappear beneath gentle blankets of swift water on other rivers. Nonetheless, kayakers should remember that larger volumes and faster currents bolster the river's power and can turn gentle rivers into powerful hazards.

GRADIENT

In North America, gradient is described in *feet per mile* (fpm) or *meters per kilometer* (mpk). Both ratings measure a river's average descent over a given distance.

To determine a river's gradient you will need to know three things: the *elevation at the put in*, the *elevation at the take out*, and the *distance between the two points*. Here's an example of how these numbers work: If the put in is at 3,000 feet elevation and the take out is at 1,200 feet, the river drops 1,800 feet in that section. If the section to be kayaked is 36 miles long, the river drops 50 feet per mile. (1,800/36 = 50). (Put-in elevation – take-out elevation) / distance in miles = gradient. The same formula works with metric numbers—just use meters

California's Dry Meadow Creek provides a dramatic example of a pool-drop river. Note the kayaker in the middle drop! (Photo by Scott Harding)

for the elevations and kilometers for distances to obtain the gradient in meters per kilometer.)

Rapids appear where the gradient of one section of river exceeds the river's average gradient, and *pools* form where the gradient dips below the overall average. So, if a river descends evenly over its entire length, the rapids might be long and constant. But if the river alternates between pools and drops, the rapids might be short but intense. The most severe example of a *pool-drop river* would be one that descends very little in its placid stretches, then plunges violently over giant waterfalls.

As with the other descriptive factors, gradient gives you some clues about the character of a river. Most whitewater rivers have an average gradient of 10 to 100 feet per mile. However, it is becoming quite common to see expert kayakers boating rivers with gradients upward of 200 to 300 feet per mile. Still, one rule of thumb should be kept in mind, especially when exploring new rivers: *The steeper the river, the more difficult the whitewater.*

Surface Features

River structures are seldom uniform. Riverbeds descend more steeply in some places than others, cliffs narrow and confine channels, and obstacles clutter and obstruct the main current. Each of these structural changes has profound effects on the river, some of which we have already discussed: If the same amount of water is forced into a smaller space (say, between two cliffs), its velocity will increase dramatically; if the main current descends down a steep slide, the gentle laminar currents will gradually give way to turbulence or chaos; and if the river travels around a bend, the currents along the outer banks will move faster than those along the inside of the bends.

Since kayakers like to spend most of their time above the river's surface (after all, a majority of kayakers rate their whitewater success in terms of avoiding submarine misadventures and close encounters with aquatic creatures), it is the *surface* effects of changes in river structure that we are most

interested in. So, let's step away from the river, scramble to a point high up on the bank, and look at the river's surface features.

Let's begin with a calm, straight river—one that flows freely over an unobstructed channel. As obstacles enter the current, rapids begin to appear. Here you'll find chutes, waves, holes, and eddies—the things river runners call *fun*—at least if they're not too large or dangerous.

TONGUES

At the top of many rapids, the main current enters a slick, smooth-surfaced ramp called a *tongue* or *downstream V.* Tongues are typically V-shaped, with the tip

Washington's Money Creek provides a different yet equally dramatic example of a continuous river.

of the V pointing downstream (hence the name "downstream V"). Tongues form between rocks, cliffs, or shallows, and point out the deepest, least-obstructed channel. There may be just one large tongue or there may be many tongues of different sizes. When there's more than one tongue—when there are large boulders or islands dividing the river into many channels—the safest and deepest tongue will usually be either the largest tongue or the one that begins dropping the soonest. (The reason for this is that channels that wait longer before they begin to drop lose water to deeper channels. So, by the time the smaller channel reaches the base of a rapid, it may consist of boulder fans barely wet enough to float a kayak.)

The second type of V is the *upstream V*, which has the tip of the V pointing upstream. Upstream Vs are shock waves created by obstacles that pierce or lurk just beneath the surface. Unlike tongues, the upstream V is a warning sign—a signal to steer clear or risk damaging your boat on the partially submerged obstacle.

STANDING WAVES

Standing waves are one of the most fascinating and entertaining of all river features. From the small, erratic riffles of your local creek to the giant haystacks of large-volume rivers, standing waves provide kayakers with the ultimate aquatic roller coaster ride.

No discussion of river waves would be complete without some comparison to ocean waves. Although ocean and river waves may look similar, there are some distinct differences. First, river waves are stationary and remain at the same location as the forces or obstacles that form them. Ocean waves, on the other hand, travel toward shore, where they dissipate as they roll up the beach. Second, water travels

A tongue or downstream V often marks the deepest, safest approach into a rapid. The tongue is readily apparent in this picture as the dark V.

Tongues or downstream Vs (A and B) show deep, clear channels, while upstream Vs (C and D) show subsurface hazards. Kayakers should stay on the tongues and avoid the upstream Vs.

through river waves, releasing its energy as it goes, while the water inside ocean waves hardly moves at all. Instead, the water inside the ocean wave transfers its energy as the wave rolls toward the beach.

Many things form standing waves: subsurface boulders, changes in gradient, converging currents. But most waves are created from a change in water speed. Since water can't be compressed like air, it moves faster when it is confined by narrow streambeds or obstacles. In fact, water gains speed whenever it is squeezed *horizontally* between banks or boulders, compressed *vertically* over rocks or the bottom, or when it falls down a steeper section of riverbed. Waves are associated with all three changes in velocity.

The most common standing waves are those that form at the bottom of downward-sloping riverbeds. Here, the potential energy stored in fast, downward-moving water dissipates gradually when it hits the bottom of the slope. In the most basic example of a sloping riverbed, there are no obstacles to interfere with the formation of standing waves. As the river reaches the end of the slope, a series of waves—*a wave train*—forms, with each wave lining up

Standing waves are remarkably similar to ocean waves. Just ask this surfer in the middle of Idaho's river country.

perpendicular to the main current. The first wave in the train usually is the largest, with each successive wave diminishing in size. (*Tailwaves*—another name used to describe standing waves—are wave trains that begin at the base of a rapid.)

Standing waves also appear where cliffs, shallow gravel bars, boulder piles, or other obstacles force a broad river into a narrow channel. Since the river has less space to occupy, it is forced to travel faster. The moment the channel reopens the energy stored in the fast-moving water dissipates in the form of standing waves.

Submarine boulders or ledges can also form waves. Here, the current picks up energy as it travels faster over the top of the obstacle, then releases it downstream in a series of waves. A *hump* or *cushion*—not a standing wave—forms above the obstacle, followed by standing waves downstream. Since waves formed by rocks and boulders frequently stand alone, their solitary presence indicates the obstacle beneath the surface.

Standing wave forming after a boulder.

Still another cause of standing waves is converging currents. *Convergence waves* often form where two channels meet or where a tributary spills its current into the main stream. Water piles up and gathers energy at the convergence, then releases the excess energy gradually as standing waves. If the cause of the convergence is a deflection of the main current back upon itself by cliffs or steep banks, the waves that bounce off the cliffs are sometimes called *reflection waves*.

DIAGONAL WAVES

When a submerged ledge or boulder cuts diagonally across the main channel, surface waves won't line up

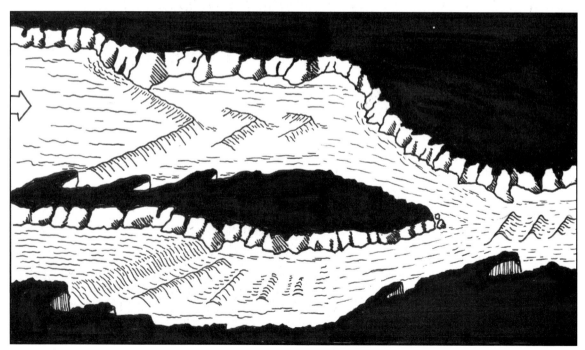

Diagonal waves (top *and* bottom left) *come in a variety of shapes and sizes but often straighten out as they roll downstream.* Standing waves (right) *can form where two channels collide.*

perpendicular to the main current. Instead, the first wave or two below the ledge will lunge upward at an angle to the main current, forming *diagonal* or *lateral waves*. Diagonal waves also appear wherever submerged boulders, converging currents, and constricted channels deflect waves at an angle to the main current. No matter what forms the diagonal waves, the waves following the first few diagonal waves realign themselves with the main current just like any other standing wave.

HAYSTACKS

Haystacks are the mountain peaks of the riverscape. Although they look like towering, peaked standing waves, they're actually formed from converging standing waves, each contributing its energy to force the haystack higher. With all of this energy packed into one wall of water, haystacks are rarely stable—they tend to dance around on the river's surface and surge randomly.

BREAKING WAVES AND STOPPERS

When a wave becomes too large to support its own weight and shape, it starts spilling the highest water down its upstream face. Like standing waves, breaking waves have their counterpart in ocean waves: The foamy break on ocean waves is similar to that found on a river's breaking waves. In any event, whether they're called *curlers, curling waves, breaking waves,* or *reversals*, these waves can be very powerful. If enough water is falling down the upstream face, it can carry sufficient force to stop and flip your kayak—hence the name *stopper*.

PILLOWS

When the current collides with an obstacle, some of the current flows vertically up the obstacle's upstream side and forms a mound of water called a *cushion* or *pillow*. These mounds stand higher than the surrounding river and disclose the presence of boulders and other obstacles. As pillows grow, they eventually

When a standing wave gets too big to support itself, the crest spills down the face of the wave, forming a breaking wave. (Photo by Jed Weingarten)

become too large to support their own weight. When that happens, the highest water spills down the upstream face, creating a hydraulic much like a breaking wave.

A pillow—or, rather, the lack of a pillow—also reveals a major river hazard: *undercuts*. To spot an undercut from your kayak, watch the river. Whenever the current collides with an obstacle without forming a pillow, beware! It is a certain indication that the obstacle is undercut and that the current is diving under the obstacle—*where you don't want to be!* Since powerful currents can carry kayaks and swimmers beneath undercut ledges, banks, and boulders, they are to be regarded as some of the worst hazards found on whitewater rivers.

ROOSTERTAILS

Roostertails are pillows gone berserk. Like pillows, roostertails form when a fast current piles into the upstream side of a rock or boulder. However, rather than building smoothly upon the shoulder of the rock, the rock slices through the current and deflects water into the air, creating an aerial fountain in the shape of a rooster's tail.

There are two types of roostertails: upstream and downstream. Upstream roostertails form when the rock is tilted upstream; they're identified by the fan of water deflecting through the air in an upstream direction. Downstream roostertails are caused by downstream-tilted rocks—they fan water through the air in a downstream direction.

Pillows form when currents collide with the upstream side of an obstacle. The current rises upward on the obstacle, forms a cushion, then settles back down as it slips around the side of the obstacle. Here, pillow A *forms on the upstream face of an exposed boulder, while the adjacent pillow* B *forms on the upstream side of a barely submerged boulder.*

Kayakers should steer clear of undercut rocks and shelves, such as the large slab rock shown on the left side of this photo.

Kayakers should avoid any kind of roostertail—the exposed rock and fast-moving currents can combine to tear or wrap the kayak in an instant.

BOILS

Boils are upwellings in the river current caused by things like underwater boulders, undercut ledges, and converging currents. Here, the river surface looks like a giant boiling pot of water.

HOLES

When water pours over a rock or ledge, the water plunges down a *falls* toward the riverbed, then flows downstream along the bottom of the river. A deep cavity appears in the river surface just downstream of the falls. In an effort to fill this cavity, the river grabs surface water from downstream and pours it in a reverse direction back into the cavity. (This zone of upstream currents is called the *backwash* or *pile*.)

Viewed from the side, the hole's currents rotate like a wheel, with the surface rolling upstream and the bottom rolling downstream. This rotating liquid vortex goes by many names, including *hole, reversal, souse hole,* and *stopper.*

Holes, like waves, come in all shapes and sizes. Large holes—sometimes called *keepers*—can hold and flip a kayak with ease, while small holes can be crashed or avoided. Getting to know the difference between friendly and unfriendly holes is one of the most important skills any kayaker can have.

Fortunately, there are four factors that reveal the intensity of a hole: the *height, angle,* and *volume* of the falls; the *shape* and *width* of the hole; the hole's *depth*; and the *length of the backwash*. These factors mix and match in countless ways, but understanding how they work together will reveal a lot about a particular hole. Let's start by looking at the falls.

This diagram shows an upstream roostertail (left) *and downstream roostertail* (right), *formed where an obstacle pierces the current near the surface. Roostertails should be avoided.*

Water plunges downward at the upstream side of a hole. Generally, the steeper and taller this falls the more severe the hole. In *vertical falls*—often called *pourovers*—water plummets toward the bottom of the river and can create a deep hole with a small pocket of violently opposing currents, especially if the pourover is more than a few feet high. *Sloping falls*, on the other hand, can create long zones of backwash—a perilous hazard for kayakers.

Falls with a lot of water usually create stronger holes than low-volume falls. In a tight, constricted channel, the whole river might plunge over a sharp ledge. This can create a nearly impenetrable hole that can easily trap and hold kayakers. On the other hand,

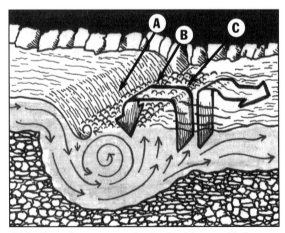

Holes form downstream of rocks, boulders, and ledges. They consist of a falls (A), *seam* (B), *and backwash* (C). *Though these names may vary, the hole's currents always act similarly.*

a small boulder in the middle of a broad stream might only create a small hole—one barely big enough to be noticeable or just big enough to splash your face. In any case, the addition of more water to the falls generally makes for a more powerful hole.

There are four different shapes that could describe almost any hole: *smiling, frowning, horizontal,* and *diagonal.* Each shape describes the hole's appearance from an imaginary perspective upstream.

In a *smiling* hole, the middle of the hole is the farthest upstream, while the hole's outer edges curl downstream and away from you. This lets some of the current—and anything floating on it—escape laterally out of the hole. Because of this, smiling holes are the safest holes to run. If the outer edges curl back at you, the hole is frowning.

Frowning holes focus much of the current's energy toward the middle of the hole, creating a powerful magnet for anything stuck in its grasp. For kayakers, this can spell disaster. Large frowning holes can make lateral escapes nearly impossible and can hold kayaks and swimmers indefinitely.

Horizontal holes show up in two places: at the base of artificial dams, and at the base of wide ledges. If the volume of water flowing over the ledge is even all the way across the river, the resulting hole forms a foreboding, bank-to-bank obstacle for kayakers. Like frowning holes, these types of holes can be powerful and dangerous, making escape very difficult.

The final type of hole—a *diagonal* hole—appears wherever an obstacle or ledge cuts across the channel at an angle to the current. Diagonal holes have one side farther upstream than the other and contain a current that slides downstream across the face of the hole. A kayak moved to the downstream end of the hole will eventually slip free of the hole and back into the main current—upright, ideally.

Hole width and *hole depth* are the next factors that indicate the strength and danger of any hole. Hole width is measured perpendicularly across the current. Wide holes are much more difficult to exit than are narrow holes and usually should be avoided. Hole depth describes how far beneath the surface the recirculating current extends; the depth is determined by the speed and volume of the falls. In deep holes, the falls force water all the way down to the riverbed. From there, the current climbs back toward the surface and repeats the cycle without letting much water escape—on large-volume rivers, a kayaker trapped in its grasp could be in real trouble. Not only can the downward current behind the rock slam swimmers against the river bottom, there is only a narrow zone of escape directly along the bottom of the river.

Shallower holes don't extend all the way to the bottom of the river and usually are much safer for kayakers (all other factors being equal). Since the hole's rotating currents only reach part of the way to the riverbed, swimmers can easily swim out from under the upstream currents by utilizing the free-flowing downstream current.

BACKWASH

The term *backwash* describes the zone of upstream current that forms downstream of a hole. In some holes, an object floating on the surface 20 or more feet downstream of the falls can travel back upstream on the backwash only to find itself caught in the swirling maelstrom again. Kayakers can follow an easy rule of thumb: *The longer the backwash, the more difficult and dangerous the hole.*

LOWHEAD DAMS AND WEIRS

Lowhead dams and *weirs* include a variety of artificial structures. Many lowhead dams were originally designed to divert water into grain mills or irrigation networks. Now they are built for flood control and power generation.

Fabricated from cement, asphalt, rebar, and riprap, most lowhead dams are installed straight across the river channel, with walls rising out of each end of the dam. As the water drops over the top of the dam, it slides down a smooth face, spilling onto a flat or *angled* apron. Then, as the water plummets into the pool below the dam, the currents form *incredibly dangerous* holes.

Holes below lowhead dams can extend all the way across the river, are very straight, display a lot

Holes come in a wide variety of shapes and sizes. This diagram shows, from left to right, a smiling hole, a frowning hole, a horizontal hole, and a diagonal hole.

The arrows indicate the direction of the kick (the direction in which the currents will try to deflect your kayak).

HOLE

Smooth humps in the river surface often disguise the presence of holes, such as the one waiting just downstream of this kayaker.

of power, and have a long zone of backwash. Any one of these factors could create a very dangerous hole in its own right. When combined, they form one of the most hazardous obstacles known to whitewater enthusiasts. In fact, a great number of river-related fatalities are due to lowhead dams. For kayakers, I've got only two words of advice: *Steer clear!* Even runnable-looking lowhead dams contain dangerous currents, and many contain nasty piles of submerged rebar, trapped logs, and construction debris.

When on the river, watch for artificial structures and smooth, river-wide horizon lines. These signs can tell you that a dam is coming up and that it is time to pull to the bank.

SPOTTING HOLES

Holes can appear anywhere a ledge or boulder lurks beneath the surface. But since the river plunges over the obstacles, the hole itself might be hard to see from upstream. Still, there are signs that reveal the hole's presence to observant kayakers. In a rapid, look for the calm, smooth hump that forms as the water stays level when passing over a submerged rock. If you can see beyond the hump, look slightly downstream for foamy backwash. Gradually you will get better at spotting holes, and eventually you'll be able to discern fun, runnable holes from hazardous holes just by looking at them from upstream.

Lowhead dams and weirs contain killer holes with powerful backwashes. Don't run them!

WATERFALLS

When holes get too big for their britches, we call them *waterfalls*. To me, waterfalls include pourovers, slides, or any type of drop that's high and steep enough to make me think twice before I kayak it. In many ways, waterfalls are no different than holes. Each waterfall has a downward-plunging current, a zone of backwash, and can be any of a number of shapes or sizes. Accordingly, everything we just learned about holes applies to waterfalls.

Waterfalls can be detected from upstream by their distinctive horizon lines. When you first start kayaking, keep a keen eye downstream. If the river seems to suddenly disappear without going around a bend, pull over and walk downstream. It may be that the gradient has simply increased or it could be that the river is about to plunge over a waterfall. As you start to learn the differences between rapids and falls, things like nearby trees and large boulders (or even the sound of the water) will give you clues as to whether the river is about to pour over a dangerous waterfall.

EDDIES

I've waited until late in this chapter to discuss eddies for two reasons. First, eddies combine almost everything mentioned so far about currents and river features: They have oppositional currents, appear opposite of pillows behind obstacles, and contain both laminar and turbulent currents. Second, eddies are the most important hydraulic formations for kayakers to know and understand: They provide gentle parking zones for loading and unloading kayaks, safe havens for scouting or resting before the next drop, and they can make cross-river maneuvers easier. They even provide great social spots before and after rapids and a place to trade notes when getting ready to play in hydraulics.

Waterfalls—like this behemoth in Washington—captivate and enchant expert kayakers. (Photo by Jed Weingarten)

Eddies are found behind any obstacle that deflects the main current—boulders, bank protrusions, even bridge abutments and logs. No matter what the obstacle is, it has the same effect: When the main current collides with the upstream face of the obstacle, it works its way around the obstacle and accelerates. This leaves a depressed zone of low pressure behind the obstacle. Water from downstream actually flows *upstream* toward the obstacle to fill in the gap, creating a pocket of current moving in the opposite direction to the main current.

A feature called an *eddy line* marks the narrow divide between the oppositional currents of the eddy and the main current. Here, the currents of the eddy and main channel mix and swirl. On powerful, large-volume rivers, the eddy and main current might rise to two different levels, causing the currents of the eddy and main channel to wrestle violently along the transition zone. When there is a visible wall of water blocking the entrance or exit from the eddy, kayakers call the eddy line an *eddy fence*.

Two factors affect the intensity of an eddy: the *size and shape of the obstacle*, and the *velocity of the current*. If the obstacle has chiseled, well-defined edges, it will sever swift currents sharply from the eddy, creating a crisp eddy line and stable eddies. On the other hand, rounded obstacles and slow currents allow the currents to mix, weakening the eddy and melting the eddy lines. Shallow obstacles can create eddies even if they don't pierce the river's surface. As the river slides over the top of the obstacle, it loses its momentum and swirls in an aerated pocket. The foamy eddy that is formed behind the obstacle is called a *white eddy*, while more solid eddies are called *green eddies*. The last type of eddy contains powerful, vertical boiling currents. For lack of a better term, call these *boiling eddies*.

FUNNY WATER

Funny water is a product of Mother Nature's warped sense of humor. It doesn't fit any of the definitions we've already used for other surface features—waves, holes, and eddies—and doesn't fit into any simple description. Most paddlers use the term funny water to describe low-gradient anomalies like strange swirling currents, migrating eddies, and unpredictable whirlpools rather than foamy, plunging rapids. In summary, funny water is anything *but* funny—

Eddies will form where peninsulas jut out from the bank or pockets form to the side of the main channel.

Eddies also form behind boulders. The eddy lines (white swirls) are clearly visible in this photo.

paddlers have to stay alert and react quickly just to figure out what's going on.

The Big Picture

The thing that makes kayaking so exciting is that no two rapids are alike. The river features we've discussed vary not only in size and intensity from river to river, they mix and match in myriad combinations. Some rivers might contain long series of gentle waves interspersed with calm pools; others might display steep boulder gardens punctuated by steep holes; still others might have giant haystacks bordered by vicious eddy fences.

As you move from one river to another, the same distinctive hydraulics will be found again and again, and their distinguishing characteristics will become familiar. You'll soon associate solitary waves or pillows with submarine boulders, strange water fountains with surface-piercing rocks, and smooth humps of water or foaming backwash with holes. Eventually, each feature will direct you to safer channels or forewarn you that any attempt at running some rapids could be risky.

Rating the Rapids

There are two universal systems used by kayakers to classify the difficulty and intensity of rapids. The most common system is the International Scale of River Difficulty, which grades rapids on a scale of I to VI (I being the easiest). In the Southwestern United States, another system, known as the Deseret Scale or the Grand Canyon System, is sometimes used. This system rates rapids on a scale of 1 to 10.

Unfortunately, neither system is perfect. Rapids change constantly, affected by water-level fluctuations and shifts in the riverbed (a Class III rapid at 500 cfs can become a nasty Class 5 drop at 1,500 cfs). Kayakers might rate rapids differently depending on their attitude or skill level. Also, the pursuit of difficult whitewater has resulted in a downgrading of many rapids: Rapids that used to be considered Class VI have been downscaled to Class V after many successful descents. And kayakers keep getting better—what was rated Class 5 10 years ago may be rated Class IV today, and today's Class IV may be the Class III of the next decade.

So, even the best rapid- and river-rating systems are subjective, and river classifications are little more than a starting point for finding out about any river. You should gather as much additional information as you can find about rapids you plan to run. Rely on your own skills, observations, and judgment to determine ratings, and don't let anyone—or any system—tell you what you can or can't do!

THE INTERNATIONAL SCALE OF RIVER DIFFICULTY

This is the American version of a rating system used to compare river difficulty throughout the world. This system is not exact; rivers do not always fit easily into one category, and regional or individual interpretations may cause misunderstandings. It is no substitute for a guidebook or accurate first-hand descriptions of a run.

Paddlers attempting difficult runs in an unfamiliar area should act cautiously until they get a feel for the way the scale is interpreted locally. River difficulty may change each year due to fluctuations in water level, downed trees, recent floods, geological disturbances, or bad weather. Stay alert for unexpected problems!

As river difficulty increases, the danger to swimming paddlers becomes more severe. As rapids become longer and more continuous, the challenge increases. There is a difference between running an occasional Class IV rapid and dealing with an entire river of this category. Allow an extra margin of safety between skills and river ratings when the water is cold or if the river itself is remote and inaccessible.

Class I: Easy. Fast-moving water with riffles and small waves. Few obstructions, all obvious and easily missed with little training. Risk to swimmers is slight; self-rescue is easy.

Class II: Novice. Straightforward rapids with wide, clear channels which are evident without scouting. Occasional maneuvering may be required, but rocks and medium-sized waves are easily missed by trained paddlers. Swimmers are seldom injured and group assistance, while helpful, is seldom needed. Rapids that are at the upper end of this difficulty range are designated "Class II+".

Class III: Intermediate. Rapids with moderate, irregular waves which may be difficult to avoid and which can swamp an open canoe. Complex maneuvers in fast current and good boat control in tight passages or around ledges are often required; large waves or strainers may be present but are easily avoided. Strong eddies and powerful current effects can be found, particularly on large-volume rivers. Scouting is advisable for inexperienced parties. Injuries while swimming are rare; self-rescue is usually easy but group assistance may be required to avoid long swims. Rapids that are at the lower or upper end of this difficulty range are designated "Class III–" or "Class III+" respectively.

Class IV: Advanced. Intense, powerful but predictable rapids requiring precise boat handling in turbulent water. Depending on the character of the river, it may feature large, unavoidable waves and holes or constricted passages demanding fast maneuvers under pressure. A fast, reliable eddy turn may be needed to initiate maneuvers, scout rapids, or rest. Rapids may require "must" moves above dangerous hazards. Scouting may be necessary the first time down. Risk of injury to swimmers is moderate to high, and water conditions may make self rescue difficult. Group assistance for rescue is often essential but requires practiced skills. A strong Eskimo roll is highly recommended. Rapids that are at the upper end of this difficulty range are designated "Class IV–" or "Class IV+" respectively.

Class 5: Expert. Extremely long, obstructed, or very violent rapids which expose a paddler to added risk. Drops may contain large, unavoidable waves and holes or steep, congested chutes with complex, demanding routes. Rapids may continue for long distances between pools, demanding a high level of fitness. What eddies exist may be small, turbulent, or difficult to reach. At the high end of the scale, several of these factors may be combined. Scouting is recommended but may be difficult. Swims are dangerous, and rescue is often difficult even for experts. A very reliable Eskimo roll, proper equipment, extensive experience, and practiced rescue skills are essential. Because of the large range of difficulty that exists beyond Class IV, Class 5 is an open-ended, multiple-level scale designated by Class 5.0, 5.1, 5.2, etc. Each of these levels is an order of magnitude more difficult than the last. Example: Increasing difficulty from class 5.0 to Class 5.1 is a similar order of magnitude as increasing from Class IV to Class 5.0.

Class VI: Extreme and Exploratory. These runs have almost never been attempted and often exemplify the extremes of difficulty, unpredictability, and danger. The consequences of errors are very severe and rescue may be impossible. For teams of experts only, at favorable water levels, after close personal inspection and taking all precautions. After a Class VI rapids has been run many times, Its rating may be changed to an appropriate Class 5.x rating.

Class I

Class II

Class III

Class IV

Class 5

Class VI

THE DYNAMICS OF RUNNING WATER

7

Running the Rapids

Heraclitus once said, "You cannot step twice into the same river, for other waters are continually flowing on." Few words capture river-running's mystique as eloquently as those. With each bend in the channel, rivers reveal new facets of their personalities—sometimes tranquil, sometimes tumultuous. The personalities of individual rapids also transform as water levels rise and fall or as streambeds erode and shift. But, while rapids shift freely from one mood to another, the skills and techniques needed to read and run them remain constant.

By now you've learned the strokes that kayakers use to harness a kayak's capabilities. It's time to combine those strokes into definite maneuvers, to expand your knowledge of river features, and to learn the fundamental techniques necessary to run rapids. This is your next big step toward becoming a whitewater kayaker!

Heading Downriver

To novice kayakers unfamiliar with the distinctive components of rapids, whitewater rivers exemplify nature in chaos. Liquid furies. But to the seasoned river runner, rapids share common features, each one a road sign to routes of safe passage. *Reading rivers* is

Running rapids is always exciting, whether you're a beginner paddling Class II or an expert paddling Class 5.

the art of interpreting those road signs, recognizing the pitfalls of ill-chosen routes, and envisioning the maneuvers that will be necessary to float rapids safely.

BASIC CONCEPTS

While reading the rest of this chapter, keep three important concepts in mind:

- Think of paddling as a means of changing your kayak's speed and direction in relation to the *current*, not in relation to solid obstacles such as rocks or cliffs.
- Always have a *contingency plan* in case you miss a stroke, spin off a wave, or bounce off a rock.
- Remember that whitewater is ever changing and that your ability to *adapt* is more important than learning the names or categories of each technique.

Keeping these three concepts in mind is easy when paddling within your skill level. The moment things get tough, however, theories tend to fly out the window. So, let's use an analogy: Think of paddling rapids like shifting lanes in freeway traffic. In traffic, you need to be aware of everything going on around you, even though things are moving at 60 mph. Your eyes remain wide open while you scan the road for hazards; your mind plans your next move; you make sure you have a back-up plan in case that idiot in the red sports car decides to hog your spot. Those same thought processes

> "**R**eading water is like learning a new language. The more rivers you run, the more you scout, and the more you watch other people run rapids, the more you'll become fluent at this new language. There's even something to be learned while portaging rapids. It's all a matter of experience, and as long as you keep experiencing rivers, you'll never stop learning.**"**
> —**JAMIE SIMON**
> **WATERFALL RECORD HOLDER**

> "**W**hen running rapids, I like to live by the wide-eye, long-neck theory where I'm really keeping my head up and I'm looking ahead. Beginners often look at their bow; intermediate boaters tend to look about five feet ahead; advanced boaters look a few feet ahead of that; and expert boaters look downriver as far as they can see. If your head is up and your eyes are looking ahead, you'll see where the river is going, what rocks are in the river, what's going to happen when the water hits those rocks, and so on.**"**
> —**JAMIE SIMON**

go into running rapids: The traffic flow is the current; your back-up plan is your way out of trouble; and you're ready to adapt to an ever-changing situation.

LEANING REVISITED

As you move downriver and into bigger rapids, you'll find yourself spending more time turning your kayak to the current. To overcome the unstable feeling that generally goes along with being sideways, you must learn to lean (tilt) correctly.

First, remember to use the J-lean—not an upper-body lean—as your primary lean. (This tilts your boat, not your body.) Next, use a lean *in the direction the current is going* as your preferred lean. This means leaning downstream in the main current and upstream in eddies. (If you don't do this, the effect will be very much like having a rug pulled out from underneath you: Your boat will roll upside down into the current.) Finally, a correct lean will also be critical when paddling amid things like rocks, big waves, or holes. Always lean *toward* these obstacles—aggressively if necessary—to avoid flips and pins.

KAYAK MANEUVERS

Amazingly, every maneuver known to kayakers falls within one of five categories:

- maneuvers that keep you parallel with the current
- ferries
- turns and spins
- sideslips
- eddy turns and peel outs

Each of these maneuvers either *moves* the kayak in a new direction or *rotates* the kayak around its pivot point.

As you learn these maneuvers, think of how they'll work in moving currents and visualize the two components that make up each one: your kayak's *momentum* and its *angle* in relation to the current. Some maneuvers, like ferries and eddy turns, rely heavily on current to drive the kayak across the river's surface. Other maneuvers, such as turns and side-slips, rely little on currents but have to overcome them to be effective. The same current that assists one maneuver may hinder another.

RIVER DIRECTIONS

As you read through this chapter, you will see references to things like *river left* and *river right*. Rivers have descriptive directions, just as maps are labeled north, south, east, and west. When describing river direction, one of four terms is used:

- *upstream* (where the current is coming from)
- *downstream* (where the current is flowing to)
- *river left* (to your left as you face downstream)
- *river right* (to your right as you face downstream)

These terms will help you understand the movement of the kayaks in the diagrams in this chapter and will make your descriptions of rapids understandable to fellow river runners.

Staying Parallel with the Current

One of the fundamental techniques all kayakers learn is how to keep the kayak *parallel* with the current. This not only helps when it comes time to slow your kayak down, it continually expands your understanding of river currents, and it provides a starting point for many other river-running techniques.

STARTING EASY

Since rivers rarely flow in a straight line, keeping your kayak parallel with the current can be trickier than it sounds. There are bends to contend with, eddies and slack water that try to spin your kayak, and obstacles that interfere with your strokes. Still, you can

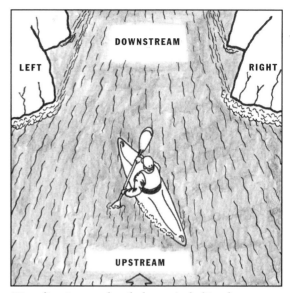

River directions are described as you're looking downstream. This diagram shows upstream, downstream, left, and right.

practice these techniques on a straight, obstacle-free section of river where it will be easier to work on basic river-running techniques.

To slow your kayak on a straight section of river, point your bow upstream and line up the kayak's long axis with the current using subtle, gentle, turning strokes. At the same time, slow your kayak using forward strokes. The more you practice this the easier it becomes. Once you're comfortable slowing your descent while facing upstream, point your bow downstream and backstroke against the current. (Paddling backwards will feel funny at first, but so did getting in a kayak for the first time!) Given some practice, you'll soon be able to paddle backwards as easily as you paddle forward.

CHANGING CURRENTS

The current's velocity often changes when a swift, deep channel collides with the slow waters of a shallow shoal. As the kayak crosses the interface between faster and slower currents, the slower current drags on the bow at the same time that the faster currents push on the stern. If your kayak turns even slightly to the current, the river will try to twist it sideways. To avoid getting turned sideways, you must turn your kayak in the opposite direction with stern draws and well-gauged turning strokes.

Eddies have the same kayak-twisting effect as changes in the current, only worse: Eddies flow opposite to the direction of the main current. The added force of these oppositional currents can frustrate even the best kayakers. If it becomes impossible to turn the kayak back in the direction of its original course, just spin your kayak in the opposite direction with a turning stroke and realign the kayak with the current.

Ferrying

Ferrying techniques date back to days when cable-guided ferry barges transported people, horses, and wagons across swift rivers. Attached to a cross-river cable by one or two strong chains, these barges could be turned at an angle to the current either by adjusting a rudder or changing the length of one chain. Once the barge was turned at an angle, the current would build up pressure on the barge's upstream side and force it toward the opposite bank.

Kayakers push against the current with forward and back strokes instead of cables, but they use the

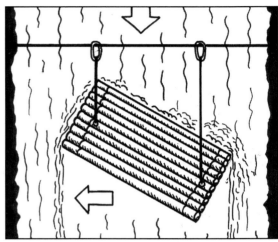

Old-time ferries relied on strong cables and river currents to move back and forth across a river. With one cable longer than the other, currents would build up on one side of the ferry and push it toward the opposite bank. Kayakers use the same principles when executing their own brand of ferrying.

same angles and forces to help move back and forth across the river.

TECHNIQUES

There are two types of ferrying techniques: *forward ferrying* and *back ferrying*.

To forward ferry, point your bow upstream, align your kayak parallel with the current, and begin forward paddling. Once you slow your descent, begin ferrying toward the left bank by turning the bow 30 to 45 degrees to *your* right (toward the *left* bank). If you continue forward paddling while maintaining that angle, your kayak will move sideways toward river left (the left bank as you look downstream). To reach the right bank, angle the bow 30 to 45 degrees toward the right bank and forward stroke again.

Back ferrying relies on the same principles as the forward ferry, only in reverse. To back ferry, point your bow downstream, angled *away* from the bank, and use back strokes to counteract the downstream current. Since you're not looking at the water coming at you, it takes a little practice to get the feel of back ferrying. Stick with it until it is second nature.

> "**W**hen running rivers, you're often trying to make it from point A to point B as efficiently as possible. The most simple way of doing that may be to put yourself on the piece of water that goes where you want to go. As the rapids get harder, you have to fine tune your interaction with the water and learn other choices for moving about the river. But ultimately you'll end up with a huge repertoire of skills, and you'll be able to call upon whichever skill is most appropriate for any given situation. **"**
>
> **—CATHY HEARN**
> **WORLD CHAMPION MEDALIST**

BETTER FERRYING

There are a few tips that will improve your ferrying techniques—especially in fast currents or swirling hydraulics.

First, match your boat angle to the current: The faster the current, the less angle you'll use to maintain your position. If you turn too far sideways, a fast current will force you downstream before your ferry is complete.

Second, avoid using back strokes on your upstream side when forward ferrying. They'll slow you down and cause you to slip downstream with the current. A stern draw on the downstream side will help you maintain your ferry angle without giving up any momentum.

Finally, use the river's surface features to help your ferries. You can ferry on the upstream face of small waves to add power to your ferries. Here, gravity holds your kayak on the wave as you surf it across the river.

When all else fails, it is often best to err on the side of pointing more upstream—that will buy you extra time to adjust your ferry angle and ferry where you want to.

APPARENT VERSUS REAL COURSE

The first few times you try ferrying across a current you're likely to notice that it may take a stroke or two to stop your downstream momentum and start you moving across the river. Even if you execute a ferry properly, you may notice that you often drift or sideslip downriver a bit. This means that the cross-river route you imagined you would follow may not be the same route you really follow. By anticipating

Before learning to ferry, learn to stay in one place parallel with the current (left). *Paddle upstream against the current, using corrective strokes to help maintain your angle. When you're ready, angle your bow a few degrees toward one bank and keep forward paddling* (center). *Not only will your descent remain slow, you'll slowly ferry toward one bank. To speed up your cross-river ferry, increase your angle to the current* (right)*, but be aware that you may begin to drift downstream faster. These same techniques can be done facing downstream while using back strokes.*

the difference between your *apparent* and *real* courses, you can adjust early and make the moves you desire.

FERRYING AROUND BENDS

As you already learned, currents don't curve around bends, they flow along a straight line from the inside to the outside of bends. To compensate for the river's tendency to push you toward the outside of the bend, you often should enter bends from the inside corner and turn your kayak at a greater angle to the inside bank than you would expect. (Remember, you want to stay parallel with the current, not with the bank.) If the inside corner is strewn with obstacles, just remember that the outside currents will be fast and strong.

Turns and Pivots

Let's take a fresh look at some familiar strokes. The same sweep strokes, rudders, draws, and duffeks you learned earlier will now help you set a ferry angle

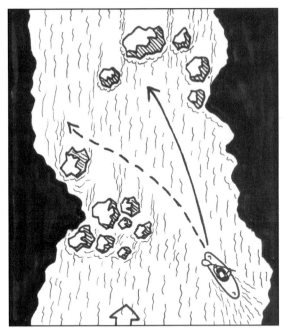

Since the main current will cause you to drift downstream at the same time you're trying to move across the river, your real course (solid line) may be different from your apparent course (dotted line) unless you compensate for the current.

around a big boulder or aim toward a fun wave. The only difference between your flatwater and whitewater techniques will be the *water movement:* Whitewater is a three-dimensional world of waves, holes, chutes, and eddies. Understanding rapids lets you anticipate the river's effect on your kayak and tailor your turns or spins to it.

As you learned in the section on ferrying, downstream currents sometimes make where you actually go different from where you think you're going to go. As long as you anticipate the effects of the current, you can adjust to the river.

STANDING WAVES

As your kayak reaches the crest of standing waves, the bow and stern become unweighted. For this split second, your kayak will spin more easily than when it's compressed into a trough between standing waves. Experienced kayakers can execute fast turns on wave

crests by anticipating the moment of weightlessness. On the other hand, a poorly timed stroke can send your kayak spinning off the crest and out of control. Accordingly, beginners are sometimes better off forward paddling through wave trains until they become familiar with the roller coaster ride of a wave train.

SIDESLIPS

There will be times when a well-executed turn or powerful ferry is not enough to maneuver safely through a rapid. This may happen in a fast chute that slams into a boulder or in a hole-riddled rapid that threatens to flip you if you turn broadside. Draw strokes can be cure-alls for some of these situations. Done correctly, the draw stroke moves you laterally across the river in a hurry.

Eddy Maneuvers

A kayak floating on the main current has a lot of inertia. It carries not only its own weight but also the force of the main current. So, stopping the kayak

When ferrying around bends, angle your kayak to the current, not the bank. Here the kayaker is back ferrying toward the inside of the bend, since this often is the safest place to be. If there were obstacles near the inside of the bend, the paddler could quickly paddle toward the outside.

takes at least the same amount of braking force working in the opposite direction. One example of incredible braking forces are midstream boulders. If a boulder hasn't been moved for a while, chances are it isn't going to let some measly kayak push it out of the way. Other examples of braking forces are big holes or reversals. Here, the surface current is moving upstream at the same rate as the downstream current. A kayak hitting this surface current broadside might find its downstream progress violently arrested.

What you're looking for are user-friendly braking forces—things that will let you stop without broaching, flipping, swimming, or losing your composure. What you're looking for are *eddies.*

Eddies are some of the most important features on the river. Their upstream currents can provide enough braking power to gently (or violently) stop your kayak. A mild eddy provides a calm haven when

> **"O**ne of the most important things you can do in a rapid is to keep paddling. As soon as you're not paddling through a rapid, you're not doing anything except putting yourself at the mercy of the water. But if you keep paddling and you always have a stroke in the water, it kind of acts as a brace: You'll not only feel more stable, you'll be able to get where you want to go. The more you develop this skill, the better you're going to be able to make moves and learn the rest. **"**
>
> —SAM DREVO
> OLYMPIC FESTIVAL MEDALIST

you're weary, a parking area for boarding and exiting your boat, and a placid platform from which rapids can be scouted. Conversely, large, tumultuous eddies can trap and flip you, and they can make any trip across an eddy line difficult.

LEANING

Whether entering or exiting an eddy, you'll have to contend with strange currents at the eddy line. The overlapping currents found here not only slide horizontally past each other—speeding up and throwing your maneuvers off—they drive *downward*, building within themselves strong capsizing forces. On large-volume rivers, giant eddy fences can generate enough capsizing force to suck down your edges and cause you to flip.

Even on mild rivers, capsizing forces can wreak havoc. When you exit a fast-moving eddy, your upstream edge is exposed to the main current. Here, the main current drives against—then under—the upstream edge. As it does, it tries to drag the upstream edge under with it and can flip you in the process.

Whether entering or exiting eddies, kayakers can avoid flipping by leaning away from the oncoming currents. (That's a J-lean, folks! Not a body lean.) In other words, J-lean *upstream* to lift your downstream edge when entering eddies; J-lean *downstream* to lift

It is much easier to turn your kayak on top of a wave (bottom) *then in the trough between waves* (top).

your upstream edge when exiting eddies. Once a vulnerable edge has been unweighted, the river has little chance to do any harm.

WHERE TO ENTER EDDIES

The best way to enter a clear, friendly eddy is to paddle into it *high* (upstream, where the maximum current differential is located), and *deep* (directly behind the center of the obstacle). Entering high and deep brings the river's friendly forces into full effect—upstream currents that will brake your momentum and bring your descent to a halt. (If you're wondering why you shouldn't enter eddies low, here's an answer: The powerful upstream currents found higher in the eddy begin to disappear downstream. So a kayak entering an eddy low is left with nothing more than its own paddle power to stop its descent.) Keep in mind that all eddies are different. Some are shallow, others are deep; some are weak, some are powerful. Adjust your plan to match the nature of the eddy and be ready to adjust your approach whenever necessary.

SPEED AND ANGLE

There are two things to think about when entering an eddy: your *speed* and *angle* of entry. Both concepts help you accomplish one goal: to get across the eddy line quickly—upright!

The most important step when entering an eddy is establishing a good angle upstream of the obstacle. Since currents jet along eddy lines faster than they do either inside the eddy or out in the main current, eddy lines create hydraulic shields that deflect any kayak that approaches the eddy with too little angle. On the other hand, a kayak that approaches

When exiting an eddy, tilt your kayak downstream (right). *Tilt your kayak upstream* (left) *when entering.*

the same eddy line with too much angle will succumb to the main current before it has a chance to cross the eddy line. The idea is to cross the eddy line at a 45-degree angle. (Later on, as your eddy skills improve, you can tailor your angles to meet the demands of the river.)

Speed is one of those vague terms that varies from person to person and from eddy to eddy. The second key to entering an eddy is to get across the eddy line—fast! The slower you try to cross an eddy

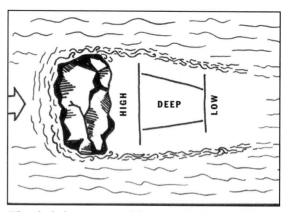

The ideal place to enter eddies is usually high and deep. That is where the eddy is the strongest.

Approaching an eddy with too little angle will cause you to miss the eddy, while a proper approach angle makes catching eddies a snap.

line the more likely you are to flip or miss the eddy altogether; if you enter a small, mid-river eddy too fast you're likely to blow out the other side. So *match your speed* with the eddy's power and *choose an angle*

that will quickly expose your kayak to the eddy's upstream current and drag it to a halt.

Once you've made it into an eddy, look around. Are you at a standstill, or are you still moving? Since eddies have their own set of currents, they will carry you upstream toward the confluence with the main current. Since this confluence marks the most powerful transition point between the eddy's current and the main current, you'll probably prefer to relax in the calmer waters deep in the eddy. To stay in the heart of the eddy, use small correction strokes or lean against the wall or boulder that formed the eddy and hold on.

EXITING EDDIES

There are three ways to exit an eddy: *peel out; ferry across the eddy line;* or *exit downstream.* Downstream exits are only used in mellow eddies with weak currents—all you have to do is paddle downstream until the eddy releases you. The first two exits—peel outs and ferries—take a little bit of finesse. Each exiting technique requires the same proper leans as do entries: Use your downstream J-lean to avoid flipping upstream, and lean more aggressively downstream if the currents make this necessary.

In this first of a series of four photos, a kayaker executes one last forward stroke on his left side to obtain the proper eddy entry angle as he approaches an eddy.

As the bow touches the eddy line, he gets ready to lean upstream and to plant a duffek stroke in the eddy.

As he pierces deeper into the eddy, the kayaker uses the duffek stroke and the turning power of the eddy to pivot the kayak upstream. Note that the kayaker is still leaning upstream.

The kayak is totally in the eddy and pointed upstream.

Peel outs

A *peel out* is an exciting maneuver that spins your kayak downstream as you exit the eddy. To start your peel out, accelerate upstream and across the eddy line but point your bow 30 to 45 degrees to the main current and lean downstream. As you cross the eddy line, lean downstream and do a forward stroke, bow draw, or duffek stroke on your downstream side. If you've executed a peel out correctly, the main current will pile beneath your upstream edge and spin you around to face downstream.

Ferrying out of eddies

Ferrying out of an eddy is little different than ferrying across the main channel, except that the transition between currents tends to take novices by surprise. The moment the bow hits the main current the kayak will try to spin downstream. To avoid spinning out, anticipate the main current, build up some upstream momentum as you paddle to the top of the eddy, and cross the eddy line pointing 10 to 25 degrees to the main current. Place your last stroke on

> **"N**inety percent of the time, the thing that's going to flip a beginner is not going to be a wave or little hole—it will be moving from slow water to fast water, or vice versa. It's a transition of speed that they haven't done and it will feel strange. However, when entering or exiting eddies, beginners can translate the movements they need to do into something they already can relate to, like riding a bike around a corner. If you're riding a bike around a right-hand corner, which way do you lean the bike? *Into the turn!* Kayaking is the same way. As soon as you enter or exit an eddy, your boat is gonna turn. And as it does, you want to lean the boat—not your body, but the boat—into the turn, much like you're on a bicycle. As soon as you're done turning, flatten the boat out and you'll be balanced and upright. **"**
>
> **—JOHN "TREE" TRUJILLO**
> **OLYMPIC FESTIVAL MEDALIST**

the downstream side of your kayak to compensate for the main current, and concentrate. Although a stern draw on the downstream side may be the preferred corrective stroke, the only way to tell what strokes you'll need next will be to watch your ferry.

The SAFE System

Now that you understand all of the basic maneuvers, just plug them into a system—one with regular routines that simplifies the way you run a river. Before running any whitewater rapid, kayakers can follow a preset game plan called the SAFE System. I designed the SAFE system to be an easy way to evaluate any rapid while providing a safe and simple approach to whitewater travel. It is based on four steps:

- **Scout** rapids fully before entering them. This may be done from either bank or, if there is an eddy or slow pool, from your kayak.
- **Analyze** the rapid and your ability to run it. Where are the obstacles? Where are the safest channels? Is there a safe line through the rapid? Which way will you swim if you fall out? Are you and your equipment capable of running the rapid safely?
- **Formulate** a plan. Which route will you follow? What is your back-up plan? What maneuvers

will you have to execute? Should you portage instead? Should a rescue team be stationed along the banks?

- **Execute** your plan. Run the rapid or carry the kayak along the bank.

To start a peel out, the kayaker accelerates up the eddy and takes one last stroke on his right side. Notice that his kayak is tilted slightly downstream.

After crossing the eddy line at a 45-degree angle, the kayaker continues leaning downstream while relying on a duffek stroke to control his speed and direction.

SCOUT

Unless you know what is around a bend or over the horizon—or you feel that you have the skills to pull to shore in an emergency—scout! Pull ashore well above the lip of rapids and long before strong currents drag your kayak places you don't want to go.

Starting from your landing point, walk all the way to the base of a rapid or all the way around a bend so that you can see the entire section of river you'll be running. This may take some scrambling to reach the best vantage point, but a clear line of sight usually is well worth the extra effort. While scouting, make mental notes of easily recognizable landmarks and distinctive hydraulics—if you decide to run the rapid, you can use them as signposts to tell you where you are and where you need to turn. Remember that rapids are areas of *falling water* and your landmarks might not be visible from upstream. Keep looking over your shoulder as you walk back to the kayak to see if your landmarks disappear. If they do, walk downstream again and pick new ones.

ANALYZE

By now you have learned about the most common hydraulics and obstacles you'll see in a typical rapid. You've learned that tongues and wave trains signify

To ferry out of an eddy, the kayaker already has accelerated up the eddy and is in a position to use a stern pry on his right side to control his boat and prevent spinning downstream.

He also could use a stern draw on his left side to control his boat angle. Better yet, he could maintain forward strokes with subtle corrections to maintain a perfect ferry angle.

safe channels, while sharp ledges, roostertails, and undercuts are hazards to be avoided. It's now time to apply your knowledge of river features—together with your knowledge of kayak maneuvers—to analyze a rapid before you.

When scouting a rapid, look for two things: *obstacles* and *safe routes*. On smaller rivers, the hazards will probably be solid obstacles like rocks or logs. Large-volume rivers, on the other hand, might not have any solid obstacles that cause you concern, but they can have minefields of keeper holes and menacing haystacks.

To find safe routes, try walking upstream from the bottom of the rapid and play *connect the dots*. Can safe routes be connected or are they broken up by major hazards? (The more broken and twisted the route, the harder the rapid will be.) Your goal is to discover at least one *clean line* through the rapid—one that you can maneuver without putting yourself in serious danger. If you are scouting a particularly difficult rapid, note where you can exit the current if you flip, and where *not to be* if you find yourself swimming.

Once you find a runnable line through the rapid, decide whether you and your equipment are up to the demands posed by the river—if not, take a look at the bank and figure out whether it is better to portage.

FORMULATE

If you think you *can* run a rapid, run it mentally first. Imagine each move you'll make as your kayak descends the rapid from top to bottom. Again, keep in mind the landmarks you scouted out and correlate them with moves you'll make in the rapid. As you imagine each maneuver, think of what could go wrong and what you'll do in the event of a mishap. Finally, discuss your plan with your fellow kayakers: If there's any chance you'll have problems, station rescuers at key points along the bank to assist you.

EXECUTE

The entry into the rapid is the most critical maneuver. Unless you have to punch a big hydraulic right at the top of the rapid, consider approaching the lip as slowly as possible to glean a last glimpse downstream. Remember that the rapid is going to look quite different from your new vantage point—especially if the rapid is steep—and that you're probably going to have pre-rapid butterflies.

As you enter the rapid, relax and look around. It is amazing how many kayakers experience tunnel vision in whitewater, emerging wet and excited in the pool below but totally unable to remember what just happened upstream.

Run the rapid methodically, sticking to your main plan, and adjusting it whenever the river proves to be too cunning. Make each move by adjusting your kayak's momentum and angle, and be ready to celebrate your trip when you reach the

> **"T**hree things will improve your boating quickly: *posture, planting* and *vision*. Good posture helps your balance, rotation, and your ability to do all of your strokes. Planting means taking the time to do your strokes correctly. Pause at the plant to feel your blade solidly grab the water before you rush into pulling it back. If you feel your blade bite the water, you'll gain some extra power in your strokes.
>
> **"**Vision has three parts: *Pre-vision*—or looking ahead—involves thinking about where you want to go, deciding where you want to be, and making a plan for running a rapid or surfing a wave; *vision* is what you see as you enter the rapid—look where you want to go and allow your boat to follow your vision; *re-vision* is what you do after you run the rapid—look back, see what you did right, analyze what you did wrong, and spot the problems that you need to work on so your next trip through the rapid will be even better.**"**
>
> —SHANE BENEDICT
> KAYAK DESIGNER/INSTRUCTOR

safety of the pool downstream. If all goes well, you'll have plenty of reason to rejoice!

Honing Your Skills

As your basic skills improve, you may find yourself longing for wilder rapids or contentedly returning to the gentle rivers you have become accustomed to. No matter what your aspirations, you can vastly improve your kayaking skills by looking at the river you're on *right now* in a different light.

Up until now you have been taught to look for the safest, easiest routes through rapids. At the same time, you learned that many rapids have several runnable channels. Now it's time to shun the obvious passages and to test your skills by using the river to challenge yourself.

Rather than taking the cleanest line through a Class II or III rapid, look for an imaginary slalom course, using boulders, holes, or logs to mark a serpentine route. Ferry back and forth around boulders and try to connect the eddies behind rocks, stopping in each one as you go. Soon you will be able to paddle exactly where you want it to go rather than just going wherever the river carries you. With just a little bit of practice, your skill level will skyrocket and prepare you for greater challenges to come.

> **"I** think one of the best ways to learn to be a better paddler is take small rapids and do every move possible. Catch all of the eddies, surf little tiny waves over to the next eddy, go up behind rocks, and just look at every feature in the rapid. Instead of trying to avoid everything, try to drop into everything and see what you can do. If you can make hard moves in easy rapids now, then you'll soon be able to make hard moves in harder rapids also. **"**
>
> —DUSTIN KNAPP
> FREESTYLE KAYAKER, TEAM DAGGER

8

Safety and Rescue

Keeping Your Head and Gear above Water

Today's kayakers find themselves in a unique quandary. Equipped with top-quality equipment and a wealth of intellectual know-how, modern kayakers are able to tackle rapids that would have sent previous explorers scurrying in search of portage routes. Also, the techniques that took our predecessors many years to learn now can be acquired by zealous novices in just a few weeks or months.

The rush toward more exciting and difficult whitewater carries with it greater risk and increased perils. The difference between a Class III and Class 5 swim can be astounding, yet many newcomers find themselves on expert runs without even having perfected their offside rolls. And fundamental rescue skills—such as those necessary to retrieve a pinned kayak or tired swimmer—frequently elude the eager novice who moves on to harder and harder rivers.

As in any outdoor sport, uncontrolled risk invites calamity. Accordingly, safety should be the primary concern on any river outing, whether it involves a peaceful, scenic float or a heart-pounding Class 5 descent.

Using Your Brain

The best rescue tool you have in your entire safety arsenal is your brain. It carries all the information you possess on first aid, rope rescues, swimming techniques—plus, it keeps working whether you're on the river or not. So keep it in shape. Check out the best safety and rescue literature you can get your hands on—like *Whitewater Rescue Manual* by Charles Walbridge and Wayne Sundmacher—and take rescue classes through Rescue 3, the ACA, or your local paddling school. When it finally comes time to use your brain in a *real* rescue situation, you'll be well prepared.

Pre-Trip Preparedness

One of the most important pre-trip considerations is to select a river your entire group is capable of running. Use the *weakest* members of your party as a reference and pick a river that is within the entire group's skill level. There are scores of outstanding guidebooks, maps, and other resources to assist you in your search for the ideal river.

Pre-trip meetings provide a perfect opportunity to discuss your river itinerary, potential river hazards, paddling strategies and river signals. Once you're at the river, *gather again on the bank or in the first eddy to confirm your trip plans, then go have fun!*

Be sure to adequately research the location and distance between put ins and take outs, the time it will take to run the river, the classification and location of major rapids, and the recommended water levels for safe trips. Pay particular attention to road access and shuttle information—important factors on any trip, since shuttles frequently consume a lot of valuable time and daylight. Also keep in mind that any guidebook is only a reference source and that rivers change constantly. Seek the recommendations and advice of more-experienced kayakers whose first-hand knowledge of the river exceeds that of any guidebook author.

The next step in your pre-trip agenda is to survey water levels and local weather forecasts. Gentle streams can become angry, dangerous torrents at high water, and bone-chilling winds or driving rains can dampen even the liveliest spirits. A number of governmental agencies provide prerecorded river-level readings and weather reports. Another source of information is a local whitewater shop or an outfitter located near the river.

TIME ON THE RIVER

Rivers flow (dams notwithstanding) on their own schedules. Veteran kayakers can guesstimate how long a trip will take by comparing the current's average velocity to the distance between the put in and take out. Beginner and intermediate kayakers can avoid this kind of guesswork by consulting a guidebook or a knowledgable kayaker to find out how long a particular trip usually takes.

Once on the river, you can try to beat the clock by paddling faster than the river's average flow, but that expends a lot of energy and cuts down on the quality of the experience (unless, of course, you're racing). Also, rivers tend to hold time-consuming surprises for the wary and unwary river runner alike. An unexpected swim or torn spray skirt can easily delay your take out, or an unexpected rise in water level might increase the river's difficulty, leading to more scouting or portaging.

To make sure you have enough time to safely enjoy your whitewater trip, expect the unexpected and leave enough time to handle ordinary mishaps.

Here are some commonly used river signals. Whatever signals you use, make sure everybody in your group understands them ahead of time.

PRE-TRIP DISCUSSION

Before leaving the put in, take some time to gather the group and discuss the day's plans. During your discussion, you can select a group leader (usually the most experienced or knowledgeable member of the group), cover the day's itinerary, form a plan for known hazards, and decide in what order the group ought to travel. It's also a good idea to cover river signals at this time.

River signals—arm signals or paddles pointed in the right direction—can point upstream paddlers in the right direction or beckon assistance during a rescue situation. Take some time to familiarize yourself with the signals and make sure that the entire group knows what signals paddlers will be using.

Safety and Rescue Equipment

Top-quality equipment often makes the difference between enjoyable river excursions and whitewater fiascoes. On the other hand, you don't have to dump all of your hard-earned money into the finest gear available. Simply put, it is important to utilize equipment designed to withstand the rigors of whitewater use.

In addition to the equipment described earlier, kayakers should carry an assortment of essential safety gadgets—*carabiners, knives, whistles, prusiks, pulleys, throw bags, web slings,* and *first aid kits.* Also, whenever there's a chance of someone breaking a

paddle on a remote river, someone should carry a *two-piece paddle* (also known as a *breakdown paddle*). These paddles split in half and can be stored in the stern of your kayak until needed.

The downside of carrying rescue gear is that it will add weight to your kayak and make it harder to maneuver. However, if an emergency arises, its presence will bring peace of mind. Carry it along and just hope that the gear collects waterspots while you enjoy the river.

CARABINERS

Carabiners are the river runner's multipurpose tool: They can be used to clip in gear, attach lines to kayaks, or they can be substituted for pulleys in an emergency. Experienced river runners carry two or three carabiners in a life-jacket pocket or clipped to the shoulder or waist of their life jackets so they'll be

Rescue gear can help keep your trip safe and enjoyable.

readily accessible when needed. (If you don't carry your carabiners in a pocket, it is important to keep the carabiners *tucked flat* against the life jacket with the gates *facing inward* to prevent injury or accidental clipping into stray ropes or branches.)

KNIVES

Knives have many applications on the river. They can quickly sever any lines that imperil a kayaker in danger and can be used for a variety of inventive purposes in other situations. Quality river knives have solid sheaths of plastic or stiffened leather and can be worn on the chest or shoulder of your life jacket for quick access. If you have a thumb-release sheath, check the release frequently to make sure your knife will still be there when you need it.

WHISTLES

Whistles are real attention-getters in almost any situation. Signal an emergency by giving three short blasts.

PRUSIKS

A prusik is a short loop—about 4 or 5 feet long—made of 5- to 7-mm kernmantle rope. It can be used to tie off kayaks or to set brakes in Z-drag rescues (discussed later in this chapter). When making your own prusiks, decide if you'll be wearing them around your waist like a belt—if so, measure your waist with your river clothes on, then double your waist width and add 1 foot to get the length of rope you'll need. Next, tie the ends of the rope together with a double fisherman's knot to form the loop. Now the prusik is ready to be worn around the waist like a belt, clipped in with a carabiner.

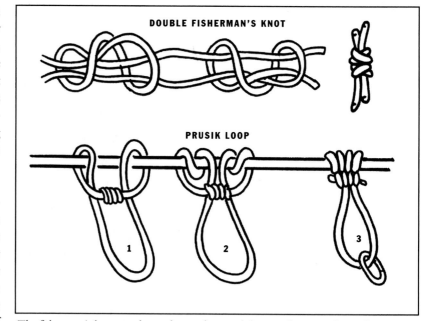

DOUBLE FISHERMAN'S KNOT

PRUSIK LOOP

1 2 3

The fisherman's knot can be used to make prusik loops—short rope loops that are often used in Z-drags and other rescue systems.

PULLEYS

Pulleys are handy friction-reducing tools that can be used in Z-drag rescues to increase the efficiency of the system. For river use, select sturdy aluminum-alloy pulleys designed to accommodate half-inch (11mm) rope.

THROW BAGS

Throw bags—also known as *throw ropes, rescue ropes,* and *rescue bags*—are remarkable rope-retaining tools designed to freely spool out rope when the bag is tossed to a swimmer. It simplifies the rope-throwing process and makes it easier for swimmers to see the rope coming—especially when the bag is filled with brightly colored, high-floating rope. When not in use, the throw bag neatly stows rope out of harm's way.

While a throw rope may be strong enough to unwrap a kayak or free a stranded swimmer, there may be times when a rope with superior strength and minimum stretch is needed. High-quality static lines have incredible tensile strength—far more than found in most throw-bag ropes. In some instances—such as a remote first descent—you may want to safely store 100 feet of 11-mm static rope in your kayak. Note, however, that the static rope's bulk and weight often make this impractical.

WEB SLINGS

Web slings—made of 1- or 2-inch-wide nylon webbing—are used as anchors in Z-drag systems, can be used as rappel anchors, and provide makeshift harnesses for vertical extrications. By carrying a few slings of varying lengths (10 to 20 feet) in your rescue kit, you'll be prepared to set up anchors in most any type of canyon environment.

FIRST AID KITS

A first aid kit should be standard equipment on any river trip. Minor injuries are inevitable, even on easy rivers, but they often can be treated immediately by someone trained in first aid. Take the time to consider the type of trip you're undertaking and the location of the nearest medical assistance when assembling the first aid kit. (See the Appendix for a list of suggested items to fill your first aid kit.)

Group Travel

River trips are safer when three or more kayakers paddle together. The extra boats and paddlers can provide assistance in emergencies and can make the difference between a successful rescue and a disaster.

In any group trip, it may be helpful to choose a *lead* boat to run at the front of the pack and a *sweep* boat to bring up the rear. The lead kayak usually contains the most experienced and knowledgeable

Anatomy of a throw bag.

paddler, acts as a scout or probe in rapids, and renders assistance to other kayaks when pulling over to scout. The sweep boat also contains an experienced paddler but lags slightly behind the pack so it can render assistance if a problem arises.

It is often helpful to scout difficult rapids as a group and follow the SAFE plan discussed in the previous chapter. Try to get everybody involved and listening to the group discussion—that way everyone will know the group's plan.

In easy rapids, a rescue plan is rarely needed. However, more difficult rapids demand special consideration and extra precautions. If the rapid is too difficult for your skill level, portage around it. If you plan to run it, position a couple of kayakers with throw bags at key points along the rapid to render assistance in case someone flips or swims. Practice *redundant safety*, which simply means that you should have both a main plan and a contingency plan for everything that could go wrong.

Self Rescues

River-based rescues fall into two categories: *self rescues* and *assisted rescues*. In self rescues, kayakers are essentially left to attend to their own well-being, while in assisted rescues, land- and water-based rescuers contribute to the relief efforts with throw lines, extra boats, and physical support. In both types of rescues, one aspect of river safety reigns supreme: *People come first!*

ESKIMO ROLLS

You don't have to look far to find the most basic form of self rescue: the Eskimo roll. Been slammed over by a wave? Roll up! Come up upside down after a big ledge? Roll! The better your roll, the less you'll swim; the less you swim, the happier you'll be! But if you're heading upside down toward a rock sieve and you don't have time to roll and get out of there, bail! Wet exit and swim like a salmon for the safest spot you can find.

SWIMMING

Swimming a rapid, much to the surprise of many beginners, is nothing like swimming in a lake or pool. Strong currents can overwhelm and fatigue even experienced swimmers. However, once swimmers understand the forces involved—either by swimming easy rapids or from prior experience—they can relax and rationally set out to swim to safety.

Unless you intentionally jumped into the river, your first reaction to swimming can range from mild frustration to outright panic. The first thing you have

to tell yourself is to *relax*. The more energy you exert underwater, the faster you'll need air. Fortunately, most wet exits let you pop back to the surface instantly. Once there, you should aggressively survey the river and banks for hazards, look downstream for calm pools and eddies that may offer safe harbors, and formulate a plan.

The human shock absorber

The first part of your self-rescue plan involves deciding *how* you're going to swim. One way to swim is to lay back in the *human shock-absorber* position (on your back, butt held high, feet downstream on the surface). In this position, you can fend off rocky collisions with your feet and back-stroke with your arms and legs to ferry toward safety. When floating in the human shock-absorber position, however, a new hazard presents itself—*foot entrapments*. To avoid the perils of foot entrapment, never jam your feet into cracks or slots or try to stand up in rapids. Instead, wait until the current has subsided or you are in the calm of a gentle eddy.

Active swimming

No matter how—or when—you apply the human shock-absorber technique, it's only temporary. Your primary goals should always be to *protect yourself, get enough air,* and *aggressively swim to safety* when an opportunity arises.

In active swimming, you start off (again) by relaxing, getting yourself to the surface (head toward light or follow the direction of the bubbles if you're disoriented), and surveying the scene. If you have to ball up in a steep, bone-bruising rapid, the *cannonball*

PORTAGING

Rapids evoke a broad spectrum of emotions—from excitement to outright fear. Your mind's inner voice usually provides a good gauge for your chances of success. For those of us who like to ignore our mind's inner voices, we can listen to our *bodies*—a sudden desire to urinate or inability to spit are pretty good indicators that an upcoming rapid's going to present one heck of a challenge. *Portaging* is common on whitewater rivers. Whenever the river exceeds your skill level, shoulder your kayak and start walking. Don't let your peers, ego, or disdain for portaging put you in whitewater that exceeds your skill level.

---

position—pulling your knees into your chest—may be a good short-term way to protect your limbs and other vital parts from injury. Still, when a safe opportunity arises, turn onto your stomach and swim aggressively toward a safe harbor (this can be the bank, an eddy, or even a midstream island). Once out of the rapid, you can breathe, restore your confidence, and decide what to do next.

The human shock-absorber position can save you from injuries. However, you must keep your feet and butt high to avoid entrapment. Tuck into a cannonball position when plunging over steep drops and actively swim toward safety when a safe opportunity arises.

Holes and dams

The upstream surface currents of large holes and lowhead dams can recirculate swimmers indefinitely, and once caught in these traps your life jacket may not have enough flotation to keep you above the aerated water. Accordingly, holes and dams sometimes demand special techniques for quick escapes.

Keep in mind that most holes are too small or irregular to be "keepers." So, if you find yourself stuck momentarily in a backwash, relax for a second, breathe when you can, and try to swim sideways out of the hole. If you can't escape sideways, remember that falls contain a powerful downcurrent that can be used to push you under the hole and out. Swim right into the falls, ball up in the cannonball position, and hang on for the ride. If you come up on the boil line, be sure to recover quickly and swim aggressively downstream to avoid being recirculated.

Lowhead dams contain the most difficult to escape and the most deadly of all holes. *Don't run them!* If you ever *do* find yourself swimming a dam, you may recirculate in the backwash many times. Try to save your energy and work your way toward shore. Swimming into the falls may be enough to push you out under the backwash, but be prepared to make many attempts at self rescue. Above all, *don't give up!*

Sweepers and strainers

Some of the worst hazards facing kayakers are downed trees (sweepers) and boulder sieves (strainers) that don't impede the current entirely. Sweepers can snag a life jacket and hold a swimmer underwater, while strainers can wedge a swimmer into tight subsurface pockets.

If you find yourself swimming toward one of these hazards, try to *swim around it* with all the power you can muster. If a collision with a downed tree or log is inevitable, turn onto your stomach and face downstream, concentrating on the approach: A split second before you reach the log, begin kicking with your legs, then pull your body *over* it *head first* using any handholds you can find. Give it all you've got! If you can't make it over the log, try hanging on until you can be rescued. If you absolutely have to go under the strainer, first feel for snags with your legs. Remember, *going underneath a strainer is the last thing you want to do!* Do it only as a last resort.

SWIMMING WITH YOUR BOAT AND PADDLE

Having paddled all types of inflatable craft (rafts and inflatable kayaks) in addition to traditional kayaks, I've become quite adept at swimming after my boat, pulling myself into an entry position, and climbing back aboard.

Traditional kayakers, on the other hand, have a bear of a time mastering these skills: Kayaks become heavy and burdensome when filled with water, and they can flatten you like a pancake if you're ever caught between them and a rock.

Still, swimming with your kayak is a necessary skill. But first let's talk about two important rules. Rule one: You're more important than your new boat. Rule two: Whenever you're swimming with your boat, refer back to rule one. Swimming with your boat can save you from having to search for it downstream later in the day (or even coming back next weekend to find it) but it has its perils. If you're going to stick with your boat, learn how to do it correctly, and learn when to leave well enough alone.

Boats and swimmers can ferry in the same manner paddlers ferry: Work across the current by slowing yourself down and angling toward one bank. To do this swimming with your kayak, grab an upstream end, angle it toward the bank you want to reach

If you are recirculated by a hole, you may be able to follow the green water and exit beneath the hole.

(maintain an *upstream angle*), and swim for all you're worth. You may make painfully slow progress, but perseverance and aggressiveness often pay off.

Even if your swim starts perfectly, though, swimming with a boat sometimes requires creativity. Let's say you're heading toward a slot with lots of pinning potential. Jam your boat in the chock, push off it and swim away. Heading toward a boulder or undercut? Keep your boat between you and the hazard, and it'll provide excellent body armor.

Paddles are a lot easier to deal with than are boats: They're smaller, lighter, and they don't hold 60 gallons of water when full. If you can safely hold your paddle, do it! You'll save your friends from chasing it downstream (and you from having to buy a new one). If you learned to wet exit without releasing your paddle, you'll be good at retaining it on the river. If your paddle is a burden—whether it is stuck between some rocks or making it difficult to execute a fast, safe rescue—ditch it! You're more important.

Water-Based Assisted Rescues

Water-based rescue skills are an essential part of every paddler's repertoire. They come into play any time land-based rescues can't be established (see page 98) and allow you to execute fast rescues in a wide variety

DUMPING OUT YOUR BOAT, REVISITED

Do you remember how to dump out your boat? Turn it upside down (cockpit facing the ground) and rock it end to end to get the water out. Use rocks, ledges, a knee—anything you can find to help support the boat off the ground and make your job easier. If you're lucky and have a drain plug installed in the stern, just unscrew it and let the water drain. What could be easier?

of situations. Most importantly, they put you where the action is, without making you waste any time setting up complicated rescue schemes.

THE ESKIMO RESCUE

Remember the Eskimo rescue? (For those of you who said *yes,* super!) You can use it on the river from time to time: For example, you're stuck against a slightly undercut wall and can get your head up enough to breathe, but you can't quite nail your roll. An Eskimo rescue can save the day, as long as the rescuer, too, doesn't get intimate with the undercut.

(Did you say *no?* Head back to page 41 and check out the Eskimo rescue techniques again. They'll come in handy some day!)

TOWING SWIMMERS

A kayaker in his boat can often assist a swimmer by offering a tow or a place on the stern to rest. In many situations, swimmers can grab stern grab loops with one hand, hold the paddle with the other hand, and kick while the rescuer tows. (On rarer occasions, the swimmer can hold on to the bow while the rescuer

> **"T**here are a lot of great swiftwater rescue programs that teach paddlers how to do a variety of rescues. However, in-boat rescue skills are often the most important to have. A lot of times there's only limited assistance you can give from shore. A lot of rescues happen from the boat. For instance, somebody that's pinned on a rock or swimming in the middle of a wide river or narrow, steep-walled canyon will need help from somebody already in a boat. Work on all of your rescue skills, take rescue classes, but pay special attention to water-based rescue skills. You'll need them the most.**"**
>
> —JOHN "TREE" TRUJILLO
> 1992 WORLD MEDALIST

paddles to safety. This latter technique is difficult, however, because it usually knocks the rescuer's kayak way out of trim and makes it extremely difficult to paddle effectively.)

Swimmers can be towed on the back deck of a kayak. However, the swimmer should allow the rescuer ample room to paddle and avoid pulling on the rescuer's body or spray skirt.

BULLDOZING BOATS

You've seen it before. A paddler flips in a ledge, wet exits, and bee lines it for the bank. The empty boat, on the other hand, takes off downstream while you and the rest of your group evaluate your moral obligation to save it. Boat rescues call upon the same ferrying and river-running principles already discussed, but you now have to apply these principles to a new technique affectionately known as *bulldozing* or *snowplowing.*

Bulldozing is just what it sounds like: You bulldoze

your friend's boat toward safety, as if you were pushing a pile of dirt with a 2-ton Caterpillar. Start by knocking the loose boat into alignment parallel with the current using your boat's bow (this helps it to slip through narrow slots and to avoid pins). Next, assess where you're going to try to push it: Look for big eddies and pools, and wait for an opening if necessary. Finally, bulldoze the boat into the eddy or the pool when the opportunity arises.

There are a lot of ways to make the bulldoze technique easier. Here are a handful of tips:

1. It is often easier to bulldoze boats from upstream since that negates powerful downstream currents.

2. Avoid letting an empty boat pivot. Once it does, you may have to reset your angle or chase it down.

3. If possible, slide your bow into the empty boat's cockpit.

4. Call your fellow boaters into action and use teamwork to rescue the boat.

Bulldozing a kayak.

5. Always come at the empty boat from the side opposite the eddy or pool you're driving toward.

USING BOAT-TOW SYSTEMS

Boat-tow systems are quite different from traditional throw bags and rescue ropes. They can be easier to employ than bulldoze rescues since they free up both hands for paddling and keep the empty boat closer at hand.

There are three popular boat-tow systems: *hand-held webbing loops, boat-mounted systems,* and *harness systems.*

Hand-held webbing loops

Some kayakers keep a loop of webbing around their waist and buckle it into place with a carabiner. When needed, the carabiner is clipped to the loose boat's bow loop and the web loop is strung over the rescuer's arm or shoulder. As long as proper caution is taken to avoid entanglement, the rescuer can paddle effectively and escape the loop if necessary.

Boat-mounted systems

Ropes can be attached to the decks of boats in a variety of ways, and they can be employed whenever boat rescues are necessary. On the other hand, some systems work better than others. My favorite—which involves tying one end of a short rope to the stern, looping and wedging the other end into a jam cleat mounted just behind the cockpit—allows for both easy rescues and quick escapes when needed.

To pull off a rescue, release the rescue rope from the jam cleat, thread it through the bow loop of the loose boat, and jam it back into the cleat. Once you're set up, paddle the empty boat into position. If you run into trouble, pull the rope out of the cleat and paddle to safety.

Harness systems

There is now a great selection of specialty life jackets (*rescue jackets*) with harness systems built right in. Tow tethers are one of the options available on these life jackets, and they can provide great rescue tools in the event of a swim.

Some tow tethers simply attach to a webbing belt on the rescue jacket with a solid ring and a carabiner. The webbing threads through the ring end of the belt, and the carabiner clips into a handy loop on the front of the jacket. During a rescue, the carabiner is unclipped from the jacket and re-clipped to the loose boat. Then, if matters take a turn for the worse, the webbing belt can be released with a quick-release buckle so the tow tether breaks free.

Sounds great, huh? The only problem is that the tow tether doesn't break free unless enough pressure is exerted. That can make rescue jackets somewhat hazardous in the hands of unskilled rescuers. Still, rescue jackets are invaluable tools—especially on steep creeks and on demanding Class 5

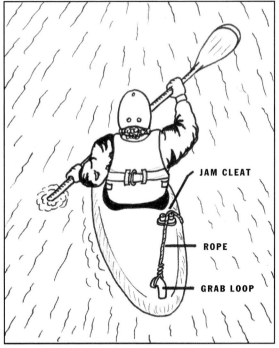

Kayaks can be retrofitted with a variety of rope-rescue systems. In this simple system, a jam cleat holds the loose end of the rope while the other end remains tied to the stern grab loop. If needed, the rope can be released from the cleat, threaded through the grab loop of the other kayak, and jammed back in the cleat. If the rescue goes awry, the rope can be released from the cleat so the rescuer can paddle freely.

Some modern rescue jackets have tow tethers that can be clipped to the free kayak or quickly released if the rescue goes awry.

rivers. Learn to assemble them properly, follow the manufacturer's recommendations, and they'll come in handy time and time again.

Land-Based Assisted Rescues

Land-based rescues differ from water-based rescues in one significant way: they put the rescuer on dry ground. Freed from currents and tippy boats, the land-based rescuer can frequently execute more precise and powerful rescues than water-based rescues, especially if the rescue situation was predicted before it ever arose.

ROPE RESCUES

Throw bags can provide life-saving umbilical cords linking swimmers with rescuers, but it takes a lot more than just aiming and tossing a rope to carry off a good rescue. It takes frequent practice to land a throw rope where a swimmer can reach it, and it takes keen knowledge of currents and river forces to finish off a rescue once a swimmer actually grasps the rope.

GETTING ROPES TO SWIMMERS

Before throwing a rope to a swimmer, evaluate the situation. The most effective rope rescues are those that were anticipated *before* the swim. By stationing themselves where a swimmer actually has an opportunity to see a throw bag coming, rescuers have a chance to establish the *first goal* of rope rescues: *eye contact* with the swimmer. By stationing a rescuer slightly downstream of where a swim might occur, a swimmer will have a chance to get back to the surface and clear his or her vision before the rope toss is made. Then, with a strong yell from the rescuer *(ROPE!)*, the swimmer has a chance to look at the rescuer and see the rope coming.

The rescuer's *second goal* also involves proper bank positioning, this time taking into account the power of the main current and downstream obstacles. Position the rescuer so that the first toss angles *45 degrees upstream* toward the swimmer. That way, the current can actually help push the swimmer toward the rescuer as the rope is pulled in. (Also, by throwing the rope upstream to the swimmer, the rescuer may have a chance

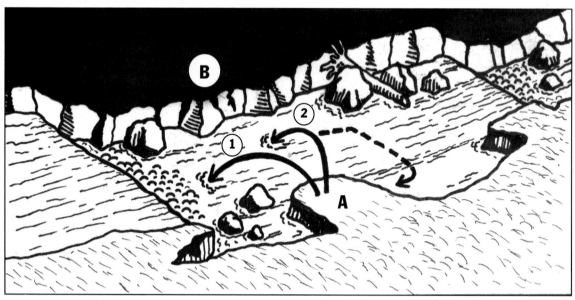

Position rescuers where they'll do the most good. Rescuer A can toss a throw bag 45 degrees upstream to a swimmer (or get in a second toss before the swimmer heads downstream). Rescuer A also has a good eddy nearby so the swimmer can *exit the current safely. Rescuer B, on the other hand, is in a dangerous position since the swimmer could be pulled into a log jam just downstream.*

An underhand rope throw.

An overhand rope throw.

at a second toss if the first one misses the mark.) If there are calm currents or gentle pools below a likely flip spot, the rescuer can use the rope to pendulum the swimmer into shore.

Never, however, pull swimmers into a worse situation than they're already in: make sure the rescue path is free of boulder sieves, sweepers, and other hazards that might be best avoided by letting the swimmer swim a few more yards downstream.

The rescuer's *third goal* is to actually get the rope to the swimmer. Depending on your dexterity and the surrounding obstacles (like overhanging cliffs or branches), your best toss may be underhand, sidearm, or overhand. Though it helps to be adept at all three types of throws, most rescues are done with an underhand toss. When aiming your throw, try to land the rope *at* or *just downstream* of the swimmer. That way, the swimmer can reach the rope even if it is a few feet away. (If you aim upstream of the swimmer, the slower surface current will slow the rope's descent while the swimmer accelerates downstream in the deeper, faster currents.)

Swimmers have to be able to help themselves just as much as rescuers help them. Presuming that the rope reaches the swimmer, the swimmer must be prepared to grab the rope with one or both hands

Swimmers should hold the rescue rope over their shoulders and lie on their backs. This lets them plane toward the surface and creates an air pocket around their face. Never wrap the rope around arm, wrist, or body. If you're a swimmer in need of help, try to actively assist your rescuer if it is safe to do so.

and turn onto his or her back, face up. (It is important to grab the rope, not the bag—review this during your pre-trip planning session.) In this position, the swimmer's body will plane toward the surface and offer less resistance to the current. A swimmer should never wrap the rope around hands, limbs, or body.

BELAYS

Once a rescuer and a swimmer are holding each end of a rescue rope, it is time to work the swimmer toward shore. Both should work to pull the slack out of the rope and prepare for a powerful jolt as it pulls tight.

There are two ways to pull the swimmer ashore: The rescuer can either pull the swimmer in from a stationary position with a *static belay* or can run downstream with the swimmer in a *dynamic belay.*

In a static belay, the rescuer pendulums the swimmer toward the shore from a stationary point on the bank. The rescuer can step on the end of the rope if he or she is worried that it will pull free, or a belay anchor, such as a tree stump or boulder, can be used. In using a *belay anchor,* the rope is wrapped one-half to one full turn around the anchor. (If you wrap the rope more than once around the anchor, it will take longer to unwrap it, and it may jam! Be careful!)

In strong currents, a dynamic belay is better since it reduces the counteracting forces that could yank the rope from the swimmer's hands. In a dynamic belay, the rescuer walks or runs down the bank with the swimmer, pulling in gradually with light rope pressure. This technique, as you can imagine, only works if there is an open corridor along the bank.

There are a few more tips that will make rope rescues easier. First, don't pick a rescue position too high above the river (this will make the working length of rope shorter and less versatile). Second, use the best type of throw you can (depending on where you're standing, the throw bag or rescue rope may have to be thrown underhand, overhand, or sidearm).

Rescuers can use a static belay (left) *or a dynamic belay* (right) *to assist swimmers. Never wrap the rope more than one turn around the anchor in a static belay in case a dynamic belay becomes necessary.*

OTHER ROPE RESCUES

There may be times when a swimmer is caught against a midstream boulder and a throw rope or boat-based rescue is impossible. If someone has to reach the swimmer to render assistance, one technique that might work is the *strong-swimmer rescue.*

The strong-swimmer rescue is a paradox in rescue procedures—by placing the rescuer inside a rope loop while working in the current, it increases the risk that the rescuer could be hurt or drowned. Nonetheless, there may be times when nothing else works and the risk is worth it.

The strong-swimmer rescue requires—at a minimum—a swimmer, a belayer, and a strong rope. A large, *very loose* loop is tied into one end of the rope and placed around the rescuer's chest. (The loop must be loose enough to push free if the rescuer encounters any trouble.) Once in the loop, the rescuer can be swung to the victim from the far bank (this only works in narrow streams) or lowered downstream to the victim from an upstream boulder or island.

A slightly safer alternative to the strong-swimmer rescue is something called the *fixed horizontal line.* The fixed horizontal line is a rope that is stretched taut just a foot or so above the river surface with one or both ends firmly anchored on shore. If both ends are anchored, the rescuer stands upstream of the fixed line, holds the rope against his or her waist, and walks sideways across the river. If something goes wrong, the rescuer somersaults over or swims under the fixed rope to break free. If only one end is anchored, the rope can be slowly let out from the loose anchor so the rescuer can walk downstream, waist against the line. If an emergency arises in this rescue technique, the rescuer can be set free by somersaulting away from the line or having a belayer release one end of the rope.

Since there is always a possibility that the in-water rescuer could snag a life-jacket buckle or carabiner on the line, it is generally best *not* to have the line anchored on both banks. Instead, use belay points on both banks or just tie one anchor off while belaying from the opposite bank.

A horizontal line supports the crosser but allows him to dive over or under the line in an emergency. Don't anchor the ends of the rope—you may have to let one end go if the crosser gets caught in the rope.

Strong-swimmer rescues: The rescuer can be swung downstream from the bank or lowered downstream from an island.

River Crossings

It is sometimes necessary to walk across shallow rivers without a rope. This can be done solo in gentle currents or as a team in stronger currents. No matter which technique is used, the same basic concepts apply: All shallow-water crossings are premised on maintaining *three points of contact* with the river bottom and are done slowly and methodically to avoid foot entrapments. Also, one crossing method may take precedence over another depending on the speed of the current and the depth of the river.

SOLO CROSSINGS

When crossing a river by yourself, use a sturdy paddle, pole, or tree limb as a brace. (The paddle—together with your two feet—provides the third point of contact.) Face upstream, jam one end of the paddle into the river bottom, and tilt it 30 degrees back toward your shoulder. At the same time, brace your shoulder against the paddle and lean your body 30 degrees upstream against it. Now, maintaining this 60-degree triangle, you can slowly sidestep your way across the river, *moving one point of contact at a time.*

GROUP CROSSINGS

The most basic group crossings are variations of solo crossings: The solo crosser carries someone piggyback from one bank to another, or a second individual follows the lead person across the river, pressed tightly against his or her back and legs.

If more people are to be added to the group, each new person can step toward the outboard shoulder of the person in front, effectively forming a wedge. A *line astern* formation works by placing additional people directly behind the point person. The secondary people add stability to the system by pressing down on the point person's shoulders, effectively increasing the pressure on his feet and the river bottom.

If there are three people in your group, arrange yourselves in a triangle and lock your arms around each other's shoulders. With the heaviest person on the downstream end of the triangle, *facing upstream,* the group members can lean into each other and form a pyramid. Moving one person's feet at a time, the group can work across the river.

Another way to shuttle people across the river is to use a technique discussed earlier in this chapter—people can walk back and forth across shallow streams along the fixed horizontal line.

Pins and Broaches

Pins and broaches—the things grandma leaves you in her will, right? Well, not by kayakers' definitions. Pins and broaches are river ordeals that you'll never forget. They can last seconds, giving you something to talk about at the bottom of a rapid; they can provide an exciting opportunity to apply all of your rescue skills and ingenuity; or they can leave you tapping your booties together and chanting, "There's no place like home, there's no place like home, there's no place . . ."

When a kayak vertically *pins* in a ledge or horizontally *broaches* across boulders, hundreds of pounds per square inch of water pressure hold it securely in

When doing a solo crossing, use a paddle, pole, or oar to steady yourself. The paddle and your feet provide three points of contact with the riverbed. By leaning forward and moving just one point of contact at a time, you will be more stable than you would be otherwise.

place. Overcoming such forces takes muscle, sturdy equipment, and a bit of stream-side engineering.

Some river runners look at pins and broaches as opportunities to whip out all of their rescue paraphernalia, blanket the landscape in ropes and hardware, and set up intricate retrieval systems. While some situations require just that type of action, it usually is more desirable to select the most basic system that will work quickly without any complication. Otherwise, any kayaker still aboard the trapped boat could quickly tire or drown while the rescuers work on their engineering skills. There are a few basic steps needed to set up a rescue from a pin or broach.

SURVEY THE SCENE

Before setting up any ropes, survey the scene. Is there a paddler in the trapped boat? Can he or she be freed before attempting to rescue the boat? *Always rescue the person first!* Use throw bags to give the paddler some leverage to pull against the current, and try to drop ropes down from above if the kayaker is pinned vertically. (This lets the paddler pull upward against the current while exiting the boat.)

Next, assess which bank the kayak is facing: What obstacles await downstream once the kayak is freed? How much of the kayak is left showing? How accessible are anchor points on the kayak and along the banks? Will the kayak be easier to remove from one direction than another?

Appoint someone to direct the rescue operation. The director should be a member of the shore crew (unless the only person who knows how to unwrap the kayak is still sitting in the middle of the river). By putting one person in charge, rescuers can work together as a team under the guidance of one coach.

Finally, keep in mind that the rescue process is flexible and should be tailored to meet the needs of the situation.

THE ANCHORS

Start the rescue operation by securely attaching one end of a strong rope to the kayak. If the kayak is left in a precarious position after its occupant washes

Pins and broaches can happen in a variety of ways, including entrapment between two rocks (left), in a vertical drop (center), or against a single obstacle (right).

free, reaching the kayak could be very difficult. Proceed with great caution and choose the approach with the lowest risk. That might mean you'll have to set up a horizontal line or a strong-swimmer rescue to reach the boat. Once at the kayak you may be able to stand on the obstacle holding it in place. If an anchor point (such as a grab loop or broach loop) is submerged, try to have an assistant hold on to the rigger to avoid getting pinned or swept beneath the surface.

BASIC ROPE SYSTEMS
The first way to pull a kayak loose is to simply join your fellow paddlers in a riverbank version of tug-o'-war. This develops only a 1:1 mechanical advantage, but it can pull trapped kayaks free. (A variation on this is the *vector pull:* Rather than pulling on the end of the rope, the shore end is tied to an anchor point and a second rope is attached to the center of the first rope at a 90 degree angle. Depending on which direction the second rope is pulled, a slightly higher power ratio can be transferred to the kayak.)

To double the power of your pulling system, anchor a couple of carabiners or a pulley to the kayak and run the rope through them. Then, with one end

of the rope tied to an anchor point on shore, you can pull on the loose end of the rope and create a 2:1 mechanical advantage.

Z-DRAGS
The Z-drag is one of the most popular rescue systems available. In a simple Z-drag system, a 3:1 mechanical advantage is developed, while more complex Z-drag systems can generate much greater leverage.

It takes little more than some strong rope to build a rudimentary Z-drag system, and carabiners and pulleys will lower rope friction any time the rope makes a turn. (If you don't have carabiners or pulleys, use a figure-eight or butterfly knot instead. These knots are illustrated in the Appendix.)

The three most basic ways to pull a pinned kayak free (from weakest to strongest) include the tug-o'-war (left), the vector pull (center), and the 2:1 system (right). The tug-o'-war provides no mechanical advantage; the vector pull can generate some mechanical advantage depending on the angle of pull. The 2:1 system, in which the rope runs from a shore anchor through a carabiner attached to the kayak and back to shore, doubles your pulling power.

The first step in setting up a Z-drag involves anchoring the rope to the kayak just as you would for a tug-o'-war or vector pull. At the same time, tie a sturdy tubular webbing sling or rope around a shore-based anchor and clip in a carabiner and a pulley (if they're available) to the webbing.

Next, tie a figure-eight or butterfly knot in the rope between the kayak and the anchor loop. Since this knot will move toward shore when you start pulling on the rope, it is important to set the knot close enough to the kayak so that it won't jam into the shore anchor. (If you're standing on the shore far from the kayak, you might want to tie the knot *before* you anchor the rope to the kayak.) If you have another carabiner and pulley handy, clip them into this knot.

Now it's time to complete the system. Take the rope's loose end and thread it through the shore-anchor carabiner or pulley, back through the figure-eight or butterfly knot, and back to shore. If set up correctly, the system will form a backward Z. To operate the system, just pull the free end of the rope.

Some rescuers add a *brake prusik* (see the prusik loop illustration at the top of page 90) to the shore-anchor loop. The brake prusik lets rescuers re-rig the system if a knot approaches the anchor loop and stops the rope from traveling backward through the system. Additional lines to the kayak can be used to ease the burden on the Z-drag.

Z-drags can be rigged in many ways. By adding a 2:1 pull to the system, the mechanical advantage grows to 6:1; by doubling the Z-drag, the mechanical advantage increases to 9:1. Familiarize yourself with multiple Z-drags—and hope you'll never have to use them!

First Aid

As with any other form of outdoor recreation, kayakers may get injured during a river trip. Fortunately, small cuts, bruises, or bouts with poison ivy are about as bad as any first-aid provider will likely see. But it is important to be prepared for any type of situation, from broken bones to near drownings.

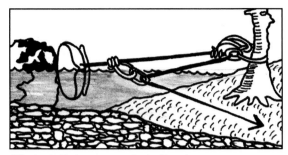

The basic Z-drag system, including the rescue rope, carabiners, and prusik loops. For every pound of pull exerted on the end of the rope, 3 pounds of pull will transfer to the kayak.

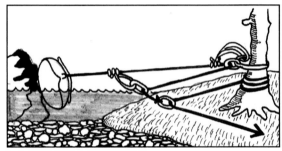

By adding a second line to a Z-drag, the mechanical advantage can be increased to 6:1.

Take the Red Cross Basic First Aid and CPR courses and strive for higher levels of certification. Know your physical limitations before embarking on a trip, and inform others of any medical conditions that may affect patient-care decisions. Also, have at least one member of your group carry a first-aid kit on every trip. On longer wilderness ventures it is not only important to have every item necessary to administer care but also to *know how to use them effectively.*

HYPOTHERMIA

The same water that provides a thrilling roller coaster ride can become a dangerous enemy for swimmers or underdressed passengers. *Hypothermia*—a cooling of the body temperature—can happen whenever a swimmer is immersed in water for any length of time or when cool air and spray drain the body's ability to stay warm. Hypothermia affects your judgment and it can be life-threatening in advanced stages. So, it is important, first, to avoid hypothermia with proper preparation and, second, to know how to reverse its effects if it sets in.

Warm clothing, adequate food consumption, and constant activity provide the first line of defense against hypothermia, but one quick swim can drain even the hardiest kayakers of internal warmth. If a kayaker winds up in the river, get him or her out *quickly*. Water can drain body heat 20 to 30 times faster than air can, making even a short swim in cold water very dangerous.

It is important to know the warning signs of hypothermia and how to treat victims if these signs are present. In the initial stages of hypothermia, victims may shiver vigorously, act cold, and appear pale. Treatment is easiest and most effective at this stage: Get victims away from the river, into dry clothes, and near a source of heat such as a warm car or a campfire. If nothing is available, walk victims along the bank until the cold and shivering go away. Left untreated, victims will progress into the next stage.

As the body's core temperature drops to 90° to 95° Fahrenheit, victims may become confused, clumsy, sluggish, and shivering may slow down. Their speech may become slurred and their eyes dull. By the time these symptoms appear, the body has lost its ability to rewarm itself and the basic treatment regimen won't work—an external source of heat is necessary. In a fix it may be necessary for a couple of people to climb into a sleeping bag with the victim and establish full-body, *skin-to-skin* contact, letting their body warmth gently warm the victim. If a strong fire is available, seat the victim close to the heat with a backdrop of blankets or sleeping bags for insulation. Whatever is done, it has to be done *before* the victim loses any more heat.

As the victim's core temperature drops further, muscles will become rigid, the patient will become unconscious and may suffer a cardiac arrest. *Immediate* evacuation and hospitalization is *mandatory* in this situation.

9

The World of Advanced Kayaking

Steeper and Deeper

How many times have you stood above a rapid, shoulder to shoulder with fellow kayakers, saying things like, "I'm going left of that hole, then to the right of the big boulder, then back to the center of those waves"? With minor variations, I've heard myself talk like that hundreds of times. The myopic thought process of scouting rapids always was *two dimensional*, locked into directions like *upstream* and *downstream, left bank* and *right bank.* Advanced paddling forces you to explore new paddling techniques. It forces you beyond the two-dimensional world you've become accustomed to and into whitewater's *third dimension.*

Whitewater's third dimension is the river's vertical world—a world of steep waves, sharp holes, exposed rocks, and swelling boils. Up to now you've thought of many surface features as obstacles—things to be avoided or overcome. But now you can

begin to think of these things as natural tools that provide an extra link with gravity, friction, or hydraulic forces—tools that enhance your ability to out-maneuver a tough rapid, and tools that can make seemingly impossible rapids runnable.

In this chapter we explore the techniques and mindset necessary to kayak difficult rivers, specialized techniques for running everything from steep creeks to giant rivers. To novice and intermediate kayakers, a lot of these concepts will sound insane. After all, who in their right mind would *intentionally* slide a kayak over rocks, drop off the lip of waterfalls, or surf holes to stop and scout a rapid? But to the advanced kayaker, these techniques not only exist, they work! If you're willing to step beyond conventional wisdom and use every part of the river to its fullest potential, you'll walk away with a broadened perspective of your kayak's capabilities—and your own.

Class 5 rapids are the playgrounds of adrenaline addicts. (Photo by Jed Weingarten)

Preparation

Class IV and 5 rivers present challenges rarely found on gentler streams. Whether these challenges manifest themselves as endless boulder labyrinths or minefields of boat-swallowing holes, the consequences of human miscalculations or the failure of inferior equipment can be catastrophic.

Accordingly, Class 5 rivers mandate that paddlers and their equipment be up to the rigors the river will present. Any kayaker preparing to run a Class 5 river already should have the skills and confidence borne of many hours on the river—not just skills suited to a particular river or set of rapids but skills that will translate well in any river situation: the ability to quickly read and run confusing currents; full knowledge of rescue systems; the ability to roll under any condition; experience in swimming rapids; and an understanding of emergency medical procedures.

A Class 5 rapid is *not* the place to learn about advanced kayaking. Instead, practice advanced techniques as you paddle Class III, then Class IV rapids, by taking more challenging lines than usual. Force yourself to roll in some challenging (not dangerous) spots. Swim Class II rapids, trying to catch eddies by swimming back and forth across the current. Do everything that *could* happen in a Class 5 rapid in a controlled setting and get *good* at fast rescues long before your first Class 5 adventure.

In addition to the obvious skills needed to survive difficult whitewater, advanced kayakers should be in good physical condition. By being in shape your body will withstand the stresses of powerful rapids. You'll have the strength to power swamped kayaks around in pushy hydraulics, the ability to hold your breath during long swims, and the dexterity to lean and brace if your kayak collides with a menacing boulder.

Advanced kayakers should surround themselves with top-quality equipment. Today's kayaks provide an enormous safety margin for intrepid river travelers, but paddles, helmets, life jackets, throw bags, and rescue gear should also be able to stand up to the rigors of the most demanding rapids. Kayakers should check and re-check gear for flaws. Spare equipment should be carried whenever possible in order to replace whatever breaks down, and enough rescue and first aid gear should be carried to meet or exceed the needs of any emergency situation. This means carrying throw bags, carabiners, pulleys, expeditionary medical kits, and any other gear you anticipate will be needed on or about the river.

Finally, consider wearing face masks and elbow guards whenever paddling difficult rivers. You're bound to flip sometime, so why not keep a solid cage between your face and the bottom of the river? Even if you don't flip, collisions with rocks can chip away at your elbows and leave you unable to rest your arms on a table for weeks after a trip (a common story among dedicated Class 5 paddlers). You may look like a gladiator heading for battle, but you'll survive rapids day in and day out using that extra body armor.

STOWING GEAR

The combination of extra gear and difficult rapids can be lethal. Trying to maneuver an overloaded kayak through a Class 5 boulder slalom may be all it takes to turn an adventure into a disaster. Pack gear behind your seat as lightly and compactly as possible, remembering to leave safety gear readily accessible.

THE CLASS 5 ATTITUDE

The first sentence of the definition of Class 5 rapids says, "Extremely long, obstructed, or very violent rapids which expose a paddler to above-average endangerment." Scary, huh? You bet! Try paddling a long Class 5 rapid—even after scouting it thoroughly—and you're likely to be on the edge of your seat until you're resting safely in a pool below.

Class 5 rapids take a keener mindset and a more confident approach than do Class III drops. First, don't stare at one or two objects in the river, such as a big rock or wave. You'll end up getting tunnel vision and lose sight of everything that is going on around you. Strive to broaden your peripheral vision and expand your senses. Relax, take a couple of deep breaths above the rapid, and try to breathe normally once you're in whitewater. You'll have a much better feel for the rapid and be able to react better if things go wrong.

It is important to never give up trying to navigate your kayak upright through a rapid. If you're suddenly confronted by a big boulder or the largest hole of the day, it is often better to keep maneuvering rather than to hold on. Your last-ditch effort might provide just enough momentum to bust through a hole or just the right move to slip through the tight spot unscathed.

Finally, don't just run Class 5 rapids in one mad dash—dissect them into bite-sized portions. Rather than blasting downstream every time, consider using a zig-zag approach: Jump from eddy to eddy, concentrating on the next eddy as you head downstream, then regroup and reassess your plan once you arrive in the eddy. Use powerful ferries in the main channel to counteract the current and avoid turning broadside to the current. If you use this piecemeal approach to rapids, you'll have more control, more time to react, and additional time to mold your strategies.

Helpful Hydraulics

We've looked at standing waves, holes, and eddies with an eye on how to maneuver through them (or how to avoid them). Now that you're more comfortable on the river, let's look at how you can use these features to make your river ride more fun.

WAVES

The same gravitational forces that pull rivers downhill help kayakers surf in place on a standing wave. By pulling your kayak against the current on the upstream face of a wave—or in the trough between two waves—the kayak will *stall out* dramatically and *surf*. This is not only fun, it can buy some extra time to execute maneuvers.

The first time you use a wave to slow down, keep your kayak parallel with the current. This will give you an extra second to make your next move. Once you get used to the feel of stalling on a wave, turn your kayak slightly, set a ferry angle, and ferry away. The wave will magnify the intensity and trajectory of your ferry—in fact, by using medium-sized waves, some seemingly impossible ferries can be achieved.

Waves can also act as *turntables*, making turns much easier. As your kayak approaches the crest of a wave, the bow and stern become unweighted, and for a split second the kayak will spin more easily than it does in wave troughs. Since a turn started in the trough between two steep waves often produces nothing until the kayak reaches a balancing point on the tip of the wave anyway, start your turns high on the wave to save a lot of unnecessary effort.

Once you get comfortable with wave moves, it will be easy to use them on other vertical features—large pillows, surging boils, and small, breaking waves. Gravity acts like a turbocharger in all these situations.

HOLES

Your first trip through a hole may have brought some big surprises. The powerful upstream current of the backwash may have kicked you sideways or stopped you in your tracks. However, experienced paddlers can tell which holes to run and which ones to avoid. They

know they can bob over small holes—and that they have to hit big holes with precision and momentum.

Since small holes (smaller than your kayak) rarely meet the textbook definition of a *keeper* (since most provide an easy escape route at one end or the other) they can be surfed in place or cross river just like waves. In fact, small holes sometimes present the only stopping point in the midst of a long rapid.

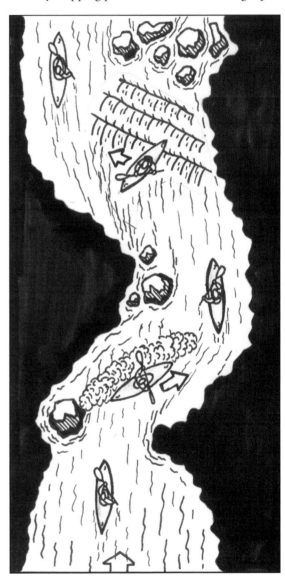

You can surf diagonal holes and ferry on the upstream face of waves to make dramatic cross-river moves.

The same concepts you use for wave surfing apply equally to hole surfing, with some minor modifications. As you approach a hole, look for the direction of its *kick*—the direction it will toss your kayak as you plow into its backwash—then be prepared to brace to keep the kayak upright. If you are going to hit the hole fairly sideways, you can brace on the backwash for stability; if you plan to hit the hole straight, reach through the backwash and grab the solid current flowing downstream.

Remember, not every hole is runnable. If you think that impeccable bracing is all that stands between you and a swim, you probably shouldn't run the hole in the first place.

EDDIES

You have already acquired the basic skills needed to enter and exit eddies. You have also learned that eddies house a variety of useful currents—some of which flow upstream, some of which swirl downstream faster than the main current, and some of which suck downward. Now you can expand your knowledge of eddies and tap into these currents for some dramatic maneuvers.

A kayak that begins ferrying in the main current will find its lateral momentum greatly magnified by maneuvering into conveniently placed eddies. As the kayak crosses the eddy, the eddy's upstream current will hurl the exiting kayak upstream against the main current faster than when it entered the eddy. The turbocharged effect of the transition from one side of the eddy to the other and back into the main current is very exciting, and can make some big, powerful moves possible. Try practicing it in a familiar rapid until you can get the kayak to make S-turns back and forth across the river.

Steep Creeking

Steep creeks are small, high-gradient streams that combine big drops with extremely difficult rapids. Most steep creekers categorize creeks as *steep* when the gradient begins to exceed 100 to 150 feet per mile, even though much steeper creeks have been

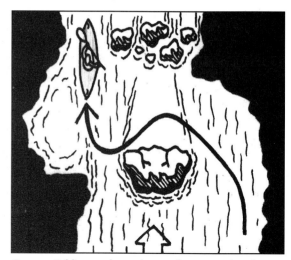

S-turns: Eddies can be used to accelerate your kayak cross river or upstream. By linking eddies, you can even use S-turns to turn around and ascend rapids.

"There are many ways to deliver energy to your kayak while minimizing the work you actually have to do. Many kayakers discuss aiming your head where you want to go as one way to do this. However, you can also aim your chest where you want to go and use your pelvis or legs to deliver power to your boat. Your chest is a bit more bulky than your head, so there's more power in it. Aiming your chest before you do, say, a draw, is a perfect way to set up because it orients your hands properly. At the same time, it helps power your boat in the direction you want to go. Initiating with your pelvis involves even bigger body parts, but it can be used for things like angling your boat off a wave. There are many ways to efficiently deliver power to your kayak. If you choose one of these techniques, learn how to do it properly and wisely and take the steps necessary to protect your shoulders."

—CATHY HEARN
OLYMPIC ATHLETE AND INSTRUCTOR

paddled. Also, the *creek* part of steep creeking denotes rivers in the 150 to 1,500 cfs range, although a few larger streams still fit the definition of steep creeks.

Steep creeks are a haven for adrenaline addicts. Though I've hammered kayaks over scores of waterfalls, I've yet to figure out a way to suppress the butterflies I get staring out over a thundering, foam-spewing horizon line. In fact, all that has occasionally stood between me and predrop hysteria was the right choice of runnable waterfalls and the techniques described in this section. This hasn't stopped me from being eaten alive in a couple of big drops, but it has increased my confidence in my kayak and has gotten me through a couple of close calls.

You already have learned how to use small holes, waves, and boulders to run hard rapids. Those same techniques apply on steep creeks. Now, it's time to take the vertical world of three-dimensional paddling to the extreme—it's time to learn about the tactics steep creekers use to run big ledges and waterfalls.

SCOUTING

The first key to successful steep creeking is knowing which ledges and falls *not* to run. Check out the face of the falls. How far does it drop?

Creekin'!

Do the falls pour freely off a ledge or do they slide downward at an angle? Are there rocks in the falls that are going to throw the kayak off course before it even hits bottom? (A tall, free-falling waterfall might flip your kayak end over end, while a slanted falls might feel like little more than an exciting carnival ride.)

Next, check out the hole at the base of the falls. Is it free of boulders and debris? Will the kayak have enough momentum to break through the backwash, or will the river be too powerful? What if you're swimming? Can you break free of the hole or will it be a keeper? Examine all these features carefully before you decide to run any waterfall—and always have a rescue team set up in case anything goes wrong.

WATERFALLS

Ask yourself how you're going to know where to enter the falls. After all, you're going to see nothing but a big horizon line from your kayak. Pick distinctive landmarks along the bank that will help tell you where your line is (for example, "I'll enter 10 feet left of that big boulder"). Other useful signposts are obvious hydraulic features ("I'll nick the right of that hole with my left edge, then drop over the falls") or downstream landmarks that can be used as a gunsight ("Paddle straight toward the tree"). No matter what signposts you use, make sure you can see them from upstream or they won't do you any good! Walk upstream and look back down at the falls from a distance. Is your landmark still visible? If not, consider picking another one.

Remember that there's more to a waterfall than paddling over the lip. You have to *land* safely, too. Sometimes that means paddling straight off the falls with a lot of power; other times it may mean paddling diagonally into softer hydraulics to the side of the falls.

ANGLING AND BOOFING

Shallow landings and powerful holes await at the bottom of many waterfalls. However, you can sometimes avoid these obstacles by angling your bow one way or the other, jumping out over the shallow landing, or keeping your bow high enough to land fairly flat.

Each of these techniques keeps your bow from penciling toward the river bottom and will help get you into safer water.

Angling works in two ways: It keeps your bow from diving straight down and it effectively shortens the length of your kayak. This may help you avoid crashing into shallow river bottoms and may help keep your kayak from stalling out and flipping in big holes. Keep in mind, however, that you'll have to paddle hard to jump out past recirculating hydraulics.

Boofing off falls—also called *pancaking* or *airplane jumping*—is a technique used to achieve a flat

Angling your kayak off the lip of a waterfall allows you to run shallower drops. You can even angle away from the falls and into eddies to avoid sticky holes. (Photo by Jed Weingarten)

landing. To boof properly, you must combine forward speed with a steady upward pull of your legs to hold the bow up as you leave the lip of the falls. One of the keys to a great boof is to take your last power stroke right at—or barely over—the lip of the falls. This gives your bow some extra lift as you begin your descent. Some kayakers boof by leaning back as far as possible. That technique may also work for you, provided you keep your legs up as you start your descent. However, it leaves you with less control of your boat and pastes you to the back deck as you enter the water. A more upright position, on the other hand, lets you lean forward or backward

The key to boofing—whether executed at a rock, ledge, or waterfall—is the timing of the last stroke. Here, the paddler has placed his last stroke at the lip of the falls to help keep his bow high and dry. (Photo by Jed Weingarten)

during your descent to adjust the angle at which you'll pierce the surface of the pool.

Whichever way you decide to run a waterfall, decide how you're going to handle your paddle. Although your paddle will give you the power you need to clear the falls, it can cause injuries if it gets caught in the fall's hydraulics. Most paddlers hold the paddle slightly to one side and stab the base of the falls; others hold it squarely in front. Either technique may work fine for you—just experiment on smaller falls first and see what works best. Whatever you do, avoid the over-the-head technique that looks cool on magazine covers: It increases your risk of shoulder dislocations dramatically.

BOULDER-CHOKED RAPIDS

Early in my kayaking career I treated solid obstacles as enemies—the nemeses of ill-fated kayakers. I respected and avoided rocks and boulders and portaged rapids that were too boulder-choked to be considered runnable. It took a bona fide Class 5 kayaking adventure to change my perspective on these notorious river features.

Boulders can be used to help make quick turns by carefully angling and sliding off their shoulders. (Also, shallow, wet boulders might provide the only feasible route through an otherwise impossible rapid.) If the main channel is hopelessly boulder choked, it would be senseless to try to kayak it. On the other hand, wet boulders can be boofed with some momentum—paddle full speed across the tops of wet boulders and into the safety of the eddies below.

READING AND RUNNING

When I first started kayaking, I scouted *everything*. I didn't care whether a rapid was Class II or Class IV—I wanted to see exactly what I was getting myself into and which way I was going to go once I was in it. Later on, as my river-reading skills developed, I spent less time on the bank and more time in my kayak. Piloting a kayak through Class II and III rapids became as comfortable as piloting my feet along rocky forest trails, but Class IV and 5 drops still kept me ferrying toward the bank.

While shoreline scouting is the best way to go in any rapid, it isn't always possible. In fact, on some really high-gradient, steep-walled rivers, scouting from the bank might be plum out of the question. So, a whole new set of river-reading skills has to come into play—skills that will let you read blind drops without scouting them from shore.

An unbroken horizon line followed by standing waves will give hints as to the cleanest path over a falls. As you learned earlier, the waves usually show up wherever the current flows clear and unobstructed. So, if you had to bet on where to run the drop, the best bet would be to head straight for that part of the drop that leads into the waves. If there's a hole visible beyond the horizon line, see if one end angles downstream: The current will kick toward the hole's downstream end, which may provide an easy escape route. (Remember to brace into the hole!)

Low-Water Techniques

Low-water trips demand a special style of river running—one that won't leave you high and dry on a

> **"T**he most important thing when setting up for a boof is to time your last stroke so it takes place right on—or just barely over—the lip of the drop. One way to practice this is to cruise down a mellow river, find a rock in the water, and think to yourself, *OK I want to take a right-hand stroke the instant my body is directly beside that rock.* You can also do this with a wave train, an eddy line, a rock, or any little feature, and actually try to boof over small rocks, ledges, and boulders as you start to improve. These sessions let you practice the timing and placement of your strokes and will make your bigger boofs much better when you need them.**"**
>
> —BRANDON KNAPP
> FREESTYLE KAYAKER, TEAM DAGGER

gravel bar trying to bribe anglers to help you hike out of a canyon. Rivers change at low water—the river moves slower and has less push, there are more obstacles to avoid, and there may be many shallow channels to select from. Slow currents decrease the power of the river but the extra obstacles increase your need to maneuver. There are many ways to make low-water kayaking enjoyable. Start by picking a river that actually has enough water to float your kayak, not one that is bone dry. Even if you are forced to portage a few rapids, pool-drop rivers are more fun at low water than rivers with continuous gradients since the pools hold water. Low-water trips also are easier when you use small, stubby kayaks—ones that fit through tight slots and are

There may be times when the only safe route through a boulder-choked rapid is over a rock. Here, the kayaker lines up for a boof over a barely submerged boulder to avoid potential pins in the boulders to his left and right.

As your river-reading skills improve, you'll be able to sneak up to the lip of some drops, peer downstream, and choose your line without ever exiting your boat. Still, if you're ever in doubt, scout.

3. Lean to one side to lessen the amount of floor actually touching the water. The unweighting of one edge might be just enough to get the kayak through a narrow slot.

4. Don't be afraid to spin or pivot your kayak to and fro. Since the kayak will inevitably snag rocks and shallow obstacles, pivots might get your kayak off a rock before you have to jump out and pull the kayak free.

easy to pull over shallow bars. Finally, think about your feet. Sooner or later you'll run aground and will have to pull your kayak free. A solid pair of booties or river shoes—even if worn over neoprene socks—will save your feet from the inevitable bashing inflicted by slippery rocks and hidden potholes.

When running rivers at low water your primary goal is to stay on the deepest channels. Here are a few hints that will make your task easier:

1. Look for slick surfaces or long, even waves among smaller, choppier waves. These features reveal deeper, more forgiving channels.

2. Use the deep eddies behind big boulders to make cross-river maneuvers around shallow shoals. When a shallow bar is impossible to avoid, build up some momentum to help you slide over it and into deeper water.

Big-Water Techniques

When rivers bloat and swell after heavy rains or snowmelts, their moods can become downright cantankerous. The current speeds up while eddies disappear, and holes become deeper while waves surge higher. It takes a dedicated paddler, a level head (figuratively speaking, of course—my friends have oval heads, just like yours), and strong river skills to match wits against big, powerful currents.

Low-water descents often require technical maneuvering through shallow boulder gardens.

Big-water rivers can really pack a wallop.

High-water runs demand some additional safety precautions. You should be a good swimmer, experienced in self-rescue techniques, and there should always be kayaks close by to help in rescue situations. You also should consider paddling rivers with roads nearby and easy evacuation routes in case the river turns out to be too dangerous.

On the river, the techniques used during high water are the same as those used during any river trip, only they're more exact. Keep your paddle moving to keep your senses tuned to the river's moods, and paddle hard through waves and holes to avoid stalling out in the troughs. If you find yourself on a collision course with a mighty hydraulic, try to hit it straight on. Also, avoid trying dramatic ferries in front of big haystacks or holes—you're likely to drift broadside into the hydraulics and get thrashed.

High-water kayakers need to know when to paddle and when to portage. You are much more likely to spend some time swimming during high-water runs than you are during ordinary trips, so your ability to recognize long, dangerous rapids can keep you alive.

Another difference between high- and low-water rivers involves scouting. During high water, rocks and shoreline landmarks might be invisible or moving by too fast to be of much help. However, things like individual holes or waves become more significant—they can be as effective signposts as riverside landmarks are.

No matter what you do, *avoid rivers at flood stage.* Flooded rivers are unpredictable and dangerous. Powerful downcurrents can hold you under for dangerous periods of time, and tree-lined banks can pose a serious threat to swimmers attempting to escape the river's grasp. If the river has water in it now, it will have water in it another day. But if you run it now, you might not be around to run it another day!

Flood-stage rivers can be wild and chaotic. Avoid them!

10

The Art of Playboating

Dances with Rivers

Look how far you've come! Your kayak feels like an extension of your body and you're paddling whitewater with style and poise. Kayaking is a blast, whether you're floating big, meandering rivers or darting through steep boulder gardens. Along the way, you've seen other kayakers surfing waves, riding holes, or popping up out of ledges. Now that's what *you* want to do.

Welcome to the world of *playboating*. A world where surfing, spinning, cartwheeling, and blasting are the norm. A world where hydraulics turn into amusement parks—and you control the ride.

In this chapter we're going to discuss standard playboating tricks and build the foundation for more advanced tricks. You can take this stuff with you every time you paddle a river and spend the rest of your days honing your playboating skills.

No matter what you do, this chapter will add to your paddling repertoire, improve your under-standing of rivers, and open a new realm of kayaking opportunities.

Equipment

The best playboat is the one you're in. It'll surf and do lots of tricks just fine. But if you *really* want to get the biggest bang for your playboating buck, check out the latest designs at your local kayak retailer. Playboats evolve and change so quickly there's always a boat that'll do something better than the boat you're paddling today. Some surf like surfboards, others cartwheel like pinwheels. Talk to your friends, see what they like, and try some boats before you buy. There's undoubtedly a boat out there with your name on it!

Surfing

Surfing a river wave utilizes the same gravitational forces that drag a surfer down the face of an ocean wave. But while the surfboard is streamlined and light, your kayak is heavy and creates a lot of surface drag. So, to surf a wave, you first have to overcome the friction created by the kayak.

An ideal beginner's wave will be about 2 to 4 feet high and close to a large eddy. Your goal is to ferry out of the eddy, cross the shoulder of the wave, and slide into position on the face of the wave. If you don't catch the wave on your first attempt, the eddy gives you a chance to paddle back upstream and give it another try.

Check out the current between the eddy and the wave. You'll often find a small diagonal wave or depression that feeds off the eddy line into the trough of the wave. This diagonal current is the "swinging door" that either lets you enter the wave or pushes you back toward the eddy. Start paddling forward up the eddy, matching your speed and ferry angle to the intensity of this diagonal current. As you cross out onto the wave, keep a shallow upstream ferry angle to avoid spinning downstream. When you find the magic balance between your boat and the current, you'll stall comfortably in the trough with your kayak gliding endlessly down the face of the wave.

ARE YOU READY TO RUMBLE?

Before you think about playing around on waves and holes, learn to distinguish forgiving hydraulics from nasty keepers. You may be able to link 30 cartwheels in a giant hole but you may also be unconscious during the last 10! By knowing the nature of holes and what the river is likely to do to your kayak, you'll be able to seek out safe play spots and avoid the rest. Understanding holes and waves also helps you anticipate the river's actions and adjust accordingly. You'll know where to pull off tricks, which direction your boat will travel, and which side will be easier to roll on. Rolling, flipping, and rolling are part of playboating, so practice enough to become comfortable rolling on both sides. You'll spend more time at your play spot that way, and less time paddling back upstream to it!

If you start veering one way or the other, use sweep strokes and stern rudders to keep yourself aligned with the current. If you have a fast boat and are planted on the wave, stern rudders may work; with stern rudders, slower kayaks may slow down and slide off challenging waves, so keep some strong forward sweeps in your stroke repertoire.

Once you've established your position, keep your boat flat or lift the upstream edge slightly. If you lean too much, your boat will dig into the wave and you'll peel off downriver. If you rudder, rudder on the downstream side so that your paddle doesn't catch against the upstream edge. Finally, watch

Many top play spots are flanked by large eddies that allow paddlers an opportunity to go back and play in one spot time and time again.

the water in front of you: If your bow starts diving, lean back; if you're sliding backward off the wave, try leaning forward and paddle forward to see if you can maintain your position on the wave.

Once you have front surfing figured out, you can try it anywhere you find waves. If there are no eddies nearby, you can drift down to a wave, point your bow upstream, then stall on the wave by paddling hard forward. It's tougher to catch a wave this way because you can't see where you're going and your momentum becomes your enemy. On the other hand, mastering this technique will open up a whole new realm of surfing opportunities.

BACK SURFING

Back surfing is the same as front surfing—just backward. But while the principles are the same, the technical aspects of back surfing are a lot tougher: Your pivot point moves toward your bow as you lean forward, the river disappears from view behind your back, and the most familiar strokes begin to feel backward when done in reverse.

"When you're surfing on a wave, pay close attention to your rudder stroke. If your blade isn't vertical, you're using a braking stroke that will often pull your back off the wave. You can minimize drag by putting your paddle in parallel to the flow of the water and keeping it vertical. (Keeping your boat flat and calm can help a lot, too.) On the other hand, if you surf down to the bottom of the wave, then you may need some braking strokes so your bow doesn't pearl (dive). In this case, you can use a hard rudder, crank your boat back and forth from one edge to another, and avoid getting back to the bottom of the wave. Finally, if your bow starts to dive into the trough in front of you, edging will help again: Just slice your boat onto one edge and that may help the bow rise back to the surface. "

—DUSTIN KNAPP
INTERNATIONAL KAYAKER

Front surfing a breaking wave. Note the paddler's hand position as she executes a rudder stroke. (Paddler: Jamie Simon)

To start your back surf, either ferry out of the eddy backward (stern pointed upstream) or stall out midriver while floating downstream by back paddling hard against the current. Practice this every chance you get, and your back-surfing skills will advance quickly.

Back surfing a breaking wave. Note how the paddler keeps her weight toward the bow in order to keep her stern high and dry. (Paddler: Amy Wiley)

SIDE SURFING

The techniques used for entering holes are similar to those used on waves, with some minor changes. To reach the hole, start parallel or just upstream of the hole and ferry across to it. As you near the hole, turn your kayak sideways and get ready for some excitement. As you drop into the trough, lean just slightly downstream (remember that J-lean) and brace on the backwash if you lose your balance (low brace, or keep that high brace low). If you plan to do vertical tricks, ferry across the shoulder of the hole and position yourself high on the pile. This will allow you to drop upstream into the trough in preparation for whatever trick you're planning to execute.

What you do *in* the hole depends on its size and shape. First, find your balance point and wait until you feel pretty stable in the hole. In almost any small to medium-sized hole, you should be able to sit upright while shifting your weight slightly downstream. Sitting sideways in the hole and bracing on the backwash is called *side surfing*. It's the most basic trick in the book and great way to learn hole riding.

> "**M**any beginners lean back and stand on their pegs when their bow starts to pearl during front surfs. I encourage paddlers to lean forward and lift one thigh up or to tilt their hips when their boat pearls. This lets water shed off the front deck so the boat can pop back to the surface. Once it's back on the surface, however, they must quickly flatten their boat again so they don't carve off the wave. On steeper waves, I try to think like a skier by using quick turns to slow my downhill momentum. As my kayak slides down the face of the wave, these same quick turns can be used to avoid diving into the trough."
>
> —DAN GAVERE
> 1993 WORLD FREESTYLE MEDALIST

PICKING HOLES

Small holes make perfect play spots: Their backwash creates natural kayak catchers and eliminates the need to keep the perfect angles you need on waves. In holes, all you have to do is stabilize your kayak, then focus your attention on spinning, side surfing, and eventually busting free of the hole.

SPINNING

Once you get the feel for side surfing, move toward the shoulder of the hole and try to spin. Keep your boat flat (with planing hulls) or edged just slightly downstream (with displacement hulls), then let the downstream currents out past the shoulder of the hole grab your bow and spin you around 180 degrees. Rotate the stern back into the middle of the hole, and *voilà*—your first 180! Next time, try to spin 360 degrees by staying high up on the backwash until your bow and stern spin all the way around. Once you get the feel for 180s and 360s, you can start linking them up in quick succession and spin until you've had enough.

> **"O**ne good way to improve the feel you need for back surfing is to run as many easy rapids as you can backwards. You'll soon understand how your stern interacts with the current and sense the adjustments you need to make near the bow to keep yourself on the wave. **"**
>
> —JAMIE SIMON
> WORLD FREESTYLE CHAMPION

Crossing a small diagonal wave to enter a play spot. Note how the paddler is using a stern pry to maintain a proper boat angle. (Paddler: Dunbar Hardy)

Side surfing a hole using a low brace. (Paddler: Erin Miller)

EXITING HOLES

When you finally get weary of surfing a hole, exit by slipping sideway over the shoulder of the hole. If you're really getting worked over by the hole, the only way to exit may be to rock back and forth across the face of the hole until you squirt free. Use alternating forward and back strokes to get your sideway momentum going, and keep working until you slide out over the shoulder of the hole. If all else fails, have someone on shore toss you a throw bag and pull your kayak free.

Aerial Tricks

If the river is deep, safe, and has a big pool below in which to reclaim your gear, you can try a classic play move—the *ender*. Whether called an *ender*, *endo*, or *pop up*, this move uses a hole's hydraulic power to sink the bow and shoot the kayak straight up in the air.

FRONT ENDERS

The best ender spots don't have to be big holes. Any hole or small ledge with a powerful, vertical falls and deep pool will work. When you find a spot like this, paddle straight upstream into the falls and let the water falling over the ledge submerge your bow. Your stern will fly upward as the buoyancy stored in your bow provides the energy to launch your kayak

To initiate a 180 or 360, let your bow intercept the downstream currents slipping past the shoulder of the hole while keeping your boat flat (with planing hulls) or edged just slightly downstream (with displacement hulls). Rotate the stern back into the middle of the hole for your first 180.

Once you master the 180, try to spin 360 degrees. Let your stern catch the same downstream current slipping past the shoulder of the hole that helped you spin 180 degrees. Keeping your stern high (so you don't flip or ender out of the hole), look back into the seam of the hole and let your boat spin back upstream. Forward and back sweeps complement the movement of your boat to help keep you spinning in the hole.

> **"T**he most basic and most important skill to learn for rodeo would be 360s, for a couple of reasons. First, in order to get really efficient 360s you have to have good posture, balance, and a feel for your edges, and you must have really efficient forward sweeps and reverse sweeps. Second, all of the cartwheel tricks are essentially based on 360s. Work on your 360s every chance you have, and they'll help with your rodeo repertoire in the future. **"**
>
> —SAM DREVO
> OLYMPIC FESTIVAL MEDALIST

skyward. You may pop up at a 45 degree angle, ender at 90 degrees, or cartwheel forward into the falls. (If you want to stay upright, lean back hard before your kayak reaches 90 degrees. Otherwise, be prepared to land on your face and get ready to roll.)

The key to clean enders is *alignment:* Aim for the deepest, most powerful part of the hydraulic and keep your kayak perpendicular to the falls. (All your wave-surfing practice comes into play here.) As your kayak launches upward, use your paddle and body to stay straight. It may take some practice and experimentation to get it right, but it'll be exciting when it finally clicks!

BACK ENDERS

Back enders are simply front enders in reverse: You bury your stern in the falls to shoot your bow up in the air. The trick to back enders is getting lined up properly. Look over your shoulder as you approach

the falls and lean back as the stern catches the down current. If you keep leaning back, your kayak can cartwheel wildly overhead; you can lean forward to stall your ender and land upright.

PIROUETTES

Once you get the feel for enders, you can move on to the next level of aerial acrobatics—the pirouette. A pirouette starts like an ender but adds a spin when the kayak becomes vertical.

There are a couple of different ways to execute pirouettes: the *reverse-sweep pirouette* and the *cross-draw pirouette.* In the reverse-sweep pirouette, you use a short, powerful reverse sweep across the bow of your boat while twisting your head and shoulders into the direction of the spin. The cross-draw pirouette also calls upon an aggressive twist of your head and shoulders in the direction of the spin, but it uses a cross-bow draw to initiate the spin.

A front ender. (Paddler: Eric Jackson)

A back ender. (Paddler: Eric Jackson)

The best place for the cross-draw pirouette is at an eddy line. Just plant the cross draw in the main current to help initiate your spin and keep the stroke going until you're flat on the water again.

VARIATIONS

Playboating is a form of self expression: One paddler and one kayak flowing together in controlled motion. Once you learn the basics of playboating, you can perfect your moves and fire up your imagination. Here are just a few ideas:

Paddle twirls. Just about any one of the classic tricks that can be done with a paddle (enders, side surfs, front surfs) can be done while twirling your paddle.

Rail grabs. Adapted from a snowboarders' move, this trick looks cool whenever you're airborne. It works in playboating tricks as well as when going off falls. Just reach across your deck and grab the front right edge of your boat with your left hand (or vice versa) and hold the paddle high with the opposite hand.

Hand tricks. You'll be amazed how little you need your paddle in some holes and waves. Try jumping in a friendly side-surfing hole and throwing your paddle back to a friend. You can side surf without a paddle—as long as your hand roll can save you when you're done.

Shudder rudders and grinds. If you want to try a crowd dazzler on a clean-surf wave, lean back and hold your paddle high in the *shudder rudder* position, or press your downstream blade flat onto the face of the wave and slide sideways down the face of the wave to execute a *grind*.

Loops. Here's a brain bender: This one's a somersaulting front or back ender that ends in the hole,

Pirouettes can be initiated with reverse sweeps (as shown here) or with cross-bow draws. The key to fast, tight spins is to keep your head and upper body tight against the back deck.

avoids any edging (like cartwheels), and contains no rotation or direction change. It helps to weigh less than your boat to pull these off.

Retentive pirouettes. This is a 360 (or better) pirouette that lands back in the hole without the paddler washing out. It's not only impressive, it's hard to do!

Retentive Tricks

The world of *rodeo boating* and *hole-riding competition* evolved at a rocket pace in the 1990s as new boat designs, classic rodeo tricks, and squirt-boating maneuvers collided in grand fashion. Cartwheels, splitwheels, loops, and a variety of other tricks that had appeared by happenstance in years past became staples of the rodeo-boater's diet. Today, the tricks have been mastered so well that they can finally appear in a book!

HOW RETENTIVE TRICKS WORK

Retentive tricks—which are often lumped under the old name *retendos*—not only start in a hole, they end

Many of the tricks that are done with paddles can be done without relying upon paddles for support. (Paddler: Ron Blanchette)

hole's trough, starts an off-vertical trick, then switches into a lightning-fast stern move while staying in the hole. *Voilà!* Another retendo. The basic theory behind any one of these retentive maneuvers is simple: The paddler presents the kayak's profile (the side of the bow or stern) to the current while going vertical so the current releases its clutch on the boat, increasing the chances of staying in the hole.

in the hole, too. They're fun to master and are essential for any rodeo boater and serious playboater.

Whether you know it or not, you may have already seen retendos during your paddle trips. Your buddy starts a vertical move in a hole but twists and lands on a side surf. There you have it—a retendo. A more experienced paddler tosses his bow toward the

CARTWHEELS

Let's put the basic retendo theory into practice with our first retentive trick: the *cartwheel*. The term cartwheel has come to mean a lot of things today: There are vertical cartwheels (between 70 and 90 degrees vertical) and off-vertical cartwheels (between 20 and 70 degrees vertical). You'll pick them up in time, but for now let's just focus on a generic, fairly vertical cartwheel.

Understanding the hole
The first key to cartwheeling is understanding where it works in a hole. Work your way high onto the pile (the hole's foamy backwash) using the current near the hole's shoulders for lift. Next, imagine that you're in the middle of a giant clock: Looking upstream, 12:00 will be directly upstream against the current (think of the *current*, not the banks), 1:00 will be slightly to the right, 11:00 slightly to the left, and so on.

When you were doing enders and pop ups, you usually planted your bow or stern at the 12:00 position—that was where the current usually was the strongest and where you could get the biggest launch for your money. When cartwheeling, the 12:00 position works best for vertical cartwheels, but 1:00 and 11:00 work well for off-vertical cartwheels.

A shudder rudder. (Photo by Jed Weingarten)

Your body and paddle

Your body should act like a big axle while your boat cartwheels around it like a wheel. To accomplish this, your posture should be upright and slightly forward. You should be balanced and flexible so you're not leaning on your blade or paddle—stay this way throughout your cartwheel. Next, if you're starting your cartwheel off your bow, your paddle starts in a sort of low-brace position, the back side of the blade

Concentrating on the focal point during cartwheels helps you link ends. (Paddler: Eric Southwick)

TRICKS IN THE HOLE

To get from the top of the hole to the 1:00 or 11:00 positions for off-vertical cartwheels, *overshoot* the 12:00 mark, penetrate your bow or stern into the trough, then slice your boat back toward the center of the clock. Want to cartwheel with your body on the left side of the boat (a left-side cartwheel)? Stick your bow into the trough at 1:00, taking care not to bury too deep or to wash out. For a right-side cartwheel, aim for 11:00. (If these don't work, don't sweat it. Just experiment until you find the right place to launch your move.) Still, no matter what you do, let your bow slice from its starting position back through the center of the clock (for example, from 1:00 to 7:00 or from 11:00 to 5:00).

resting on top of the pile. As you start to go vertical, use something akin to a back stroke, pressing down lightly on the paddle to help drive the bow under the water. (This stroke actually is more like a braking or down stroke than a back stroke.) When you press down on the blade, use your torso muscles to drive the bow toward the paddle, and "close the scissors" (the paddle and boat form the two blades of the scissors). Your bow will slice through the trough, up through the pile, and into the air. You're now ready to forward sweep with the opposite blade and finish off a complete cartwheel.

Need an English translation of what I just said? Here goes:

- With your boat on its right edge, slice the tip of the bow into the trough at 11:00 just deep enough to avoid endering out.
- Press down lightly on your right blade while driving your right knee down.
- Pull on your left blade and look back into the hole as your bow slices through and out of the backwash into the air.
- Finish off with your bow pointed upstream ready for your next end.

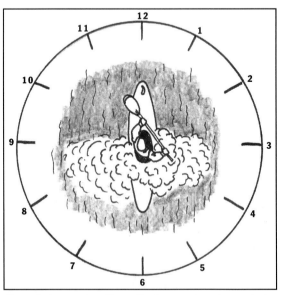

Freestyle instructors often talk about an imaginary clock lying over the top of a hole.

You've now finished your first cartwheel. Keep the sequence going and you'll start to add *points* to your cartwheels. (Add one point each time your bow or stern flies into the air.)

SPLITWHEELS

In cartwheels, you used opposing knees and blades for each end. In other words, you kept your left knee up and pressed your right blade down to start a right-side cartwheel off your bow. In splitwheels, the same knee and blade are engaged for both ends of the split. When done properly, you'll rotate more like a wobbly wheel than a top, but your friends will recognize your technical prowess.

MORE WHEELS

There are many more variations of cartwheels that can be added to the playboater's repertoire. In an *air wheel*, for example, you execute a cartwheel with your weight supported only by the first end of the cartwheel. Even if your second end is in the water, it can't be supporting your weight.

In the chapter on squirt boating, you'll discover ways to execute *stern squirts* (a distant cousin of the stern ender), *bow squirts* (a distant cousin of the bow ender) and *wave wheels* (cartwheels executed in wave trains). Stern and bow squirts can be linked to execute *flatwater cartwheels*, and wave wheels can be executed on waterfalls to make *free wheels*. Basically, the number of types of wheels you can pull off are only limited by your style, athleticism, and imagination.

Rodeos

Some time back in the golden age of kayaking, two people dared to out-shred one another on a wave. Today, scores of competitors line up to strut their stuff at holes, waves, eddy lines—even waterfalls—in the name of fun, competition, and self improvement.

Whitewater rodeos not only are awesome places to show off, they're great for learning tricks. Hang out in an eddy next to some top pro and you're bound to see things happen that you never thought a body could do. Give yourself enough time, prac-

> **"O**ne of the biggest keys with hole riding is looking with your eyes and leading with your head. A ton of people go out—you'll see them—they have their heads pointed in the right direction but their eyes are off in some other random direction. Your body and boat are going to tend to follow where your eyes are looking. So look with your eyes at exactly the point that you want to be and, as you spin, continue to look at that spot until you can't turn your head any farther. Switch to the other side really quick and still look at that one spot on the wave. While winding your head around, your boat's going to continue in that motion.**"**
>
> **—BRANDON KNAPP**
> **INTERNATIONAL KAYAKER**

tice, and physical ability, and you too may be doing those same tricks come next rodeo.

RULES RULE

If you want to rodeo to win, you have to rodeo by the rules. And, in rodeo circles, rules rule. Before every competition, judges will announce the competition formats, scoring methods, and rules stating which part of the river can be used by competitors. Formats and rules changed and evolved from one competition to the next and continued as the sport matured. It is still an ongoing process, one that will keep kayakers guessing for years.

Rodeo competitions have been divided into preliminary heats and finals. In the preliminaries, competitors are placed in heats and vie for top position by chalking up points with as many clean, exciting, controlled tricks as they can muster. If there are enough people in a class, finals will follow the preliminaries, but the finals may be scratched if too few competitors enlist in the class.

In years past, three format options have been used in preliminaries.

Setting up high on the pile for a left-side cartwheel.

Bury your bow in the seam, taking care not to go too deep (or you'll ender out of the hole). Note that the paddle blade remains to the left side and atop the pile in a sort of low-brace position.

1. **Standard Hole Riding.** Each competitor gets two 60-second runs. Both scores are added together to determine who gets to advance to the finals.

2. **Free-for-All.** This is a round-robin competition with a fixed time for each heat set by the judges (say, 5 minutes for a five-competitor heat). Competitors enter the hole one-by-one in the roster order; as one washes out, the next competitor enters the hole. Time limits are imposed for each competitor's ride, and this goes on until the time for the heat is up. To even up the field, the points given for a competitor's rides are added up, then divided by that competitor's number of rides. Each competitor is then allowed one 60-second ride, then enters another free-for-all heat. In the end, each competitor gets three scores, which are then added to determine the finals lineup.

3. **Three 60-Second Runs.** Each competitor is allowed three 60-second runs. The lowest-scoring run is dropped and the two higher-scoring runs are totaled to determine the finals lineup. The same three preliminar-

> **"T**he smart rodeo competitor watches 'homies' there before they ever get in the water. I'll go to a hole and watch the gurus of that spot—watch all the things that they do and the things that they avoid. They've felt it out. They know where all the tricky spots are and where all the cool, easy moves can be made. By watching them, I'll gain a pretty good database of what can happen at that hole. Then I just try to keep my mind open so that I can invent as well. **"**
>
> —SHANE BENEDICT
> KAYAK DESIGNER/INSTRUCTOR

ies formats can be used in finals, but the higher-scoring runs are usually the only ones counted in the *standard hole-riding* and *three 60-second run* formats. Any tie for first place will be broken with a winner-takes-all format. Lower-placing tie-breakers often are settled by combining runs and using the combined scores to determine placement.

Press down on your left blade while pulling your bow toward your blade to close the scissors and get the cartwheel going.

As your bow carves beneath the pile and back to the surface, reach around and put your right blade where your left blade used to rest. At the same time, turn your head to your left to look back into the hole.

Use a forward sweep on your right side while pulling your boat through the second half of the cartwheel with your legs and torso. Keep looking into the seam of the hole to see where you want your bow to land.

Just before your bow reenters the hole, flip your paddle back around to the modified low-brace position, with your left blade atop the pile—and get ready for another round!

JUDGES JUDGE

As with rules, rodeo judging evolves from year to year. One judging format used the combined efforts of *technical/style* judges and *variety* judges to generate overall scores. The technical judges focus on technical moves and give overall style scores for each run; variety judges note the number of different moves performed. In many competitions, technical judges verbalize the scores to a *scribe*, who records the points as they are accumulated.

This is just one way to run a rodeo. Check out the judging format before your next competition and know who to smile at when you're in the hole.

RODEOS RAGE

We've come a long way since the days when surfing a wave seemed outrageous. Soon after the advent of *freestyle through a rapid* events in the 1990s, rodeo boaters and creekers joined schools and started holding rodeos at big ledges, waterfalls—anything it took to get an adrenaline rush. (And, based upon the looks on some spectators' faces, the adrenaline surge didn't stop at the competitors' adrenal glands—the rodeos captured the fancy of people everywhere.)

Waterfall rodeos are now part of the rodeo boaters' traveling minstrel show, and water wheels, meltdowns, and moves yet to be named are quickly becoming part of the rodeo boater's repertoire.

Where will rodeos go from here? They'll just keep getting bigger and better!

Even top pros watch their fellow competitors' moves to keep up with the latest tricks.

Rodeos aren't just for waves and holes any more. Waterfall rodeos—like this one on Washington's White Salmon River—started to appear in the late 1990s. (Paddler: Sam Drevo)

11

The World of Squirt Boating

You've seen them before: skinny, edgy, low-volume boats darting about the surface of the river, magically switching from horizontal planes to vertical tricks amid the smallest changes in currents.

Squirt boats—kayaks designed to tap into the submarine, three-dimensional world of whitewater paddling—evolved from race boats into ultra-low-volume beasts that submerge with an intricate blend of technical prowess and current play. At the forefront of this evolution were guys like Jesse Whittemore and the Snyder brothers (Jeff and James). These guys fine-tuned many of the tricks squirt boaters use today, and they pushed the sport of *squirting* into the kayaking limelight.

In this chapter, we stick our toes into the big pond of squirt boating. We look at a handful of popular tricks and whet your appetite for more exploration. If you leave this chapter hungry for more information on squirting, hook up with local *squirtists* and try to dig up an old copy of James Snyder's *The Squirt Book*. It'll provide some of the best insights available on squirting and take your paddling to a higher—or deeper—level.

Squirt Boats

For years, about the only way to consistently pull off solid squirts was to use a squirt boat. While squirt boats are still the top choice for serious squirt boating, many modern rodeo boats now have low-volume bows and sterns that allow boaters to pull off basic squirt tricks. Although many paddlers would have trouble pulling off mystery moves in rodeo boats (a trick that buries the entire boat beneath the surface), they're still be able to pull off tricks like bow squirts, stern squirts, rocket moves, and screw ups with ease.

Nonetheless, dedicated squirt boaters opt for genuine squirt boats. They're the only boats that'll let you tap into the full range of squirting possibilities and impart the most intimate relationship with three-dimensional submarine currents.

The Stern Squirt

The key to many squirt tricks—stern squirts included—is the *charc*, otherwise known as the *charging arc*. Jim Snyder describes the charc as "the angle of attack of a boat's long axis as it encounters local currents/features." That sounds like a mouthful at first, but it will soon make sense.

Stern squirts are exciting to do and cool to watch, but they're also the antithesis of everything you've already learned: The premise behind the stern squirt is to do pretty much the opposite of whatever keeps you upright and happy the rest of the time. Instead of entering eddies or turns with an inside, upstream lean, squirt boaters lean on their outside, downstream edge, and intentionally sink the stern underwater. Instead of the catastrophic result one might expect, this technique sends their boats into tight, vertical pivot turns. Weird, huh? But once

Squirt boats tap into the subsurface world of kayaking.

> **"I**n squirt maneuvers it helps to use what we call *curved charcs*, our term for the charging arc, which denotes the angle of attack for the boat. You can tell if you've established the proper curved charc when you go into a squirt by looking at the bubbles behind the boat after you've done the squirt. If the bubble trail is curved, you'll know you set up a proper charc; if the trail is straight, it means you tried to put the boat up too early and you were using your arms too much. **"**
>
> **—JAMES SNYDER**
> **SQUIRT BOAT PIONEER/DESIGNER**

you get the hang of this enigmatic pursuit, it opens up a whole new world of exciting kayak tricks.

Experienced paddlers can pull off stern squirts just about anywhere there's an interface between two different currents. Beginners, on the other hand, are better off learning stern squirts on flatwater. Starting on the flats helps you get the feel for your equipment while knocking out the variables inherent in moving water.

The stern squirt is built off three strokes: the reverse sweep, the forward stroke, and the duffek stroke. Here's how each stroke fits into the stern squirt sequence:

1. **The charc.** Start with a wide, controlled, moderately fast charc.
2. **The reverse sweep.** Start the squirt with a reverse sweep on the inside of the turn. Plant your inside blade within 18 inches of your stern, lean back slightly (you don't have to lean very far!), and tilt your opposite edge 5 to 15 degrees downward into the water. Use your hip to bury the edge and to stay balanced over your boat and your stern will dive automatically.
3. **The forward stroke.** As your stern starts to dive, use your forward stroke on the outside of the turn to act as a brace and send the bow to its highest point.

The stern squirt: Start with a wide, controlled, moderately fast charc (left). Next, initiate the squirt with a reverse sweep on the inside of the turn. Plant your inside blade within 18 inches of your stern, lean back slightly, and tilt your opposite edge 5 to 15 degrees downward into the water. Use your hip to bury the edge to stay balanced over your boat, and your stern will dive automatically. As the stern starts to dive, use a forward stroke on the outside of the turn to act as a brace and send the bow to its highest point. Finally, guide the bow back down using a duffek stroke on the inside of the turn.

4. The duffek stroke. Finally, guide the bow back down using a duffek stroke on the inside of the turn.

If you have trouble following the previous sequence, take it more slowly. Isolate the reverse sweep and see how it affects the rise and fall of your bow. If you can get your bow a foot or two off the water without forward paddling to set a charc, that's super! Otherwise, keep practicing until you get the bow lifted. Once your bow is consistently rising, add some forward paddling before setting up for your stern squirt and follow through with the techniques described above.

STERN SQUIRTS IN EDDIES

Once you have mastered the flatwater stern squirt, take it out into an eddy and try it anew. A stern squirt executed in the strongest interface between upstream and downstream currents (squirt boaters call this *the squeeze*) feels surreal and takes on a life of its own. The river provides much of the power for the move: You just supply the charc, three key strokes, and the correct leans to harvest it.

SQUIRT TERRITORY

Squirting is as much an underwater activity as it is a way of paddling rivers. If you don't know what's beneath the surface now, you'll find out the moment you start squirting. *All the tricks in this chapter should be attempted only in deep water.* You'll avoid injuries that way, enjoy your down time without being stressed, and you'll be able to paddle another day and keep perfecting your techniques.

"The trick to mastering the stern squirt is to use proper form. This means peaking the move (hitting its highest point with the bow) with the second forward stroke when the cross section of the stern is lined up parallel with the grain of the current. Your hull should be facing back into the eddy—not downstream.**"**

—JAMES SNYDER

To stern squirt exiting an eddy, face upstream, set a slight ferry charc, and initiate your stern squirt by pushing your upstream hip sideways into the grain of the current. (Do this using lateral momentum to fold your stern into the current at the point of maximum squeeze between the main downstream current and eddy's upstream current.) Done correctly, your bow will peak as your forward stroke guides it skyward. You can keep this squirt going by continuing the spin with forward and back strokes until your bow finally collapses back to the surface.

SCREW UPS

If your stern squirt passes vertical and flops over backwards on your head, you can still finish it off upright by executing a fast roll in the same direction your momentum is going. Done correctly, this trick is called a *screw up*. The key to the roll is actually committing to the forward stroke *before* the bow collapses over your head: This will keep your head dry and prevent you from ever really having to roll at all.

Bow Squirts

The *bow squirt*—as its name implies—sends the bow beneath the surface and the stern skyward. Most paddlers bow squirt using one of two techniques: a *crossbow draw* to pull the kayak against its own veer; or a *back stroke* on the inside of a turn to start the bow

> **"D**ifferent squirt methods work for different people. Experiment with stern squirts by shifting your weight toward the bow. Many top pros use this technique to improve their leverage and speed up their reaction time. Staying in the front seat can also help prolong your stern squirts, giving you an opportunity to spin them 360 to 720 degrees instead of flipping early. After some experimentation, you may find a middle ground—where you're neither leaning forward nor backward—that works perfect for you. **"**
>
> —DAN GAVERE
> **1996 WKF EXTREME WORLDS MEDALIST**

diving. However, before we talk about these techniques, let's look at setting up your boat so these strokes will work.

THE INITIATION

To start a bow squirt in flatwater, paddle forward fast enough to generate a wake. Next, stop paddling for a moment and surf this wake. Once you feel your own wake surge beneath you, lean forward to get your bow to dive. Learn this technique correctly and you'll find many uses for it in a variety of bow-squirting situations.

The screw up: If your stern squirt is vertical enough to flop over backwards on your head (left), *you can finish it off* *upright by executing a fast roll in the same direction you're going. Done correctly, this trick is called a screw up.*

Going down: a bow squirt.

THE BACK-STROKE BOW SQUIRT

To start a back-stroke bow squirt, first forward paddle, then veer off in one direction. Let's say you're going to veer left in this example. Once your left veer is set, backstroke against the veer (backstroke on the right side) and tilt your right hip downward to feed water over your bow. As your bow starts to dive, your backstroke will soon lose its energy. However, you can then stop and reverse the rotation of the boat by switching to a forward stroke on the right side. By continuously adjusting your hip angles, you can keep your boat diving deeper and deeper. (To start with a right veer, just flop the stroke sequence over to the opposite side.)

THE CROSS-BOW DRAW BOW SQUIRT

To initiate a bow squirt with a cross-bow draw, start your left veer again. However, instead of using a backstroke on your right side, reach across your bow and plant a cross-bow draw on your right side. If you start with your bow pointed at 11:00, plant your paddle at 1:00 and throw your weight forward into the 12:00 position. As your bow starts to dive, pull your boat and paddle together and let your bow wing down. Once you've begun, you can finish your bow squirt by continuously switching forward, back, and cross-bow draw strokes, and feeling your way through the rest of the squirt.

Rocket Moves

Rocket moves let you launch your bow from the top of a wave during a downstream run. You start the move

The bow squirt using a back stroke: To start a back-stroke bow squirt, first forward paddle, then veer off in one direction. Once your left veer is set, back stroke against the veer and tilt your right hip downward to feed water over your bow. As your bow starts to dive, *your back stroke will soon lose its energy; you can stop and reverse the rotation of your boat by switching to a forward stroke on the right side. By continuously adjusting your hip angles, you can keep your boat diving deeper and deeper.*

by approaching the crest of the wave with some lateral momentum (this provides the opportunity to put some sideways pressure on the stern). Aim for the point where the shoulder meets the crest of the wave and hit your rocket move by executing a long forward sweep while edging on the same side of your kayak. Execute it properly and you'll squirt vertically from the top of the wave, your bow pointed high into the air.

Splats

A *splat* is basically a squirt done on the upstream side of a rock. Though the name sounds like something a bug does to your windshield, the squirtist's splat is far less terminal.

The pillow that forms on the upstream of friendly, round boulders actually deflects boats—most of the time. Choose your splat sides wisely and start with safe, well-known splat rocks before venturing into unknown territory. Also, keep your boat and paddle between you and the rock when paddling, and your hands, arms, and head will fare much better.

To splat off your stern, start a stern squirt on the upstream side of the boulder with a reverse sweep planted between you and the boulder.

The bow squirt using a cross-bow draw: The kayaker started this bow squirt by veering again, but instead of using a back stroke to initiate the squirt he reaches across his bow and plants a cross-bow draw on the opposite side. Notice the angles of his original trajectory, veer, and paddle placement. Once he's begun, he can finish his bow squirt by continuously switching forward, back and cross-bow draw strokes, or spinning.

The rocket move: Approach the crest of a wave with some lateral momentum, aim for the point where the shoulder meets the crest, and hit your rocket by executing a long forward sweep while edging on the same side.

Let the squirt peak as your boat reaches the corner of the rock, and brace on your upstream side. To finish the move, press down on that upstream brace to swing your bow out and away from the boulder, smile, and pat yourself on the back.

Once you get the stern splat down, you can do the same trick with a bow squirt.

Blasting

In *blasting,* you sink your stern beneath the recirculating foam and point the bow upstream into the air. Do it correctly and you can stall your kayak in the hole just like you were front surfing a wave. The big difference will be the wall of boiling water now crashing into your stern and over your back.

Blasting works best in well-defined holes formed by low-angle, sliding ledges. These low-angle holes make blasting easier by providing plenty of space for your bow. (In steeper holes, your bow will dive into the falls, making blasting difficult or impossible.)

Wave Moves

Wave moves provide an exciting, dynamic way to exit waves. Start by front surfing a wave. When you're ready to exit, lean forward to engage your bow. As it starts to turn, lean upstream against it and look for a supporting brace to hang on to. Your

A splat. (Photo by Scott Harding)

The splat: This kayaker initiates a stern squirt on the upstream side of a boulder with a reverse sweep planted between him and the boulder. The squirt peaks out as his boat reaches the corner of the rock and he braces on his upstream side. To finish the move, he presses down on that upstream brace and swings his bow out and away from the boulder. Once you get the stern splat down, you can do the same trick with a bow squirt.

Blasting a breaking wave.

boat will start to dive as it exits the wave, but its trapped buoyancy will soon bring it back to the surface. Look for a sustained stern squirt, a screw up, or even a long *mystery move* (see page 139) to finish off your trick.

WAVE WHEELS

Now here's a trick that leaves me slack jawed any time I see it: *Wave wheels* are cartwheels on waves. They start like rocket moves, then quickly change into mutated aquatic somersaults that are magnificent to behold.

To pull off a wave wheel, find a good-sized wave train and head straight toward the first crest with a lot of speed. As you head up the first wave, start your rocket move, but don't go fully vertical. As your bow clears the surface, shift your weight forward, edge harder than usual (your boat will practically be on

its side), and push down on your upstream blade as if you were trying to initiate a cartwheel. (If your body is on the right side of your kayak, you'll be on your right edge, pushing down on your right blade, using your left knee to drive the wheel.)

OTHER SQUIRT TRICKS

So many squirts, so little time. The squirt tricks described here are just to get you going. If you mystery move out of a hole while blasting, you're *subbing out*; doing tricks as backcut maneuvers (spinning contrary to whirlpool currents) constitutes *mush moves*; connecting bow and stern squirts in sequence sets up *cartwheels*. The tricks and combinations are endless.

The wave wheel: The kayaker heads into the first good-sized wave with a lot of speed and starts a rocket move. As his bow clears the surface, he shifts his weight forward, edges harder than usual, and pushes down on his upstream (right) *blade as if he were trying to initiate a cartwheel. At the same time, his left knee is driving the wheel around. As his bow plunges into the next trough, his stern flies into the air. From there, he finishes the rotation by forward stroking/sweeping on the opposite side while pulling that left knee through the maneuver.*

Mystery Moves

Here it is. The brass ring of squirt moves. The key that unlocks door to down time and gives paddlers an opportunity to test their breath-holding capability while trying to awe their friends at the same time. The *mystery move* involves getting your entire boat underwater by allowing your body to get caught between the eddy and downstream currents. Once in this position, your boat acts like a wing and begins to dive downward, taking you down with it.

The weight shift, increased edge, and downstroke combination will push your bow downward into the next trough while sending your stern skyward. Finish off your rotation by forward stroking/sweeping on the opposite side while pulling that left knee (for a right-side wave wheel) through the maneuver. Your bow will fly over you, completing the 360-degree circle. Not enough power to finish one whole wave wheel? No sweat— just stall on a bow squirt, pull off a pirouette, and impress your friends.

To start a mystery move from an eddy, exit as close to the rock or wall forming the eddy as possible, aiming for the point where the pillow meets the current. Let the current turn your bow, then wing down as your boat turns sideways. Weight the upstream hip to start the sinking action and let the downstream currents push against your upstream edge as the eddy supports your boat. Once your boat is underwater, level it out and use whatever braces are available to you to keep your mystery move going. This whole process takes some time to perfect, but stick with it. Down time is fun time!

12

Whitewater Racing

Fast and Wild

Whitewater racing takes common facets of river running—like reading rapids and executing maneuvers—then squeezes them into a world where speed, focus, and precision dominate. From wildwater events to slalom races, the challenge of running rivers is magnified when every move becomes critical. In the desire to go fast and minimize errors, racers become totally focused and skills are tested. Sound techniques shine, while even the most subtle deficiencies become glaringly apparent.

It is in this competitive process that another aspect of kayak racing appears: Kayakers who make good racers make good river runners! The same precision that goes into running gates and threading a fast line down a wildwater course carries into running rapids. Ask any whitewater racer—racing and recreational kayaking complement each other magnificently.

Kayak racing is more open and boater-friendly than many paddlers realize. Many races are open to all levels of paddlers and even offer different categories based on boat design. You can show up in your stubby creek boat, your low-profile rodeo boat, or your sleek slalom boat and find a slalom or wildwater category suited to your paddling style. Later, as you

improve, you'll be able to slip into high-tech boats, rub paddles with serious racers, and master many more techniques than we could ever describe in this introduction. No matter where you fall in the echelon, racing will improve your paddling skills and make river running more fun.

Types of Races

Kayak races have varied over the years as much as the rivers that have hosted them. Today, most races involve two events: *slalom* and *wildwater* races.

For spectators and competitors alike, slalom competitions can be dynamic and fascinating. They take a river's natural features and add 25 *gates* that force kayakers to follow an altered and often unnatural course through the rapids. (Gates consist of pairs of poles 1.2 to 3.5 meters apart. Paddlers must paddle between the poles to successfully negotiate each gate.) Rather than progressing straight downstream on the fastest currents, slalom racers have to maneuver back and forth from gate to gate, turn into eddies to drive through upstream gates, and ferry across powerful currents to pick up a challenging gate placed across the river.

Slalom courses take the river's natural features, then add gates to force kayakers to follow an altered course through the rapids.

Wildwater races offer the purest form of kayak racing. They are the sprints and marathons of the whitewater world, where no poles or gate judges add penalties to your time. They are simply downriver races against the clock—the fastest overall time wins. Since continuous, powerful strokes and clean, unobstructed lines must be maintained throughout the race, it takes both physical conditioning and solid river-reading skills to compete effectively.

Slalom Races

Skilled paddlers unaccustomed to the challenges of slalom courses are often surprised to find that few courses are as easy as they look. Just about every combination or series of gates is designed to challenge racers and to force skilled maneuvers in the pursuit of clean, penalty free runs. Still, looking at a course is the key to successful racing.

READING THE COURSE

When analyzing any slalom course, memorize the *placement* and *direction* of each gate. Each gate will be numbered in sequence, and gates will be marked as downstream (green) or upstream (red, with numbered plaques with a slash through the number).

As you visually connect the lines between all the downstream and upstream gates, a pattern will begin to emerge. It is your ability to follow this pattern—as well as your ability to execute all the moves and strokes it takes to stick to it—that measure your level of success.

No single gate can be analyzed independently: The way you paddle through gate 19 affects the way you paddle through gate 20. Your angle of attack on one gate can make your attack on the next gate easier or more difficult. Analyze each gate in terms of both the preceding and succeeding gate, and seek out combination moves. Look for opportunities to turn your boat early, smooth out the line you'll follow through the course, and avoid speed-draining corrective strokes whenever possible.

Finally, analyze gates in relationship to the surrounding currents. Look for strong currents—currents that will assist you with turns—and fast routes from gate to gate. By forming a mental image of the course, the currents, and every stroke you plan to execute throughout the race, you'll be on your way to improving your time.

UNDERSTANDING THE RULES

Speed is critical in slalom racing, but the pursuit of raw speed must be tempered with perfect technique. Each tapped pole or missed gate adds significantly to the kayakers' final time. If you touch a pole with your boat, paddle, your body, or any other part of your equipment, two seconds are added to your time.

Carefully review the course configuration and memorize gate placements before your race.

Fail to negotiate a gate properly—miss it, turn upside down while passing through it, paddle it in the wrong direction, or only get your head through it—will add 50 seconds to your overall time.

Read and understand all the rules of slalom racing before you race. Do International Canoe Federation (ICF) rules apply to your race? If so, the combined times (including penalties) for two runs are scored, so consistency counts. (Under older rules—which still govern at some local races—you can keep the best of two runs.) Read the rules and race hard.

USING YOUR PADDLE

The goals of the slalom racer—paddle fast and avoid penalties—are clear cut, but the ways in which these goals are achieved are less obvious. Take your paddle, for example: Even short paddles won't fit horizontally through some gates, especially when you're staying close to one pole or the other. So keep your paddle as vertical as possible to avoid frustrating pole taps. Next, think of how your paddle affects the speed and angle of your boat. It only develops power and control when it's in the water, right? So, keep it in the water as much as possible and avoid using it to apply corrective strokes.

KEEP YOUR VISION OPEN

In any athletic pursuit—especially whitewater racing—it is easy to get tunnel vision. Novice skiers stare at their ski tips; first-time mountain bikers stare at the ground inches in front of their bikes. Tunnel vision handicaps racers—it tightens your muscles, drains confidence, and closes your senses to the changes in your surroundings.

When racing, keep your head up and your eyes focused. Look where you want to go, not where you've been. (Looking back to see if you've cleared a gate won't help you clear it, but it will take your focus off the next gate.) Pay attention to surges in the river surface while focusing on the course and you'll gain more complete control over your boat.

By keeping your paddle fairly vertical and your head up you will avoid pole touches and maximize your peripheral vision. (Paddler: Scott Shipley)

There's always something new to learn in slalom kayaking. Here, Cathy Hearn passes on tips to a group of eager students.

KNOW HOW TO PADDLE SPECIFIC GATES

There are as many ways to construct race courses as there are rivers and race-course designers. Still, many characteristics of race courses remain constant. There are always upstream and downstream gates that force kayakers to paddle in the right direction, and combinations such as *offset gates* that require skillful maneuvering.

Downstream gates. Downstream gates in the middle of a clear channel are usually the easiest to paddle, as long as you move through them with the proper speed and angle so you're set up to attack the next gate and you time your stroke so you don't hit the poles.

Downstream gates in eddies. Downstream gates in eddies present new challenges. You must avoid catching an edge or allowing your bow to dive as you enter the eddy (these could cause you to turn and lose time). Depending on the placement of the gate, your best entry may be to come in with little, if any, cross-current angle. When combined with a slight backward lean and a forward sweep stroke placed in the current on your upstream side, you can carry some momentum into the gate and combat the turning action of the eddy. If you're able to keep your boat flat as you enter the eddy, that will help counteract the speed-draining action of catching an edge. Once you're in the eddy, avoid stalling by leaning forward again and keeping your boat level. Your exit from the downstream gate will depend on the placement of the next gate: You may be able to continue forward paddling to reach gates downstream or you may need to turn sharply to set up cross-current ferries or peel outs. Again, let the course dictate your actions.

Offset gates. Offset gates—two to three gates set across the current from each other—make downstream maneuvers very interesting. When approaching offset gates, it is often best to turn toward the second gate *before* you even enter the first gate (some racers call this the pre-turn). By repeating this pattern from gate two to gate three you'll establish a smooth, flowing pattern through the offset gates using forward strokes and forward sweeps to keep your speed up. If the current leading out of one gate is fast and the next gate is some distance across the river, you may have to ferry between gates to make them all. You may be able to stall after the first gate, back ferry to the second gate, then resume forward paddling through the second gate. If many back strokes are required, however, it may be faster to spin upstream upon leaving the first gate, then ferry across to the next gate. The final option is to turn backward before the first gate, run the gate backward, then forward ferry to the second gate. Watch what the top paddlers are doing and try to imitate their maneuvers.

Upstream gates. Upstream gates placed in eddies often consume time and energy since you're actually paddling *away* from the finish line and dealing with oppositional currents. However, when done correctly, upstream gates can be paddled fast. One of many ways to paddle an upstream gate in an eddy is to charge it from a fairly wide angle and enter the eddy with an angle set by a forward sweep on the downstream side, lean into the eddy, and direct your

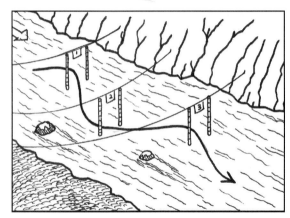

Offset gates—two to three gates set across the current from each another—make downstream maneuvers very interesting. When approaching gates with little offset, it is often best to turn toward the second gate before you enter the first one. By repeating this pattern from gate to gate you'll establish a smooth, flowing pattern through the offset gates.

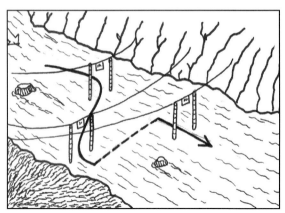

Long offsets often require different techniques—such as ferrying—than slightly offset gates do. In this illustration, the kayaker pre-turned before gate one to set his approach into gate two, then back ferried from gate two to gate three before resuming forward paddling. If he had wanted to, he could have spun upstream after gate two, forward ferried across to gate three, and turned back downstream to complete the course; or turned backward before gate two, run gate two backward, then forward ferried to gate three.

bow between the poles. As your bow pierces the gate, reach forward through the gate for a duffek stroke on the inside of the turn and flatten out your boat. Finally, sweep on the outside of the turn and duffek downstream to exit. Again: sweep in, duffek through, and sweep out. The final duffek can help set you on a proper course toward the next downstream gate. There will be times when the gate *above* the upstream gate is almost in line with the upstream gate. Still, shooting for a wider line—which provides a wider entry angle into the eddy—often saves time and energy since the same pattern described above will work here.

Other gate tricks and configurations. There are so many ways to set and paddle slalom courses that entire books have been written on the subject. Try to get your hands on William T. Endicott's *To Win the Worlds* and *The Ultimate Run*, or dig up an old copy of *Whitewater Racing* by Eric Evans and John Burton. These books provide tremendous insight to the sport.

Wildwater Races

Wildwater races have challenges not easily recognizable by many beginners. Wildwater boats are extremely narrow and have little, if any, rocker, so

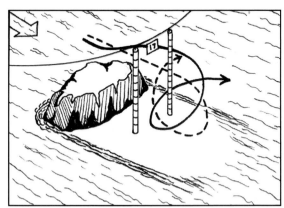

When done correctly, upstream gates can be paddled fast. One way to approach an upstream gate in an eddy is to charge it from a fairly wide angle and enter it with an angle set by a forward sweep on the downstream side, lean into the eddy, and direct your bow between the poles.

> **"O**ne of the most catchy phrases that I was ever taught in slalom racing was by my junior coach, Fritz Haller. He taught me, 'It's sometimes faster to be slower.' A lot of people want to paddle straight through a gate as fast as they can, then turn and try to get to the next gate. It's actually faster to be slower if you take the time to set up the turn above the first gate so you're already heading toward the second gate. It's all about never letting anything happen *to* you but planning it so it happens *for* you. **"**
>
> —JOHN "TREE" TRUJILLO
> **OLYMPIC FESTIVAL MEDALIST**

they're tippy and hard to turn. They can also be light and fragile, so miscalculations in rapids can have devastating effects on some boats. Still, wildwater racing is exciting and rewarding.

Prepare for wildwater races the same way you do for slalom races: review the rules, check your starting time, and scout the river. Run the course multiple times to find fast currents and clean pathways through rapids. Seek out straight routes that demand the fewest maneuvers (to avoid correctional strokes), test these routes against wider routes that rely more heavily upon current patterns for sustained momentum, and go with the fastest lines at race time.

When running the river, look for ways to avoid eddies, holes, and pockets of shallow, slower-moving water. Although wave trains generally signify fast water, run the shoulders of waves rather than their peaks, or seek places where waves cancel each other out. (Wave peaks may increase your vertical motion, slap your kayak around, and make it tougher to paddle, all of which may slow you down.) If you catch up to the kayak in front of you, overtake it carefully. Balance energy-wasting maneuvers against your overall course strategy to pick the moment to pass. Be aware: *You cannot pass racers who need to be rescued.* You *must* stop and rescue them or risk being disqualified.

Slalom paddlers use techniques not usually familiar to beginning kayakers. Here, the kayaker leans his chest and head toward the next gate while still finishing his sweep stroke. Though this leaves his shoulder in a vulnerable position, he has the experience to execute such a stroke. (Paddler: Rick Williams)

Extreme Races

Combine the aerobic capacity of a wildwater racer with the guts of a Class 5 adrenaline junkie and you have the perfect recipe for an extreme racer.

Extreme races combine the downstream sprints of wildwater races but add outrageous rapids to spice up the soup. Let's say you're a serious Class 5 paddler. Would you run the same rapids bordering on ex-

haustion? Enough paddlers have the skill and mettle to say, "Hell ya'!" and go after this sport with a fervor. Extreme races have popped up all over North America—on Washington's White Salmon River, in Colorado's Gore Canyon, and at the Great Falls of the Potomac River outside of Washington, D.C. Even if you never enter one of these races, go watch them. It's a rush just watching from the bank.

13

Surf Kayaking

Just Add Salt

For every drop of fresh water that can be paddled there is infinite more salt water available that provides a recreational wonderland for whitewater kayakers. Saltwater paddling takes on many forms. Whether paddling along a gentle coastline or riding through pounding surf, salt water can present as much variety as river running, possibly more.

Riding ocean waves in a kayak is a thrilling form of whitewater boating. It combines all the paddling techniques you've learned with some simple adjustments for surviving the surf.

But riding ocean waves can be hazardous for the uninitiated—powerful rip tides, rugged headlands, and pounding waves can take their toll on boats and boaters alike. Before jumping into even moderate surf, make sure that you have strong swimming skills and enough paddling skills to run Class III rapids. Later, you can progress to bigger, more challenging waves as you refine your skills and develop a sense of how the surf works.

In this chapter we briefly explore surf kayaking and examine the techniques that can make your next outing exciting and memorable.

Equipment

Here's some good news for the budget conscious: You can rip it up in the surf with exactly the same gear you use in the rapids. Plus, your boat will perform similarly in both environs. If you can flat spin a wave on the river, you can do the same thing in the surf. Love launching your high-volume boat into massive enders? Drop over the top of a wave in the surf and you can achieve the same result.

Though surf kayaking in your standard river-running boat may feel familiar and comfortable, elite surf kayakers have their own brand of kayaking gear. Hybridized from surfboards and kayaks, *surf kayaks* shred waves like surfboards and wave skis (a type of sit-on-top surfboard) while maintaining the closed hull and traditional cockpit designs of river kayaks. This allows for big leans, braces, and rolls, just like in your whitewater kayak.

Waves and Currents

Surf waves often begin hundreds or thousands of miles offshore where storm winds whip the ocean's surface into patches of irregular waves. Gradually, these waves transform into ocean swells as they travel away from the storm center. When these swells reach shallower waters, they begin to drag on the beach bottom (called *shoaling*) until they begin to spill shoreward.

If the beach descends steeply into deeper water, the waves will rise and plunge steeply, while gentler beaches produce gradually spilling breakers that can roll for hundreds of yards before reaching land. Tides, winds, swell size, and shoreline shape also affect the way waves behave.

The best waves upon which to learn surf kayaking are small, spilling breakers in the 2- to 4-foot range (measured from crest to trough). Bigger waves can punish paddlers and bust up gear, so start small and work your way up. If you can find waves that roll left or right from a sandbar, reef, or point, you may have found a perfect kayaking zone. By staying just in front of the breaking part of the wave, you can stay on the steep, smooth part of the wave and enjoy a long ride.

Beach currents can hold some big surprises for paddlers used to kayaking rivers. *Longshore currents* flow parallel to the shore and can travel much faster than you can paddle. *Nearshore currents*—which push surface waters toward the beach—can form from shoaling waves. Finally, *rip currents* can suck violently out to sea, carrying unwary paddlers or swimmers half a mile offshore before letting them go. Rip currents can be the most hazardous. You can identify them by choppy surface

Surf kayaking brings the thrills of playboating into an exciting saltwater environment. (Photo by Jed Weingarten)

water, turbid water, or streaks of sea foam. If you get caught in these currents, your best escape is to swim or paddle perpendicular to the current until you break free. This can take some time and perseverance in big surf.

Undertows—which aren't really currents—form at many beaches. Here, the surface water pushed up on shore from breaking waves dives to the bottom as it works its way back out to sea. This backwash can pull swimmers underwater for a short period of time, then pop them back up many yards off the beach.

Basic Techniques

The first trick to surf kayaking is breaking through the waves on the way out from the beach. Before you enter the *surf zone*, watch how long it takes each set of waves to build, break, and re-build. Also check the water for hazards like strong currents or shallow reefs.

There often will be patterns in the surf—areas of slack water and gentle highways will open up amid breakers. Watch for an opportunity when the waves are least powerful and paddle toward that window aggressively. The key to success usually involves timing and direction: Point your bow straight into oncoming waves and time your approach so you hit the waves after they have already expended their energy. Paddle all the way through the wave, grabbing as much of the solid water on the back side as possible.

DROPPING IN

Ocean waves are similar to river waves and holes, with some interesting exceptions. In the ocean, the waves move while the water stays put; in rivers, the water moves while the waves stay put. Either way, though, wave surfing is the same: You slide onto the face of the wave, let gravity pull you downward, and surf away. (If the ocean wave breaks, simply switch to the hole-riding techniques you learned in the playboating chapter and side surf, cartwheel, or blast your way to the beach.)

A good ride starts with wave selection. Relax out beyond the surf zone and watch how the waves form. There generally will be a set of nicely shaped waves followed by a series of duds. Each wave will steepen and begin to break in the same area—this is where you'll want to drop in to your first wave.

Once you find a wave you like, paddle into position. Find the location where the wave will be steep enough to carry you forward, and begin paddling toward shore. As the wave picks you up, forward stroke just enough to keep your momentum going. Use your rudder and sweep strokes to keep yourself on the cleanest part of the wave and watch that the breakers don't swallow you up. If all goes well, you'll spend your day catching the good waves and paddling back out through the duds.

Surf Tricks

Depending on the type of kayak you're paddling, you can ride just the smooth face of the waves (back off the wave before it begins to break), blast the breakers by leaning back into the whitewater, or even lean forward and paddle off the lip of a breaker to do front and back enders. All the tricks you learned for playboating apply equally well in the surf.

HANDLING BREAKERS

If a big wave is about to crash in your face, you've got two choices: paddle like mad or brace. Frequently, a series of powerful forward strokes will propel you over the face of a wave, into the air, and onto the flat water behind the wave. Other times, forward stroking is an effort in futility. If there's no way to bust through a wave, turn sideways, lean hard into the wave, and *brace into the wave*. If you're lucky, you'll squirt out in front of the wave—still sideways—and side surf the wave into shore. If you're unlucky, you'll get creamed and have to start all over again.

14

Overnight Trips

Life on the Liquid Road

Camping and kayaking make great travel companions. In fact, some paddlers say that the river is little more than a liquid highway to be traveled before finding the next campsite.

Though few kayakers would downplay the joy of river running, most kayakers agree that camping is a ton of fun. Riverside camping has a special air about it. There are no RVs parked in the next space, no pop machines or laundromats nearby, and, if you're lucky, no humans for miles around. Everything in camp was put there by Mother Nature or carried there by boat.

On the other hand, an extended camping trip is one of the hardest things to pull off in a whitewater kayak. Low-volume kayaks have little (if any) storage space, and larger kayaks become heavy and unwieldy if sleeping bags and stoves burden their hulls.

Planning Ahead

Before you start a river outing, consider what you'll need to bring. Will you be on the river one day or three? Will your entire wardrobe comprise a few pairs of shorts and T-shirts, or will you need some heavy outerwear to stay warm? What do you plan to eat?

No matter how long a trip you plan or what type of conditions you expect to encounter, the mere fact that you'll be floating your gear into camp will change the type of food and equipment you'll have to carry. The river is going to jostle your equipment and attack your gear cache. For instance, if you're carrying down sleeping bags, cotton clothing, or canvas tents, you're asking for long, damp nights in camp. Polyester and nylon gear, on the other hand, repel water and work well even when wet. Synthetic sleeping bags—filled with Hollofil, Quallofil, Polarguard, or other space-age insulators—provide some warmth if they're wet, and fleece clothing dries quickly once you squeeze out most of the water.

The more gear you carry, the heavier and less maneuverable your boat will become. That's fine in flat, swift rapids—but try maneuvering your battleship in a Class IV maelstrom. Your trip can be more enjoyable if you think like a backpacker. Consider carrying minimum kitchen gear, one-burner stoves, and dehydrated meals. Layer your clothes for efficiency and leave excess baggage at home.

Rafts

Don't get me wrong—I love rafting as much as I love kayaking. Heck, I even wrote a book on rafting (*The Complete Whitewater Rafter*) Still, I know a packhorse when I see it. As far as I'm concerned, there's no better aquatic packhorse than a raft.

One of the best ways to undertake overnight trips in your kayak is to con a rafter into coming along. Dump all your heavy gear on the raft and free yourself to play! Even if this means picking up the tab for the rafter's gas money, it'll be well worth the investment. You'll be able to give up your Spartan existence, carry a few extra pork chops, and bring that big tent that folds into a stuff sack just slightly smaller than a kayak itself.

Pack Your 'Yak

If no rafters agree to babysit your gear while you play, you're going to have to carry your own. That means packing light, packing tight, and packing right.

Pack like a backpacker. Bring the smallest, lightest tents, stoves, and clothing you can; bring polypropylene outerwear and nylon shells whenever possible. Rely on a one-burner stove and freeze-dried meals (if possible) to limit food weight. Bring a water-purifying system and renew your water supply as your trip progresses to keep heavy water bottles from adding weight to your kayak.

WATERPROOF CONTAINERS

Improperly packed gear is destined for a soaking—if only from the water that seeps through your kayak's screw holes—but a number of modern technological wonders have made kayaking drier and more enjoyable than ever. You really *can* keep your gear dry on the river.

Dry bags are durable, specially designed waterproof sacks. When properly sealed—usually with fold-over or zip-lock closures—dry bags keep their contents totally dry. Most of the time. For some extra insurance, seal gear in small plastic trash bags before placing it in the dry bag. Smaller items can be separated into sandwich- and freezer-size bags before dropping them into dry bags. (Not only will this help keep small things dry, it will make finding them in camp much easier.)

Rafts can carry hundreds of pounds of gear with relative ease.

A few manufacturers make *float bags* that open at one end to accept gear. These bags—sometimes known as *stow-floats*—fit in the bow and stern like air bags, but keep your gear dry like dry bags. After you stuff these bags with gear, you can blow air into them and gain some flotation in the event of a swim.

Some items—such as cameras and video equipment, matches, and maps—are more vulnerable to water and jostling. Accordingly, you should pay extra-special attention to packing these items. *Waterproof boxes*—such as Pelican cases—have O-ring seals and solid, foam-lined walls that provide great protection for their contents. Waterproof boxes can be purchased in a variety of sizes and are well worth their price.

STOWING GEAR SAFELY

Veteran kayakers take great pride in their ability to pack odd-shaped items within the small confines of a kayak. Why can't you just throw gear behind the seat and hope for the best? Because *some day you're gonna' swim!* Sooner or later, all the gear sitting in your hull's air pocket is going to start flopping around in a hull filled with water. The longer it flops around in there, the more likely you are to douse it or lose it.

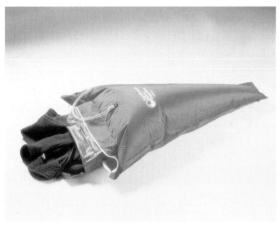

Stow-floats combine the flotation features of an air bag with the storage features of a dry bag. (Photo courtesy of Northwest River Supplies, Inc.)

When packing gear into dry bags and stow-floats, take extra care not to carry any sharp objects: They might not only tear the bags, they could help crack your hull. If your gear won't fit into the narrow confines between your kayak's pillars and the hull, consider removing the pillar to increase storage space, then using your stow-floats—or one large dry bag—for storage. (While this is not an uncommon practice, it makes your kayak more susceptible to deck collapse. Make sure you're a darned good paddler, and don't pin if you try this.)

You can put smaller waterproof boxes behind your seat or carry one between your knees. However, if you opt for the latter method (used by some photographers) you'll be increasing your risk of entrapment and making it much more difficult to wet exit from your kayak in an emergency. I've carried boxes between my knees, but I wouldn't recommend it.

Campsite Selection

Some canyons offer a wide variety of terrain and campsites, while others contain few, if any, hospitable camping niches. Before you start your trip, peruse the local guidebooks for camping opportunities or ask friends who have run the river what to expect. If the river is unexplored, check topographic maps for broad valleys that may offer level, comfortable sites. There may even be a government agency that preassigns designated campsites to river travelers. If you are able to find out about campsites ahead of time, try to preselect sites that fit your travel plans. If the trip is two days long, pick a site midway so that both river days are enjoyable.

Whether or not you've learned about campsites before leaving the put in, make sure that you find a feasible site in daylight. There is nothing more petrifying, disheartening, or dangerous than traveling downriver after dusk. If the bank offers many ideal settings, you're in luck—you can choose a campsite that will be sunny early in the morning or late in the day, one that slopes gently into the water or involves a short hike away from the river, or one that offers shade or unobstructed vistas.

RISING WATER

One thing you certainly don't want is a riverside campsite that might disappear if the river comes up! If there is *any* chance that the river will rise—from heavy runoff or dam releases—pick a site high above the waterline that offers easy escape, even in the dark.

Unload kayaks in the evening and carry the gear and kayaks high up on the shore. If the river rises a few feet, you can still spend the night resting peacefully.

WIND

There's another thing to think about when you make camp for the evening: *wind.* If you've spread your paddle jackets, drysuits, T-shirts, and hats all over the rocks to dry out, they might not be where you left them come morning. Canyons have a way of focusing and amplifying local air currents, especially late in the afternoon. Make sure you secure all of your belongings each time you make camp so that you'll still have them each time you break camp.

THE ENVIRONMENT

Conscientious kayakers strive to minimize their impact on the environment. Thick, grassy banks or beaches lined with delicate shrubs are especially susceptible to human harm. On the other hand, broad, sandy beaches and pebble-strewn bars can camouflage and erase your presence soon after your group leaves. Pick a site that has been used many times before or one that won't record your presence, and treat it with respect.

KAYAK PACKING TIPS

1. **Keep the kayak's trim as balanced as possible—stuff lighter gear back in the hull and heavier items closer to the kayaker and the bottom of the hull.**
2. **Pack items in the bow beyond your foot braces or bulkheads carefully! Leave plenty of room for your legs and feet, and beware of items that could entangle you.**
3. **Protect your hull. Keep hard-sided objects away from the hull and don't overload. Try to pack as lightly as possible.**
4. **Secure your gear. Make sure every item is secured inside the kayak with strong webbing. Use the best anchor points available—whether they're straps on the back of your backband, holes in the back of your seat, or holes drilled through the pillars.**

One trick to preserving the habitat is to use nothing but *freestanding gear*. Utilize tents that don't have to be staked out and small stoves that can be set up on a large rock. Avoid building campfires or clearing brush to make your camp more comfortable. If you must have a fire, build a small fire below the high-water mark and away from immovable boulders and logs. (Provided you dismantle the fire in the morning, the scars will vanish with the next freshet.)

Human Waste

Sooner or later you're going to have to answer the call of nature. Unfortunately, kayakers are caught between a rock and a hard spot when it comes to human waste. Many federally regulated rivers have strict rules regarding the disposal of waste, landfills are prohibited from accepting human waste in plastic bags, and river runners are often required to pack their waste out of the river. A number of companies build portable latrines that meet federal regulations, but they're too bulky to carry in a kayak; even large ammo cans often used as latrines by rafters are too big to carry in a kayak.

This leaves you with three choices: bring a support raft to carry a latrine; use a small container to capture human waste; or go *au naturel* on nonregulated rivers. Although I've dashed behind a thousand trees in my day, it's not the best way to do things. Instead, the best way to do things *naturally* is to dig a single hole 6 to 8 inches deep *at least* 100 feet from the river and dispose of human waste there.

Cookery

Kayaking—like any other form of outdoor recreation—burns calories. If you're anything like me, much of your time will be spent figuring out how to restore those calories while keeping your taste buds amused. After a long day on the river, a tasty meal provides a soothing transition into the lazy hours after dusk, while bountiful lunch spreads will give you all the energy you need to get you down the river.

Riverside meals can be simple or elaborate, depending on your budget, kitchen paraphernalia, carrying space, and gastronomic preferences. They can be simple, one-pot meals, cheese and salami, or extravagant banquets. Riverside dining is limited only by your culinary creativity.

THE MENU

Menu planning begins long before you make your first lunch stop or reach your first camp. In fact, it starts before you get to the local supermarket. Planning your river menu is only slightly different from planning your menu at home—you are only limited by weight, carrying space, refrigeration, and cooking utensils. Select a menu that will make everyone on the trip happy, and get everyone involved in selecting meals, either by having them list items they do and don't like or by having people rotate menu responsibilities for each day they're on the river.

Try to plan meals around the length of the trip, your level of patience, and the available cookware. On lengthy trips, select durable, long-lasting foods that won't spoil quickly. (Most perishables are bulky and rot quickly without a cooler, while dehydrated food items are light and long lasting.) Consider easy meals like one-pot stews, pasta, and Mexican dinners. Also consider the season and weather. Do you *really* want to stand outside in the middle of a rainstorm slow-simmering that special stew?

PACKING YOUR FOOD

Food-storage techniques depend on the length of your trip, the number of people on your trip, and the amount of food you're carrying. On a short, one-day jaunt with no more than a handful of kayakers, you may be able to get by with string cheese, apples, and high-energy bars packed into a small dry bag. More hearty eaters can pack bigger meals. On multiday journeys, even the chilly compartment of a friend's cooler might not be enough to keep food fresh and edible. In this case, some creative menu planning and packing become necessary.

River runners tend to be an inventive and resourceful lot when it comes to packing foods. The tricks are many. Since eggs break easily, they can be broken ahead of time and stored in plastic bottles, ready for use in your morning omelet. Bagels and hard rolls last longer than soft bread. Durable fruits and vegetables—such as potatoes, apples, and cucumbers—can be stored in tough bags and are easier to keep fresh and undamaged than are other types of produce. Even canned meats, powdered milk, and freeze-dried items can replace fresh goods—they'll last longer and they come in their own protective containers.

THE KITCHEN

Just about any manually powered tool you have in your home kitchen will work in your riverside kitchen. There are many compact camping stoves (powered by white gas, propane, or butane) on the market. Though all of these fuel-burning stoves work fine, some rivers restrict the types of fuel kayakers can use in camp. Check local regulations well in advance.

Once in camp, set up the kitchen away from the gear pile. (That way, people won't constantly pester the cook and make off with important ingredients before they hit the pan.)

Water

It is disheartening to think that almost every kayakable river poses a potential risk to humans if used for drinking water. Even the clearest streams can carry industrial pollutants, dangerous bacteria, and a nasty little bugger called *Giardia lamblia*.

Nonetheless, it is important to maintain your level of hydration by drinking enough water every day. So, maintaining a supply of safe drinking water demands some special attention, especially on long trips.

The most obvious way to guarantee fresh drinking water is to carry your own. However, water is heavy, so you must produce potable water during your river trip. There are three common ways to treat water and to make it safe for drinking.

- Boil the water for 10 to 20 minutes (add 1 minute of boiling time for every 1,000 feet above sea level).
- Use chemical purifiers such as halizone, iodine, or bleach. Halizone and iodine tablets come with instructions for proper dosages. If you're using 2 percent tincture of iodine, use 5 drops per quart of water and let it sit 30 minutes (double the time if the water is cold and double the dosage if the water is cloudy). Bleach is generally added to water at the rate of 8 drops per gallon; it takes about 30 minutes to kill living organisms. None of the chemical treatments is foolproof, and each requires some patience and caution. Remember that it takes time to kill the organisms and that just one drop of untreated water can spoil the whole batch.
- Filtration is the only method that can remove pesticides, solvents, and other artificial contaminants as well as living organisms. Portable filtration units strain water under pressure through microscopic pores in the unit's filter element. Kayakers should carry large enough water filters to supply adequate water for everyone on the trip, as well as replacement filter elements in case one clogs or breaks.

15

River Exploration and First Descents

Your Own River Wild

Exploring an unnavigated river can be an extraordinary experience. Some kayakers feel an irresistible draw to these types of trips, just as some travelers prefer forgotten back roads over popular highways. In many ways, exploratory descents are the epitome of whitewater endeavors. Such trips provide the ultimate test of your skill, judgment, and river prowess since many aspects of these adventures start as unknowns. First descents can combine the reverence of traversing untouched wilderness with the personal challenge of negotiating unnavigated canyons.

Having made countless descents on hundreds of different rivers and creeks, I still perk up with the rumor that an unexplored section of river exists. The competitive desire to nab a first descent and to paddle what no other kayaker has yet paddled is always present, but so are the memories of many failed descents. The potential for failure is omnipresent

during first descents, as is the risk of loss of equipment and life. This chapter provides some insight on the art and science of river exploration and is designed to help you map out your own first descents.

The Research Phase

Few exploratory descents (successful ones, at least) take place without an enormous amount of preparation. In fact, pre-trip planning often takes much longer than the trip itself, beginning weeks, months, or even years ahead of time. By learning everything possible about the river and surrounding terrain ahead of time, many of the risks inherent in wilderness exploration can be minimized.

Any exploratory descent should begin with a survey of all available information resources. Start with a copy of the region's best guidebooks, review paddling magazines and paddling newsletters, and call around to local whitewater clubs. It is quite possible that your exploratory trip is really a second, third, or twentieth descent!

Next, check out topographic maps. For North American paddlers, the United States or Canadian Geological Surveys maintain detailed topographic maps covering any river you can find, and these maps can be your single most valuable resource. When purchasing topographic maps, select the smallest scale possible. Large-area maps (1:100,000 or 1:250,000 scale) usually offer too little detail to provide much information. However, smaller-scaled maps—particularly the 1:24,000 or 7.5' maps—are quite useful. Many have contour intervals of 20 to 40 feet, which can at least forewarn of the presence of large waterfalls and box canyons.

Begin reading the map by looking at the width of the blue line denoting the river: Is it a *thick* blue line, indicative of a large-volume river, or is it a *narrow* line, indicating a small stream? Next, note the contour intervals and the mileage scale. Look at the section of river you wish to explore and break it down into half-mile or mile sections. By counting the number of times the contour lines cross the river in a mile-long section and multiplying by the contour interval, you get the average gradient in feet per mile.

Knowing how to interpret gradient is important. Many popular streams drop 10 to 100 feet per mile; more extreme whitewater rivers drop 100 to 200 feet per mile. (On rare occasions, kayakers have descended rivers with gradients exceeding 300 feet per mile.) Always keep in mind that even low-gradient rivers might descend very gradually, then suddenly drop many feet over unrunnable falls.

One way to determine whether your venture is worth the risk is to compare the river's gradient to the canyon's surrounding terrain. If the land adjacent to the river shows closely spaced contour lines, the river is in a canyon—a genuine hazard if there are waterfalls, severe whitewater sections, or unrunnable rapids. A narrow canyon with a steep gradient is not the place to be unless you've scouted everything out from the air or land ahead of time! However, put that same steep river on a map showing widely spaced

contour lines traversing the adjacent land and it may be possible to portage around unrunnable sections.

Look for obvious escape routes in the form of broad contour lines departing the river's edge. Note obvious landmarks such as peaks, cliffs, or major tributaries that will be visible from the river—these will let you monitor your progress. Also determine the total mileage between put in and take out to get a rough estimate of your expected river time.

Topographic maps are your guidebooks during exploratory descents, so take good care of them. Keep them securely fastened and stored in waterproof containers when not in use, and keep a duplicate set on another kayak in case one set gets lost or destroyed.

Once you have an imaginary picture of the river, gather more information. If you can, go to the river and scout as much of it as you can see. Many first descents started with long, arduous hikes along canyon rims to view the rapids below or with airplane and helicopter flights over the river to view hidden

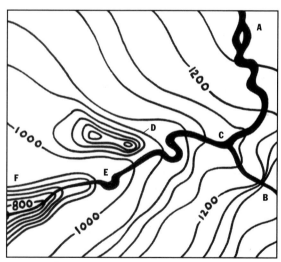

Topographic maps can provide a lot of valuable information. Here, the river winds through a broad valley while gradually descending through a braided channel (A). *A tributary descends over a big waterfall* (B) *before entering the main river* (C). *A big hill on the right side of the river* (D) *might be visible from the water. Finally, if you did your homework, you'd know that the big eddy* (E) *signals the approach to a steeper, narrower section of river* (F).

corridors. Talk to the locals—anglers, hunters, and hikers—and glean whatever information they're willing to share with you.

The final research stage is to obtain information on water levels. While the mental picture imparted by that thick blue line might be accurate, a gauge will tell you a lot more. Check with the local government or river-management offices, weather services, or water districts to see if the river has a gauge, then monitor the river level periodically. The U.S. Geological Survey can also provide historical watershed and drainage information and flow data. When combined with information on local weather patterns and a Water Supply Outlook (available from the USGS), this information gives a strong indication of the river's reaction to things like rain and snowmelt.

Putting Together a Team

In North America, almost anything that *could* be kayaked *has* been kayaked. Accordingly, usually only the most difficult and challenging rivers remain unexplored. To meet that challenge takes a *team* of kayakers compatible in both their personalities and skills.

It takes much more than just a positive mental attitude to confront and survive unknown dilemmas. Each team member should be comfortable with treacherous whitewater, and each should bring to the team a solid set of wilderness skills and useful technical abilities. By including kayakers with medical expertise, rock-climbing skills, or intimate knowledge of the adjacent terrain, the team will have a broad range of useful skills and will be more prepared to handle difficult situations.

Equipment and Supplies

Since you'll be traversing unknown canyons, portaging with greater frequency, and relying much more on your equipment then ever before, it is imperative that your equipment be top quality and in excellent shape. Take some time before the trip to double check your kayak: Examine it closely for flaws and wear spots; make sure *everything* is intact; tighten any loose screws. Grab a different boat if your kayak won't withstand the rigors of the descent. If an irreparable defect shows up in any other equipment (life jacket, helmet, etc.), don't bring those items along either! Everything you bring should be at least in near-perfect condition.

The most important part of assembling the equipment for the trip is trimming weight. It is far easier to portage a light kayak than one fully loaded with expendable luxuries. But that doesn't mean that you shouldn't bring all of the gear that is—or may be—necessary! You will be relying more on your gear now than ever before, so bring everything essential to the success of your trip.

Safety

One place you *don't* want to shave weight is in your safety gear selection. Bring extra safety gear (climbing ropes, carabiners, throw bags, etc.) in case of an emergency. Carry a fully equipped first aid kit along with a detailed medical handbook. The more remote and dangerous the trip, the more you should consider carrying a two-way radio (and know how to use it). Notify rangers, families, and friends of your itinerary before you leave (including the expected time and location of your return). That way,

> **"**If your foreign exploratory descent is more than a day or two long, bring a team that you know better than your family. A first descent on foreign soil is no place to meet your paddling counterparts for the first time, regardless of their experience or reputation. Furthermore, bringing a teammate versed in the language and culture of the area can be more beneficial than having nothing but the fastest, most skilled paddlers on your team. Choose your teammates wisely and your exploratory descents will be much more enjoyable. **"**
>
> **—LARS HOLBEK**
> **EXPLORER AND GUIDEBOOK AUTHOR**

First descents are getting more and more difficult to find. Some first descents take a lot of hard work and can involve some arduous portages around impenetrable obstacles. Be prepared for anything.

if something does go wrong, a search party can be sent to find and help you.)

Getting to the River

Many first descents and exploratory trips have been overlooked simply because of the difficulty of accessing put ins or take outs. If you're willing to carry your gear long distances over adverse terrain, you may just find a whitewater paradise awaiting at the end of the trail.

Keep in mind that additional gear—sleeping bags, riverwear, safety gear, and food—has to be carried to the river. If the hike down to the put in is only a mile or two long, consider spending one day hiking back and forth to transport everything to the river. On the other hand, if you only have time to make one hike, load your gear into backpack-style dry bags—they carry a heavy load and won't interfere with carrying the kayak on your shoulders.

Running the River

Whenever you're in a new canyon or on an unknown section of river, *run more conservatively* than you would otherwise. Make sure your gear is lashed down with bombproof straps or knots. Take a moment to ask yourself *what if* before running blindly around a bend or over a horizon line. On remote rivers, a mistake could be costly and any injury could go untreated for days. Don't succumb to paranoia, but step back from your normal river bravado. (By the time you return to civilization, the descent will take on heroic proportions anyway.)

> **"T**he most important thing to bring with you on exploratory trips and first descents is good judgment. Going for it on a marginal Class 5 rapid may be OK near home or during roadside descents, but it can have devastating consequences in the wilderness. Proceed with caution, be more conservative than usual, and you'll still have plenty to brag about when you get back home. **"**
>
> —LARS HOLBEK

16

Transporting and Caring for Kayaking Gear

Kayaks are built to withstand abuse—collisions with rocks, occasional dragging on the ground, even the damaging effects of ultraviolet rays. But owner abuse—poor maintenance, careless storage, or improper use—will greatly shorten the life of almost every item in your kayaking arsenal.

It only takes a little bit of care and common sense to keep your equipment healthy and kicking long after the warranties wear out. In this chapter we'll look not only at how to maintain kayaks and paddling accessories, we'll explore ways to repair gear once it breaks down.

Caring for Your Kayak

There are a multitude of ways to damage or destroy a kayak, but most kayak damage is the result of severe impacts, abrasion, or ultraviolet decay. Here are some simple guidelines to follow every time you use your kayak.

1. Don't beat it into submission. If you run big waterfalls with shallow landings, you're going to break some boats.
2. Don't step into or sit on grounded kayaks any more than necessary (when entering or exiting rivers). There may be rocks or sharp objects on the ground that could damage or puncture the boat. If your boat is particularly fragile, *never* place weight on it when it is out of the water.
3. Carry—don't drag—kayaks. Whether your kayak is plastic or fiberglass, ground abrasion will soon wear weak spots into your boat.
4. When transporting kayaks on roof racks or trailers, make sure they aren't rubbing against bolts or sharp objects.

5. When carrying kayaks on roof racks, take care not to compress the hull, especially in warmer climates.

6. Store kayaks away from direct sunlight to avoid long-term ultraviolet damage.

7. Store kayaks away from harmful chemicals and solvents.

8. Store kayaks vertically (standing on the bow or stern) or on edge to avoid hull distortions.

CARTOPPING

Lightweight kayaks are easy to transport on car- or truck-top roof racks. Today's roof-rack manufacturers offer accessories such as kayak saddles, stacking posts, and paddle holders that are easy to use and offer hull protection during transportation.

Kayaks can be strapped to roof racks rightside up, upside down, or on edge. However, carrying your kayak on edge is the most space-efficient method and is less likely to distort your boat. This method is difficult, however, without racks with upright bars.

When strapping kayaks into place, be sure not to tie them down too tightly as this will quickly distort the hull's shape. Be sure to secure the boat to both racks and to the front and back of the vehicle (using the kayak's grab loops).

Kayak Repairs

By just looking at the number of sharp rocks in a typical river and applying the law of averages you'll see that, sooner or later, your kayak is going to crack. Avid steep creekers are notorious for breaking boats annually, while some paddlers get their boats to last 5 to 10 years.

Cracked plastic kayak hulls are challenging—sometimes impossible—to repair. Some blow-molded kayaks can be welded by experienced technicians, but most roto-molded kayaks are permanently broken once they're cracked.

Roof racks come in a wide variety of styles, from simple cross bars to specially designed saddles and stacking posts. To ensure your kayak's safety, tie the bow and stern to front and rear bumpers (taking care not to damage your vehicle's paint).

If you crack a kayak midtrip, there may still be some ways to patch it long enough to complete your trip. Duct tape (one of the wonders of the modern world) can be used to temporarily stop the inflow of water through a crack and offer some hull support. Pick up a half dozen sticks of P-Tex to temporarily patch small cracks. (P-Tex is a type of plastic used in ski bases. When needed, you light one end of the P-Tex stick—just like you are lighting a candle—and let the plastic drip into position. Take care to ensure that the flame stays clear so that the P-Tex retains much of its original strength.)

Be aware that patch jobs—with the exception of high-tech welds—might not last more than a few minutes on a river and that big cracks are nearly impossible to patch. So, plan on *not* cracking your kayak if you plan to paddle some more.

Also, there's more to a kayak than just the hull. One of the more common problems with some kayaks is lost or broken drain plugs. Many modern drain plugs are replaceable, so carry a spare plug and a few necessary tools (many only require a screwdriver) and you'll never have to worry. Broken broach loops and bow caps also may be replaceable. Check with your local kayak retailer at the time you buy your boat.

Maintaining Equipment

Spray skirts, drysuits, wetsuits, paddle jackets and booties see an enormous amount of abuse on river trips. Twigs and snags can rip the fabric, body oils start to stink up your neoprene items, and ultraviolet rays slowly chisel away at the life span of nylon.

Spray skirts are especially vulnerable to damage. Luckily, they often can be repaired with neoprene cement or a special glue known as Aquaseal. (Just follow the directions and take care not to distort the skirt during the repair.)

Other neoprene gear—such as wetsuits and booties—should be hand washed with mild soap and water. There are even some special detergents on the market for eliminating the tell-tale neoprene smell that follows many river runners around.

Drysuits, however, demand special care. First, *never try to zip a rear-entry drysuit by yourself*—have someone do it for you. (The zippers are very expensive and can be easily damaged if tugged or bent the wrong way.) Next, take good care of your drysuit's neck, wrist and ankle seals, and cuffs, which are particularly vulnerable to drying, splitting, and tearing. Swab the seals with generous amounts of the suit manufacturer's recommended protectant before or after each trip. Don't use anything on the seals that contains petroleum and avoid spilling other solvents on the seals.

DRYSUIT REPAIRS

If a drysuit seal or cuff tears, it can be replaced by the factory or by some whitewater shops. If you want to do it yourself, here's how.

1. Tear off the old cuff, making sure to get rid of all the excess latex and glue.
2. Find a container large enough to fully expand the opening where the cuff will be mounted and stuff it inside that opening.
3. Apply a thick coat of Aquaseal to the outside of the drysuit opening where the new cuff will go, being sure to add an extra quarter-inch of Aquaseal past the cuff line.
4. Stretch the new gasket with your hands and lay it over the glued opening of the suit.
5. Hold the seal in place with tape and let it dry for 24 hours.

Repair tears to drysuits with vinyl bond—a general-purpose glue—and a small patch made from the same material as your drysuit, or use a small dab of Aquaseal to repair small holes or tears.

WETSUIT REPAIRS

Wetsuits start seeing abuse the moment you go to put them on. Neoprene can tear if stretched or pulled too hard, so use care when you're putting it on and taking it off. If a rip does develop, repair it before the tear spreads. The easiest way to repair damaged suits is to use an iron-on neoprene patch (available at dive shops); however, neoprene cement and Aquaseal work better and don't leave an elevated section of material. Both Aquaseal and neoprene cement come in small cans with simple directions for gluing the torn edges back together.

To keep a wetsuit clean and strong, wash it by hand periodically using special wetsuit detergents. (It is possible to wash your wetsuit in the washing machine on the rinse cycle, but be careful.) Once the suit is dry, sprinkle it with talcum powder and store it in a dry place.

LIFE JACKETS

Life jackets are tough if properly maintained. The key to life-jacket longevity is to not use it as a seat, cushion, or rag. Don't overpack it in small spaces, and keep it clean. When it's not in use, keep it away from ultraviolet rays and heat.

PADDLES

Most modern paddles are tough and resilient, but they can still snap from undue pressure or abuse. Don't place a lot of weight on one part of a paddle, throw it on the ground, or bang it on rocks. Blade edges can be maintained by cementing Rim Rubber (a special edge protector available at many paddle shops) in place. Wood-paddle manufacturers can provide solid advice on maintenance and repair of wooden paddles.

17

Preserving the River Environment

I have been fortunate over these past 10 years to witness the joy, the thrill, and the challenge that only whitewater rivers can bestow. While sliding down a smooth tongue, gliding toward the heart of a rapid, I feel a return to the elements, to primal forces far more powerful than the human spirit. On the river, I gain a deeper understanding of my own roots, and I begin to understand humanity's reliance upon water for the sustenance of life. When away from the river, I feel a profound sense of displacement affecting every aspect of my daily life, as if a part of me had been left at the last take out.

This sense of interconnectedness has been shared by my predecessors, captured in timeless prose for boaters of all generations. John Muir, the grand architect of environmentalism, once professed, "The rivers flow not past, but through us, thrilling, tingling, vibrating every fiber and cell of the substance of our bodies, making them glide and sing." Henry David Thoreau, writing in his journals, stated, "The river is my own highway, the only wild and unfenced part of the world hereabouts." And Chief Seattle's words have inspired many a follower: "The rivers are our brothers, they quench our thirst. The rivers carry our canoes and feed our children... and you must give to the rivers the kindness you would give any brother."

While contemporary whitewater enthusiasts look upon flowing waters with reverence and respect, others eye rivers as developable resources, a raw product to be harvested, transformed, and sold. The latter group appears in many forms—regional irrigation districts, private utility companies, the U.S. Army Corps of Engineers. They come to the rivers not to float and enjoy the wonders of wilderness but to dam and divert them, shackling eternal waters behind the transient insults of concrete and steel.

I have strained to eloquently capture my own feelings on this latter type of river use but have fallen quite short of my goal. Instead, I defer to the poetry of Margaret Hindes, whose beautiful verse I read in William O. Douglas's *My Wilderness*:

Gone, desecrated for a dam—
Pines, stream, and trails
Burned and bare
Down to dust.
Now water fills the hollow,
Water for power,
But the bowl of wilderness
Is broken, forever.

Rivers are the veins of the earth, the lifeblood of the planet. They feed and nourish the land, and rinse away the trivial monuments of man's arrogance, mindless of humanity's pride. Rivers are there for all of us to view, to float, and to enjoy. They carry our dreams and the dreams of future generations.

Whether you kayak for inner peace or an adrenaline rush, you can help preserve rivers for everyone to enjoy. Take the first step by getting involved—join a local whitewater club and support national environmental groups' efforts. Then, let the river's own wealth of inspiration kindle your energies and foster your own desires to preserve free-flowing water for everyone.

I leave you with these words, passed along by Tanaka Shozo: "The care of rivers is not a question of rivers, but of the human heart."

Put some heart into your rivers and they'll last forever.

The stagnant backwaters of California's New Melones Reservoir cover a stretch of the Stanislaus River—once one of the most popular whitewater rivers in the state.

Appendix

Safety Code of American Whitewater (Revision 1998)

This code has been prepared using the best available information and has been reviewed by a broad cross section of whitewater experts. The code, however, is only a collection of guidelines; attempts to minimize risks should be flexible, not constrained by a rigid set of rules. Varying conditions and group goals may combine with unpredictable circumstances to require alternate procedures. This code is not intended to serve as a standard of care for commercial outfitters or guides.

I. PERSONAL PREPAREDNESS AND RESPONSIBILITY

1. Be a competent swimmer, with the ability to handle yourself underwater.

2. Wear a life jacket. A snugly fitting vest-type life preserver offers back and shoulder protection as well as the flotation needed to swim safely in whitewater.

3. Wear a solid, correctly fitted helmet when upsets are likely. This is essential in kayaks or covered canoes, and recommended for open canoeists using thigh straps and rafters running steep drops.

4. Do not boat out of control. Your skills should be sufficient to stop or reach shore before reaching danger. Do not enter a rapid unless you are reasonably sure that you can run it safely or swim it without injury.

5. Whitewater rivers contain many hazards which are not always easily recognized. The following are the most frequent killers.

A. HIGH WATER. The river's speed and power increase tremendously as the flow increases, raising the difficulty of most rapids. Rescue becomes progressively harder as the water rises, adding to the danger. Floating debris and strainers make even an easy rapid quite hazardous. It is often misleading to judge the river level at the put in, since a small rise in a wide, shallow place will be multiplied many times where the river narrows. Use reliable gauge information whenever possible, and be aware that sun on snowpack, hard rain, and upstream dam releases may greatly increase the flow.

B. COLD. Cold drains your strength and robs you of the ability to make sound decisions on matters affecting your survival. Cold-water immersion, because of the initial shock and the rapid heat loss which follows, is especially dangerous. Dress appropriately for bad weather or sudden immersion in the water. When the water temperature is less than 50° Fahrenheit, a wetsuit or drysuit is essential for protection if you swim. Next best is wool or pile clothing under a waterproof shell. In this case, you should also carry waterproof matches and a change of clothing in a waterproof bag. If, after prolonged exposure, a person experiences uncontrollable shaking, loss of coordination, or difficulty speaking, he or she is hypothermic and needs your assistance.

C. STRAINERS. Brush, fallen trees, bridge pilings, undercut rocks or anything else which allows river current to sweep through can pin boats and boaters against the obstacle. Water pressure on anything trapped this way can be overwhelming. Rescue is often extremely difficult. Pinning may occur in fast current, with little or no whitewater to warn of the danger.

D. DAMS, WEIRS, LEDGES, REVERSALS, HOLES, AND HYDRAULICS. When water drops over an obstacle, it curls back on itself, forming a strong upstream current which may be capable of holding a boat or swimmer. Some holes make for excellent sport. Others are proven killers. Paddlers who cannot recognize the difference should avoid all but the smallest holes. Hydraulics around man-made dams must be treated with utmost respect regardless of their height or the level of the river. Despite their seemingly benign appearance, they can create an almost escape-proof trap. The swimmer's only exit from the "drowning machine" is to dive below the surface when the downstream current is flowing beneath the reversal.

E. BROACHING. When a boat is pushed sideways against a rock by strong current, it may collapse and wrap. This is especially dangerous to kayak and decked-canoe paddlers; these boats will collapse, and the combination of indestructible hulls and tight outfitting may create a deadly trap. Even without entrapment, releasing pinned boats can be extremely time consuming and dangerous. To avoid pinning, throw your weight downstream toward the rock. This allows the current to slide harmlessly underneath the hull.

6. Boating alone is discouraged. The minimum party is three people or two craft.

7. Have a frank knowledge of your boating ability, and don't attempt rivers or rapids which lie beyond that ability.

A. Develop the paddling skills and teamwork required to match the river you plan to boat. Most good paddlers develop skills gradually, and attempts to advance too quickly will compromise your safety and enjoyment.

B. Be in good physical and mental condition, consistent with the difficulties which may be expected. Make adjustments for loss of skills due to age, health,

fitness. Any health limitations must be explained to your fellow paddlers prior to starting the trip.

8. Be practiced in self rescue, including escape from an overturned craft. The Eskimo roll is strongly recommended for decked boaters who run rapids Class IV or greater, or who paddle in cold environmental conditions.

9. Be trained in rescue skills, CPR, and first aid, with special emphasis on recognizing and treating hypothermia. It may save your friend's life.

10. Carry equipment needed for unexpected emergencies, including footwear which will protect your feet when walking out, a throw rope, knife, whistle, and waterproof matches. If you wear eyeglasses, tie them on and carry a spare pair on long trips. Bring cloth repair tape on short runs and a full repair kit on isolated rivers. Do not wear bulky jackets, ponchos, heavy boots, or anything else which could reduce your ability to survive a swim.

11. Despite the mutually supportive group structure described in this code, individual paddlers are ultimately responsible for their own safety and must assume sole responsibility for the following decisions:

A. The decision to participate on any trip. This includes an evaluation of the expected difficulty of the rapids under the conditions existing at the time of the put in.

B. The selection of appropriate equipment, including a boat design suited to their skills and the appropriate rescue and survival gear.

C. The decision to scout any rapid, and to run or portage according to their best judgment. Other members of the group may offer advice, but paddlers should resist pressure from anyone to paddle beyond their skills. It is also their responsibility to decide whether to pass up any walk out or take out opportunity.

D. All trip participants should consistently evaluate their own and their group's safety, voicing their concerns when appropriate and following what they believe to be the best course of action. Paddlers are encouraged to speak with anyone whose actions on the water are dangerous, whether they are a part of your group or not.

II. BOAT AND EQUIPMENT PREPAREDNESS

1. Test new and different equipment under familiar conditions before relying on it for difficult runs. This is especially true when adopting a new boat design or outfitting system. Low-volume craft may present additional hazards to inexperienced or poorly conditioned paddlers.

2. Be sure your boat and gear are in good repair before starting a trip. The more isolated and difficult the run, the more rigorous this inspection should be.

3. Install flotation bags in non-inflatable craft, securely fixed in each end, designed to displace as much water as possible. Inflatable boats should have multiple air chambers and be test inflated before launching.

4. Have strong, properly sized paddles or oars for controlling your craft. Carry sufficient spares for the length and difficulty of the trip.

5. Outfit your boat safely. The ability to exit your boat quickly is an essential component of safety in rapids. It is your responsibility to see that there is absolutely nothing to cause entrapment when coming free of an upset craft. This includes:

A. Spray covers which won't release reliably or which release prematurely.

B. Boat outfitting too tight to allow a fast exit, especially in low-volume kayaks or decked canoes. This includes low-hung thwarts in canoes lacking adequate clearance for your feet, and kayak footbraces which fail or allow your feet to become wedged under them.

C. Inadequately supported decks which collapse on a paddler's legs when a decked boat is pinned by water pressure. Inadequate clearance with the deck because of your size or build.

D. Loose ropes which cause entanglement. Beware of any length of loose line attached to a whitewater boat. All items must be tied tightly and excess line eliminated; painters, throw lines, and safety rope systems must be completely and effectively stored. Do not knot the end of a rope, as it can get caught in cracks between rocks.

6. Provide ropes which permit you to hold on to your craft so that it may be rescued. The following methods are recommended:

A. Kayaks and covered canoes should have grab loops of quarter-inch rope or equivalent webbing sized to admit a normal-sized hand. Stern painters are permissible if properly secured.

B. Open canoes should have securely anchored bow and stern painters consisting of 8 to 10 feet of quarter-inch line. These must be secured in such a way that they are readily accessible but cannot come loose accidentally. Grab loops are acceptable but are more difficult to reach after an upset.

C. Rafts and dories may have taut perimeter lines threaded through the loops provided. Footholds should be designed so that a paddler's feet cannot be forced through them, causing entrapment. Flip lines should be carefully and reliably stowed.

7. Know your craft's carrying capacity and how added loads affect boat handling in whitewater. Most rafts have a minimum crew size which can be added to on day trips or in easy rapids. Carrying more than two paddlers in an open canoe when running rapids is not recommended.

8. Cartop racks must be strong and attach positively to the vehicle. Lash your boat to each crossbar, then tie the ends of the boats directly to the bumpers for added security. This arrangement should survive all but the most violent vehicle accident.

III. GROUP PREPAREDNESS AND RESPONSIBILITY

1. Organization. A river trip should be regarded as a common adventure by all participants, except on instructional or commercially guided trips as defined below. Participants share the

responsibility for the conduct of the trip, and each participant is individually responsible for judging his or her own capabilities and for his or her own safety as the trip progresses. Participants are encouraged (but are not obligated) to offer advice and guidance for the independent consideration and judgment of others.

2. River Conditions. The group should have a reasonable knowledge of the difficulty of the run. Participants should evaluate this information and adjust their plans accordingly. If the run is exploratory or no one is familiar with the river, maps and guidebooks, if available, should be examined. The group should secure accurate flow information; the more difficult the run, the more important this will be. Be aware of possible changes in river level and how this will affect the difficulty of the run. If the trip involves tidal stretches, secure appropriate information on tides.

3. Group equipment should be suited to the difficulty of the river. The group should always have a throw line available, and one line per boat is recommended on difficult runs. The list may include: carabiners, prusik loops, first aid kit, flashlight, folding saw, fire starter, guidebooks, maps, food, extra clothing, and any other rescue or survival items suggested by conditions. Each item is not required on every run, and this list is not meant to be a substitute for good judgment.

4. Keep the group compact, but maintain sufficient spacing to avoid collisions. If the group is large, consider dividing into smaller groups or using the "buddy system" as an additional safeguard. Space yourselves closely enough to permit good communication but not so close as to interfere with one another in rapids.

A. A point paddler sets the pace. When in front, do not get in over your head. Never run drops when you cannot see a clear route to the bottom or, for advanced paddlers, a sure route to the next eddy. When in doubt, stop and scout.

B. Keep track of all group members. Each boat keeps the one behind it in sight, stopping if necessary. Know how many people are in your group and take head counts regularly. No one should paddle ahead or walk out without first informing the group. Paddlers requiring additional support should stay at the center of a group and not allow themselves to lag behind in the more difficult rapids. If the group is large and contains a wide range of abilities, a "sweep boat" may be designated to bring up the rear.

C. Courtesy. On heavily used rivers, do not cut in front of a boater running a drop. Always look upstream before leaving eddies to run or play. Never enter a crowded drop or eddy when no room for you exists. Passing other groups in a rapid may be hazardous: It's often safer to wait upstream until the group ahead has passed.

5. Float plan. If the trip is into a wilderness area or for an extended period, plans should be filed with a responsible person who will contact the authorities if you are overdue. It may be wise to establish checkpoints along the way where civilization could be contacted if necessary. Knowing the location of possible help and pre-planning escape routes can speed rescue.

6. Drugs. The use of alcohol or mind-altering drugs before or during river trips is not recommended. It dulls reflexes, reduces decision-making ability, and may interfere with important survival reflexes.

7. Instructional or Commercially Guided Trips. In contrast to the common adventure-trip format, in these trip formats a boating instructor or commercial guide assumes some of the responsibilities normally exercised by the group as a whole, as appropriate under the circumstances. These formats recognize that instructional or commercially guided trips may involve participants who lack significant experience in whitewater. However, as a participant acquires experience in whitewater, he or she takes on increasing responsibility for his or her own safety, in accordance with what he or she

knows or should know as a result of that increased experience. Also, as in all trip formats, every participant must realize and assume the risks associated with the serious hazards of whitewater rivers. It is advisable for instructors and commercial guides or their employers to acquire trip or personal liability insurance.

A. An "instructional trip" is characterized by a clear teacher/pupil relationship, where the primary purpose of the trip is to teach boating skills, and which is conducted for a fee.

B. A "commercially guided trip" is characterized by a licensed, professional guide conducting trips for a fee.

IV. GUIDELINES FOR RIVER RESCUE

1. Recover from an upset with an Eskimo roll whenever possible. Evacuate your boat immediately if there is imminent danger of being trapped against rocks, brush, or any other kind of strainer.

2. If you swim, hold on to your boat. It has much flotation and is easy for rescuers to spot. Get to the upstream end so that you cannot be crushed between a rock and your boat by the force of the current. Persons with good balance may be able to climb on top of a swamped kayak or flipped raft and paddle to shore.

3. Release your craft if this will improve your chances, especially if the water is cold or dangerous rapids lie ahead. Actively attempt self rescue whenever possible by swimming for safety. Be prepared to assist others who may come to your aid.

A. When swimming in shallow or obstructed rapids, lie on your back with feet held high and pointed downstream. Do not attempt to stand in fast-moving water; if your foot wedges on the bottom, fast water will push you under and keep you there. Get to slow or very shallow water before attempting to stand or walk. Look ahead! Avoid possible pinning situations, including undercut rocks, strainers, downed trees, holes, and other dangers by swimming away from them.

B. If the rapids are deep and powerful, roll over onto your stomach and swim aggressively for shore. Watch for eddies and slackwater and use them to get out of the current. Strong swimmers can effect a powerful upstream ferry and get to shore fast. If the shores are obstructed with strainers or undercut rocks, however, it is safer to "ride the rapid out" until a safer escape can be found.

4. If others spill and swim, go after the boaters first. Rescue boats and equipment only if this can be done safely. While participants are encouraged (but not obligated) to assist one another to the best of their ability, they should do so only if they can, in their judgment, do so safely. The first duty of a rescuer is to not compound the problem by becoming another victim.

5. The use of rescue lines requires training; uninformed use may cause injury. Never tie yourself into either end of a line without a reliable quick-release system. Have a knife handy to deal with unexpected entanglement. Learn to place set lines effectively, to throw accurately, to belay effectively, and to properly handle a rope thrown to you.

6. When reviving a drowning victim, be aware that cold water may greatly extend survival time underwater. Victims of hypothermia may have depressed vital signs so they look and feel dead. Don't give up; continue CPR for as long as possible without compromising safety.

Equipment Checklist

- Kayak
- Float bags
- Spray skirt
- Paddle
- Helmet
- Life jacket
- Waterproof containers
- Rescue and safety gear
- First aid kit

RIVERWEAR

- Booties
- Wetsuit, wet shorts, or drysuit
- Paddle jacket or dry top
- Polypro underwear/sweater
- Helmet liner
- Gloves or pogies
- Nose clips and ear plugs
- Other: _____

SAFETY AND RESCUE GEAR

- Throw bag
- Carabiners
- River knife
- Pulleys
- Whistle
- Web slings
- Prusik loops
- Static rope
- Other:

First-Aid Kit

Note: Consult with a doctor or other medical professionals and take a first aid-course before assembling your first-aid kit.

- First-aid book
- Band-Aids
- Adhesive tape
- Gauze (sheet and roll)
- Compresses
- Ace bandages
- Paramedic shears
- 10 percent proridine-iodine solution
- 19 percent hydrocortisone cream
- Neosporin ointment
- Small tweezers
- Knife
- Needles
- Safety pins
- CPR face shield
- Oral glucose/sugar/candy
- Powdered sports drink
- Penlight
- Large syringe/rubber bulb
- Moleskin
- Venom-extraction kit
- Space blanket
- Aspirin, Tylenol, or ibuprofen
- Lomotil
- Ex-Lax
- Dramamine
- Robitussin DM
- Prescription medications
- Triangular bandages (optional)
- Sam splint (optional)
- Sun block
- Hypothermia thermometer
- Disposable gloves
- Alcohol swabs
- Small package liquid soap
- Waterproof carrying case
- Other: _____

Trip Planner

This list is designed primarily to be a basic guideline for inexperienced paddlers. There are many more steps that go into the pretrip agenda. As your river experience grows, so will your ability to quickly assemble groups of kayakers and plan trips.

- Assemble group
- Choose river
- Research guidebooks for best season, water levels, access points, rapids, etc.
- Talk to local paddlers about river
- Check water levels/weather
- Check permit requirements
- Obtain necessary permits
- Check for other river regulations
- Plan shuttle
- Plan menu
- Review equipment list
- Review safety/rescue list
- Review first aid kit list
- Fix/replace broken or lost gear
- Other: _____

Metric Conversions

1 cfs = 0.0283 cms
1 cms = 35.3 cfs
1 mile = 1.6 km
1 km = 0.6214 mile
1 foot = 0.3 meter
1 meter = 3.28 feet

Glossary

Baffle: a diaphragm that divides the interior of tubes into separate compartments

Bank: the river's shore

Bar: a shallow part of the river channel with sand, gravel, or small rocks

Belay: a method of slowing or stopping a rope from sliding

Big water: refers to rivers with large volume and powerful hydraulics

Blade: the wide, flat part of a paddle or oar

Boat: kayak

Boater: kayaker

Boils: ascending currents that rise above surface level unpredictably

Bony: shallow, rocky rapids

Boof: launching your boat over a rock or shallow ledge

Booties: specialized neoprene socks/shoes for kayakers

Boulder garden: a rapid densely strewn with boulders

Bow: the front or nose of a kayak

Brace: using the paddle to assist a paddler in staying in the kayak or to prevent the kayak from flipping over

Breaking wave: a standing wave that falls upstream

Broach: a horizontal/sideways pin against an obstacle

Bulkhead: a type of footbrace (see *footbrace*)

Cfs: cubic feet per second. Measures the current's velocity past a fixed point in the river (35.3 cfs equals one cubic meter per second)

Cms: cubic meters per second

Carabiner: a metal clip used to attach lines to kayaks, secure gear, or substitute for a pulley

Cartwheel: flipping a kayak end for end in a hydraulic. There are many kinds of cartwheels, including *whipits* (cartwheels more than 45 degrees vertical), *McTwists* (cartwheels less than 45 degrees vertical), *waterwheels* (cartwheels on waterfalls), *wave wheels* (cartwheels on waves), and *splats* (cartwheels executed on the upstream side of a rock)

Chute: a narrow, constricted portion of the river

Class I–VI: the international standard classifications used to rate the difficulty of rivers and rapids

Classification: a system for rating the difficulty of whitewater rapids

Clean: a word used to describe a route free of obstructions

Confluence: the point where two rivers or streams meet

Control hand: the hand that remains in a fixed position on the paddle shaft while the shaft rotates through the opposite hand (right-handed paddlers usually have a right control hand)

Creek boat: a kayak designed to run steep rivers and waterfalls

Creeking (*steep creeking*): paddling steep, technical rivers

Curler: see *breaking wave*

Current: moving water

Cushion: see *pillow*

D-ring: a steel ring attached to the kayak and used as a tie-down point

Deck: the top of the kayak

Diaphragm: see *baffle*

Downstream: the part of the river to where the current flows (also *downriver*)

Draw stroke: a stroke used to move the kayak sideways by placing the paddle out to the side of the kayak and pulling it back to the kayak

Drop: a steep, sudden change in the level of the river bottom. Drops taller than 6 to 7 feet are frequently called *waterfalls*

Dry bag: a waterproof bag designed to keep its contents dry

Drysuit: a waterproof suit that encloses a paddler in impermeable layers of fabric. Designed to be worn over insulating layers of clothing

Eddy: a pocket of water downstream of an obstacle that flows upstream or back against the main current

Eddy line: the interface between the eddy current and the main current (a high eddy line is called an *eddy fence*)

Eddy out: to stop in an eddy

Edging: tilting your kayak with a J-lean

Ender: a trick that uses river hydraulics to drive the kayak into a vertical position (also *endo, pop up*)

Entrapment: a situation where a kayak or kayaker gets pinned by the river's current against an obstacle (also *broach, pin*)

Falls: a drop where the river plummets steeply over boulders or broken river bottom. Can refer to a waterfall or to the upstream side of a hole

Feather: the offset in angle between the two blades of a paddle

Ferry: a maneuvering technique used to move a kayak back and forth laterally across the river

Flatwater: water without rapids

Float bag: the airbags installed in a kayak's hull to provide extra flotation

Footbrace: the part of the inside of a kayak against which your feet rest

Gauge: the device that measures the water level on rivers

Grab loop: the handles on the bow and stern of the kayak

Gradient: a term used to measure a river's descent in feet per mile or meters per kilometer

Haystack: a large, unstable standing wave

Helmet: rigid headgear designed to protect a kayaker's head from impact

Hip snap: the motion used to turn a kayak upright using hip and knee movements. The foundation movement for Eskimo rolls

Hole: a swirling vortex of water formed where the river pours over an obstacle and drops toward the river bottom, leaving a pocket behind the obstacle which is filled in by an upstream surface current

Horizon line: the point at which the river disappears over a drop. Time to scout!

Hydraulic: any type of rapid feature. However, many kayakers use the term hydraulic to describe holes only (see *hole*)

Hypothermia: a dangerous lowering of the body's core temperature

J-lean: the method for tilting your kayak on one edge by pinching one hip to your ribs. Your spine takes on a J shape, letting you balance over the edge of the kayak lowest in the water without using your paddle for support

Keeper: a large hole or reversal that can keep and hold a kayak or swimmer for a long period of time

Life jacket: a personal flotation device designed to float a swimmer in water (also *PFD*)

Peel out: exiting an eddy and entering the main current while allowing the bow to catch the main current and point downstream

PFD: see *life jacket*

Pillow: a cushion of water that forms on the upstream side of obstacles

Pin: to get your kayak stuck against an obstacle. Paddlers can also be pinned in boats

Pirouette: a spinning ender (see *ender*)

Pivot: to turn the kayak in place

Play: to use the river hydraulics to execute a variety of interesting maneuvers such as enders, surfs, etc.

Playboat: a boat specially designed for playing

Pool: a flat section of river with no rapids

Pool drop: a type of river that has intermittent rapids followed by long, easy sections of calm water

Portage: to carry a kayak around a rapid

Power face: the side of the paddle blade that normally pulls against the current

Put in: the place where your kayak trip begins

Rapid: a place where the river leaves its two-dimensional state and enters a three-dimensional state complete with faster currents, rocks, and various types of liquid surface features

Reversal: see *hole*

Riffle: shallow, gentle rapids caused by rocks or streambeds

River left: the left side of the river as you look downstream

River right: the right side of the river as you look downstream

Roll: the technique used to right a capsized kayak

Roller: a big, curling wave that falls back upstream on itself

Roostertail: a fountain of water that explodes in a fan pattern off a submerged obstacle

Scout: walk along a bank to inspect the river

Section: a portion of river between two points

Shaft: the long cylindrical tube between the blades of a paddle

Shuttle: the method used to get to and from take outs using cars, bikes, etc.

Sneak route: the easiest route through a rapid (also *cheat route*)

Spray skirt (also *spray deck*): the skirtlike apparatus that is worn around the paddler's waist and attaches to the cockpit to provide a watertight closure of the cockpit

Squirt boat: an extra-low-volume boat used to play in underwater river currents

Standing wave: a stationary river wave

Stern: the back end of a kayak

Stopper: a hole, reversal, or breaking wave capable of stopping, holding, or flipping a kayak or swimmer

Strainer: obstacles such as logs or boulders that let water flow freely through them but catch swimmers, kayaks, and debris (also *sweeper, logjam, boulder sieve*)

Surf: riding in place on a river hydraulic (waves, holes, etc.)

Sweep stroke: a turning stroke wherein the blade is swept in an arc pattern fore or aft

Tailwaves: standing waves that form at the base of a rapid

Take out: the place where kayak trips end and kayaks depart the river

Technical: a type of river that has many obstacles and therefore requires constant maneuvering

Throw bag: a bag that holds a long coiled rope, used as a rescue device to be tossed to swimmers

Tongue: a smooth V of fast-moving water that frequently appears at the top of a rapid

Undercut: an overhanging rock or ledge with water flowing underneath it

Volume: a measure of water in a river in cubic feet or cubic meters

Waterfall: a big, vertical drop (see *drop*)

Wave: a hump in the river's flowing water

Wave train: a series of standing waves

Whitewater: rapids. Also: *fun!*

Wrap: a kayak pinned flat by river currents against an obstacle

Z-drag: a pulley system used to rescue pinned or wrapped kayaks

Resources

Recommended Reading

Bechdel, Les, and Slim Ray. *River Rescue.*
Boston: Appalachian Mountain Club, 1985.

Dutky, Paul. *The Bombproof Roll and Beyond.*
Birmingham, AL: Menasha Ridge Press,
1993.

Gullion, Laurie. *The Canoeing and Kayaking
Instruction Manual.* Birmingham, AL:
American Canoe Association/Menasha
Ridge Press, 1987.

Nealy, William. *Kayak: The Animated Manual
of Intermediate and Advanced Whitewater
Technique.* Birmingham, AL: Menasha Ridge
Press, 1986.

Snyder, Jim. *The Squirt Manual.* Menasha
Ridge Press (currently out of print).

Walbridge, Charles, and Wayne A. Sund-
macher, Sr. *Whitewater Rescue Manual: New
Techniques for Canoeists, Kayakers, and
Rafters.* Camden, ME: Ragged Mountain
Press, 1995.

How-To Videos

Certain Squirtin'
Action Video
7503 New Market Dr.
Bethesda, MD 20817
301-229-1748

Essential Boat Control
Waterworks
P.O. Box 190
Topton, NC 28781

Grace under Pressure
Rapid Progression
P.O. Box 97
Almond, NC 28702

Just Add Water
Joe Holt Productions
P.O. Box 97
Almond, NC 28702

The Kayaker's Edge
Whitewater Instruction
160 Hideaway Road
Durango, CO 81301

Retendo
Performance Video and Instruction, Inc.
550 Riverbend
Durango, CO 81301

Periodicals

American Whitewater
P.O. Box 636
Margaretville, NY 12455
914-586-2355
E-mail RichB@amwhitewater.org
http://www.AWA.org

Canoe & Kayak
P.O. Box 3146
Kirkland, WA 98083-3146
425-827-6363
http://www.canoekayak.com/

Kanawa Magazine
P.O. Box 398
446 Main St. West
Merrickville, Ontario K0G 1N0
http://www.crca.ca/

Paddler
P.O. Box 775450
Steamboat Springs, CO 80477
970-879-1450
http://www.aca-paddler.org/paddler.html

River
P.O. Box 1068
Bozeman, MT 59771
http://www.rivermag.com/

Organizations

American Canoe Association (ACA)
7432 Alban Station Blvd., Suite B232
Springfield, VA 22150
703-451-0141
E-mail acadirect@aol.com
http://www.aca-paddler.org/

American Whitewater
P.O. Box 636
Margaretville, NY 12455
914-586-2355
E-mail RichB@amwhitewater.org
http://www.AWA.org

Canadian Recreational Canoeing Association
http://www.crca.ca/
National Organization of Whitewater Rodeos
http://www.nowr.org/

Other Internet links

Lightning Links to the World-Wide Web:
http://www.paddles.com/links/index.html
On-Water Sports: http://www.viewit.com/wtr/
Watersports_Resources.html
The Paddler's Web: http://mindlink.net/
summit/P.Net.html
Riversport.Com: http://www.riversport.com/
Rec.Boats.Paddle (newsgroup): Rec.boats.paddle

Cyber Updates and Author Inquiries

Jeff Bennett can be reached at
Steepcrks@aol.com

Index